God has gifted Art Azurdia as a trenchar
His word, and his gifts are on ready disp
Azurdia unpacks the early chapters of A
mission of the church, demonstrating th
Holy Spirit to carry out God's work. Here we find careful exegesis,
faithful theology, and powerful application intertwined together.
Take up and read, and be challenged, convicted, comforted, and
encouraged.

THOMAS R. SCHREINER,
James Buchanan Harrison Professor of New Testament Interpretation,
The Southern Baptist Theological Seminary, Louisville, Kentucky

Art Azurdia has previously blessed Christ's church with a powerful
reminder of the role of the Holy Spirit in preaching. Now he adds
to the blessing, not only by reminding us of the power of the Holy
Spirit in the church's mission, but also the priority of that mission:
transforming souls for eternity. In a day where much that claims to
be Gospel-driven can actually be Gospel-distracting, Art provides a
Gospel-focus that is most welcome and needed.

BRYAN CHAPELL,
Pastor, Grace Presbyterian Church, Peoria, Illinois

Art Azurdia is an exegetical surgeon who carefully cuts straight the
tissue of the text of Acts 1-2. This book timely attempts to awaken
the modern-day church to a Great Awakening that can only come
when the church executes the mission of God (missio dei) in
taking the gospel to humanity made in the image of God (imago
dei) for the glory of God (soli deo gloria) through the power of
the Holy Spirit until Christ returns (marantha). Azurdia is correct
in tenaciously contending that the twin pillars of the music and
practice of the church remain inextricably connected: What God
has joined together let no one put asunder. This work is a spiritual
literary success waiting to happen!

ROBERT SMITH, JR.,
Charles T. Carter Baptist Chair of Divinity,
Beeson Divinity School, Samford University, Birmingham, Alabama,

The mission is global conquest. The Conqueror is the risen,
ascended, enthroned, reigning Lord Jesus. The dynamic is the

personal presence of the Holy Spirit, indwelling and enabling His church. Arturo Azurdia's exposition of Acts 1 and 2 in *Spirit Empowered Mission* blends rich biblical interpretation with warm evangelistic passion, challenging all of us who belong to Christ's church to throw ourselves into Jesus' kingdom agenda, boldly and with joyful expectation.

DENNIS E. JOHNSON
Professor of Practical Theology,
Westminster Seminary in California, Escondido, California

The scriptural logic of Dr. Art Azurdia's *Spirit Empowered Mission* establishes in soaring, memorable terms that the central task of the church is taking the Christian gospel to the people of the world. The author's exacting exegesis and carefully wrought exposition of Luke's argument left me, a preacher of many years, informed, educated, convicted and motivated. Here are the Spirit-given "redemptive physics" for the church!

R. KENT HUGHES,
Senior Pastor Emeritus, College Church, Wheaton, Illinois
and Visiting Professor of Practical Theology,
Westminster Theological Seminary, Philadelphia, Pennsylvania

Arturo G. Azurdia III

SPIRIT EMPOWERED MISSION

Aligning the **Church's Mission** with the **Mission of Jesus**

CHRISTIAN
FOCUS

Arturo G. Azurdia III is Senior Minister of Word and Worship at Trinity Church in Portland, Oregon. He is also Associate Professor of Pastoral and Church Ministry, Director of Doctor of Ministry Program, Western Seminary and Founder and Director of The Spurgeon Fellowship. He preaches at conferences across the United States and internationally and has also written *Spirit Empowered Preaching* and *Connected Christianity* and contributed to several other volumes.

Copyright © Arturo Azurdia III 2016

paperback ISBN 978-1-78191-774-9
epub ISBN 978-1-78191-875-3
mobi ISBN 978-1-78191-876-0

10 9 8 7 6 5 4 3 2 1

Published in 2016
by
Christian Focus Publications Ltd,
Geanies House, Fearn,
Ross-shire, IV20 1TW, Scotland.
www.christianfocus.com

Cover design by Daniel van Straaten

Printed and bound by
Bell and Bain, Glasgow

CONTENTS

DEDICATION

*To the dear and faithful men of
The Spurgeon Fellowship ...
May the Spirit of the living God
empower our efforts for the advancement of the gospel
in the Pacific Northwest*

ACKNOWLEDGEMENTS

Dr. Norm Thiesen, David Thommen, and Thomas Terry ...
You are fine pastoral elders, each in your own unique way.
Thank you for the contributions you make to the congregation
Jesus has entrusted to us. I deeply appreciate the support and
kindness you display to me always, and especially during this
project.

The members of Trinity Church ...
Your enthusiasm for the gospel makes preaching on the Lord's
Day the most enjoyable ministry I have ever known. I am filled
with expectancy on our behalf, believing we have yet to experience
the most fruitful days of ministry that have been ordained for us.

Lori Azurdia ...
You are such an unusually wonderful gift—an extraordinary
combination of strength, patience, discernment, and practicality. God knew I needed you, and He gave me what I needed. Thank you for your careful editing so as to make this work
much clearer to understand.

To Dr. Randal Roberts (President, Western Seminary) and Dr. Rob Wiggins (Academic Dean, Western Seminary) ...
Your leadership expresses itself in consistent efforts to ensure the development of your students and faculty. Thank you for allowing me three uninterrupted months to write, without which it would have been impossible to complete this effort.

To Dr. Dennis Johnson (Professor of Practical Theology, Westminster Seminary California) ...
You taught me Hebrews, Revelation, and Acts. I have preached each of these books, and I am certain that the echo of your instruction is heard in everything I have said. Your influence will be found in these pages as well. Thank you, dear brother.

INTRODUCTION

Thunder Mountain Railroad ...
The Matterhorn Bobsleds ...
Indiana Jones and the Temple of the Forbidden Eye ...
The Mad Hatter Teacups ...
(and my personal favorite) Space Mountain ...

Those readers who possess a palate uniquely trained to appreciate the most urbane features of American culture will certainly identify the category into which each of these is to be placed: They are Disneyland attractions! More to the point, they are the attractions that most frequently leave their riders feeling nauseated ... especially after a big bowl of clam chowder. Most of you, I expect, are acquainted with this experience. Are you aware, however, of the laws of physics that actually ensure it? All of these attractions expose their riders to the pressures of centripetal force and centrifugal force. What are these? Centripetal force pulls a person toward the center of a rotating body, while centrifugal force pulls a person away from the center of a rotating body. In either case, the result is the same: somebody on these attractions inevitably—wonderfully!—gets squashed.

In many ways, this same dynamic illustrates the two volumes that comprise the Spirit-inspired writings of Luke. Not that anyone gets squashed, of course, or nauseated. But a careful reading of his New Testament contributions makes it nearly impossible not to feel the pressure of movement in his writing; that is, the force of being pulled in or the force of being thrust out. In his initial volume, referred to as the third Gospel, the movement is centripetal. As if a law of physics was at work, Luke inexorably draws his reader to the center—a geographical center: the city of Jerusalem (e.g., Luke 9:51; 13:22; 17:11; 19:11). Something significant is to occur there. In Luke's second volume, the book of Acts, the direction of movement changes dramatically. While Luke begins at this geographical center, his narrative quickly displays a decided movement away from it—almost as if there were centrifugal forces at work in defiance of anything seeking to resist them.

This raises the obvious question: If Jerusalem serves as the geographical pivot for this centripetal/centrifugal shift in Luke's writings, what is it that actually sets this shift in motion? A composite of salvation/historical events centered upon Jesus of Nazareth: His death and resurrection, followed by His ascension and exaltation as the universal Lord, all of which climaxes in His outpouring of the Holy Spirit on those who savingly belong to Him. *This* is the turning point for Luke, triggering an irresistible law of redemptive physics. The achievement of Jesus Christ is not to be confined to a geographical center. Rather, the entire world must realize that God's Son has brought salvation to the human race.

It is the aim of this book to reinforce this glorious agenda; but to do so, even more particularly, by displaying it as the unique and irreplaceable mission that has been given to the church by her resurrected Lord—a mission that, at present, is threatened by conscious and unconscious efforts to dissuade the church from it. My aim is not to identify and expose these efforts in detail (which are often distinct to each church setting and seemingly ever changing). It is to attempt something less subjective, more enduring, and applicable to all: to unambiguously and unashamedly define the mission of the church as articulated by Jesus Himself. At a time in which nearly everything is being uncritically heralded as 'the mission of the church,' Christians need to discerningly evaluate these claims via the light of the explicit instruction of Jesus and the apostles. Acts 1-2, specifically, provide a significant contribution to this necessary discussion. A careful exposition of these chapters can serve a conscientious pastor, council of elders, or an entire congregation by providing objective and revelatory criteria for self-evaluation. Though the process may potentially prove uncomfortable, its importance is beyond calculation—especially given the susceptibilities to which many churches are quickly falling prey, as illustrated in the following parable:

> On a dangerous seacoast where shipwrecks often occur, there was once a crude little lifesaving station. The building was just a hut, and there was only one boat, but the few devoted members kept a constant watch over the sea. With no thought of themselves they went out day and night, tirelessly searching for the lost. This wonderful little station saved many lives and, over time, it became famous. Some of those who were saved, and various others in the surrounding area, sought to become associated with the station—to give of their time, money, and effort for the support of its work. New boats were bought, and new crews trained. The little lifesaving station grew.
>
> Some of the members of the lifesaving station were unhappy that the building was so crude and poorly equipped. They felt that a more comfortable place should be provided as the first refuge for those saved from the sea. So they replaced the emergency cots with beds and put better furniture in the enlarged building. Gradually, the lifesaving station became a popular gathering place for its members. Over time, they decorated it exquisitely, using it as a sort of club. Fewer

members, however, were now interested in going to sea
on lifesaving missions, so they hired lifeboat crews to
do the work. The lifesaving motif still prevailed in the
club's decoration, and there was a liturgical lifeboat in
the room where the club's initiations were held. About
this time, a large ship was wrecked off the coast and
the hired crews brought in boatloads of cold, wet, and
half-drowned people. They were dirty and sick; some
of them had black skin and some had yellow skin.
The beautiful new club was in chaos. So the property
committee immediately had a shower-house built
outside the club where shipwrecked victims could be
cleaned up before coming inside.

At the next meeting, there was a split in the club's
membership. Most of the members wanted to stop
the club's lifesaving activities altogether, having come
to regard them as unpleasant and a hindrance to the
normal social life of the club. Some members insisted
upon lifesaving as their primary purpose, and pointed
out that they were still called a lifesaving station. But
they were finally voted down and told that if they
wanted to save the lives of all the various kinds of
people who were shipwrecked in those waters, they
could begin their own lifesaving station down the
coast. They did.

As the years went by, the new station experienced
the same changes that had occurred in the old. It,
too, evolved into a club, while yet another lifesaving
station was founded. History has continued to repeat
itself, and if you visit that seacoast today you will
find a number of exclusive clubs along that shore.
Shipwrecks are frequent in those waters, but most of
the people drown.[1]

This is a parable—and, therefore, fictional. The effectiveness
of a parable, however, lies in its proximity to reality. Its success
turns on the immediacy it shares with the person to whom
it is being told. As a pastor, this parable grips *me* with a very

---

1. This is a slightly modified story borrowed from an article by Theodore O. Wedel,
'Evangelism—the Mission of the Church to Those Outside Her Life,' *The Ecumeni-
cal Review* (October, 1953), p. 24.

real immediacy indeed. It requires no explanation because, frankly, I live in dread of just such a possibility: the creation of a missional irrelevance as the result of a congregational narcissism—or, stated differently, professing followers of Jesus who, while absorbed in the self-satisfying benefits of church life, are no longer preoccupied with getting themselves dirty searching for drowning people. It highlights one of the perennial anxieties of every discerning pastor: that a congregation would become so *self-absorbed*—with doctrinal minutiae, musical styles, political agendas, nuances of family life, social issues—that she eventually loses her preoccupation with mission. In a real sense, the *cause* of this self-absorption is immaterial. The potential reality of it is what proves so disconcerting—a reality that has not only made itself repeatedly evident throughout church history, but one that continues to make itself evident in congregations within our own respective communities. It is my prayer, then, that this book—through the means of a careful examination of Acts 1-2—will stimulate you to a fresh consideration of the mission Jesus has assigned to the church, and that as a result of doing so it would prompt you to evaluate your fidelity to this mission.

It is no exaggeration to claim that Acts 1-2 has forever changed me. Interestingly, it has done so, not only by providing me with truth I had never before considered, but by furnishing me with conviction I had never before felt. This is a most wonderful gift that the Spirit of God can give to a preacher of the gospel. I have no doubt that He can effect this same kind phenomenon within you.

It is to this end that I hope *Spirit Empowered Mission* will make a helpful contribution to your life and ministry.

1

THE APOSTOLIC DOCUDRAMA

I am fascinated by the Acts of the Apostles.
It is a book supremely relevant for our time.
MICHAEL GREEN

The Acts of the Apostles is the most exciting book
in the New Testament, probably in the whole
Christian Bible.
JAMES D. G. DUNN

Live in the book of Acts, I exhort you:
it is a tonic, the greatest tonic I know in the realm
of the Spirit.
D. MARTYN LLOYD-JONES

Awakening to the Conspiracy

It is not my wish to be curt, indelicate, or in any way
sensationalistic. It is, however, my intent to be immediate and
free of ambiguity. Permit me, then, for expedience sake, this
unadorned assertion:

> At all times and in all places, there is a frightening
> conspiracy to undermine the primary mission of the
> church of Jesus Christ.

There. I've said it ... finally. Would you allow me to say it again?

> At all times and in all places, there is a frightening
> conspiracy to undermine the primary mission of the
> church of Jesus Christ.

Do you believe this? *I do.* It is a conviction conceived, birthed,
and nurtured over three decades of pastoral ministry. The *form*

this conspiracy takes may be unique to the particular moment in history in which it expresses itself. But the *existence* of it is transcendent. Consider the following examples:[1]

In the past, this conspiracy has taken the form of *liberalism*: the undermining and, in some cases, outright denial of the major tenets of Christian orthodoxy, thus *eliminating the reason* for the church to be engaged in her primary mission. This conspiracy has often assumed the guise of *mysticism*: the insatiable pursuit of spiritual ecstasy found in the experiences of an otherworldly union with God, thereby *distracting* the church from her primary mission. Another expression of this conspiracy has manifested itself in *pragmatism*: the rabid quest for various life formulas that will ensure an existence in the present that approximates the new creation (often legitimized by a few Bible verses extracted from their contexts), consequently *obscuring the essence* of the church's primary mission. Overlooked as a form of conspiracy is the beguiling trap of *theological myopia*: a hyper-focused preoccupation with a particular theological/confessional position that ever seeks to buttress itself (including the endless search for theological conclusions that transcend biblical revelation and historic Christian orthodoxy), thus *misdirecting energies* away from the church's primary mission. A more recent vintage of this conspiracy has come through the influence of *cultural postmodernism*: the notion that since nothing is true *ultimately*, choosing to become a follower of Jesus Christ is acceptable insofar as any attempt to proselytize another person is repudiated, accordingly *invalidating the legitimacy* of the church's primary mission.

It must be said, of course, that such manifestations of conspiracy are not mutually exclusive. They frequently work in tandem. Nor are they intrinsically confined to a historical epoch. In some instances, they have been renounced by clarion gospel voices within the church and have become

---

1. This list is intended to be illustrative, not exhaustive.

dormant, only to reappear sometime later in a form more carefully nuanced and subtle. The fact is, vestiges of these conspiratorial attacks are *always* evident and at work in the church, even to this present moment.

Among the most prominent of the current expressions of this conspiracy is the renaissance of the call to *social justice*: the seemingly obvious (but rarely defended) notion that the work of the kingdom of God is to partner with Him for the purpose of overturning expressions of injustice and oppression that mar this broken world. *This* is the relevant mission of the church, many assert, and will alone restore the church's credibility in the eyes of our culture: the establishment of schools that will provide an equitable education for minorities, the launching of programs for the technical training of the unemployed, the formation of 'green teams' to raise consciousness regarding the environment, and a commitment to end the problem of malnutrition among the impoverished in our community.

Are you mindful of these ubiquitous claims? Have you felt the force of their pressure? Or, perhaps, wooed by their allure? Kevin DeYoung and Ted Kluck have summarized this phenomenon succinctly:

> Social action is hot. Evangelism is regarded as too aggressive (just a sales pitch), modern (cold, logical argumentation), and condescending ('my God is better than yours') ... A generation raised on seeker-sensitive churches where all the energy and value seemed to be on getting the unchurched into our worship services has reacted against an all-or-nothing commitment to getting people saved ... Now the emphasis is on human trafficking, AIDS, poverty, the homeless, and the environment. To bring Christ's kingdom of peace, justice, and blessing to the world is the mission of God (*missio dei*) for the church ... All Christians agree that the gospel has social implications. Most probably agree that community transformation could be a good thing. But where do we see Paul talking to his churches about transforming their communities?

> Where does Jesus, with the corrupt oppressive Roman
> Empire in full sway, seem interested in world-changing
> initiatives? It may be implied in passages about the
> cosmic lordship of Christ or living good lives among
> the pagans or praying for the king, but the concerns
> of the New Testament seem to have little to do with
> explicit community transformation.[2]

It is yet another attempt at misdirection, a subtle sleight
of hand that replaces the church's primary mission with
something less significant while simultaneously boosting her
own self-perception: 'Finally, a meaningful reason for our
existence—a place for us within this culture where we can make
a significant contribution. And as a consequence, we, too, can
be esteemed with real value.' It is a susceptibility common
to many evangelicals. Even the most insensitive Christian
recognizes the greater social acceptability of asking, 'May we
rehabilitate the public school playgrounds in this community?'
over against declaring, 'You will perish eternally unless you
repent of your sins and place your faith in a crucified and
resurrected Messiah.' How would this declaration be received
at the engineering firm that employs you? Is it embraced
enthusiastically at the university you attend? Though fellow-
members of the gym where you exercise will no doubt applaud
your efforts to end sex-trafficking in your community, how
will they respond to your winsome but accurate explanation of
the Christian gospel with all of its exclusive demands?[3]

> At all times and in all places there is a frightening
> conspiracy to undermine the primary mission of the
> church of Jesus Christ.

Moreover, the precise form into which this conspiracy in-
carnates itself at any point in time is not nearly as signifi-

---

2. Kevin DeYoung and Ted Kluck, *Why We Love The Church* (Chicago: Moody Publishers), pp. 36-39.

3. It is essential for Christians to remember that the unregenerate people of our
fallen culture will always esteem the gospel as 'foolish' (*cf.* 1 Cor. 1:18, 21, 23-24).

cant as is the failure of the church to identify its disastrous effects.

The Necessary Sequel

All of this begs the obvious question: What *is* the primary mission of the church of Jesus Christ? Ironically, it is a question that should not *need* to be asked by people who are resolved to allow the church's mission to be defined by Jesus.[4] Nevertheless, as implied by the preceding paragraphs, it remains a question that *must* be asked.

With this in mind, I invite your attention to the book of Acts where even a cursory visit to this enticing narrative will not allow for any confusion regarding the primary mission of the church. Whetting our appetite, Michael Green exuberantly writes:

> Three decades in world history. That is all it took. In the years between A.D. 33 and 64 a new movement was born. In those thirty years it got sufficient growth and credibility to become the largest religion the world has ever seen and to change the lives of hundreds of millions of people. It has spread into every corner of the globe and has more than two billion putative adherents. It has had an indelible impact on civilization, on culture, on education, on medicine, on freedom and of course on the lives of countless people worldwide. And the seedbed for all this, the time when it took decisive root, was in these three decades. It all began with a dozen men and a handful of women: and then the Spirit came. We have some hints as to how this took place from scattered allusions in the letters of the New Testament, several of them written during these same thirty lyrical years; but there is only one connected account of this astonishing, volcanic eruption of the Christian faith and that is contained in the Acts of the Apostles.[5]

---

4. This is a subject I have addressed previously in *Connected Christianity: Engaging Culture without Compromise* (Ross-shire: Christian Focus Publications, 2009).

5. Michael Green, *Thirty Years that Changed the World: The Book of Acts for Today* (Grand Rapids: William B. Eerdmans Publishing Company), p. 7.

But what should you know about the book of Acts, generally speaking? To begin with, it belongs to a portion of the Bible that has been traditionally referred to as the *New Testament*—a fact that, all by itself, may prove to be an impediment for the reader seeking to appreciate Acts as a contribution to the entirety of the Bible's historical/redemptive storyline. It was a point made graphically by Dr. Robert Smith[6] when asked by an aspiring pastoral candidate: 'What can I do to develop the ability to read the entire Bible Christocentrically?' Dr. Smith replied, 'There is one page in your Bible that you must remove immediately.' He then opened his Bible at the middle, to a page made conspicuous by the near totality of its whiteness, yet bearing a lonely heading comprised of two simple words: *New Testament*. The point was emphatic and unforgettable. Whether intentional or unintentional, theological or psychological, the white page with the simple two-word heading has served as a *separating page*, stressing an exaggerated discontinuity and thus implying that a reader of the Bible is dealing with two distinct books rather than one. Indeed, both are bound together in a single volume because they each share the quality of divine inspiration. But is this the full extent of their relationship? Writing under the inspiration of the Spirit, the author of Acts would insist, 'Absolutely not!' On nearly every page of his volume, he displays an unmistakable unity with the Old Testament Scriptures, not only citing one Old Testament text after another (in some cases multiple Old Testament passages in a single chapter), but revealing their terminus in Jesus Christ and the events surrounding Him. Revisiting Dr. Smith's illustration, the barren *'white page,'* which has functioned as a virtual brick wall between the Testaments, can impede a full understanding of the Bible's one overarching storyline. Acts, almost singlehandedly, serves to dismantle this wall.[7]

---

6. Dr. Robert Smith holds the Charles T. Carter Baptist Chair of Divinity at Beeson Divinity School.

7. This is not to deny all discontinuity as the Bible moves from Old Testament to

It is to be regarded as a strategic installment in the Bible's metanarrative that commences in Genesis and culminates in the Apocalypse.

Focusing more narrowly, it is also essential to note that Acts bears a uniquely intimate relationship to *one* Bible book in particular: the Gospel of Luke. Consider, briefly, its opening paragraph:

> Many have undertaken to draw up an account of the things that have been fulfilled among us, just as they were handed down to us by those who from the first were eyewitnesses and servants of the word. With this in mind, since I myself have carefully investigated everything from the beginning, I too decided to write an orderly account for you, most excellent Theophilus, so that you may know the certainty of the things you have been taught. (Luke 1:1-4)

Luke, a doctor (*cf.* Col 4:14) and traveling companion of the apostle Paul, is purposed to remove all shadow of doubt[8] from this man he refers to as, 'most excellent Theophilus.' How does he achieve this? He composes an ordered account of the fulfillment of the Hebrew Scriptures, an aim that requires Luke to recount the story of the person to whom the entirety of the Old Testament points. He begins, therefore, with the dramatic events of the birth of Jesus. He then advances his chronicle to encompass the ministry of Jesus, ultimately culminating in Jesus' sacrificial and vicarious death—a death that, in turn, is answered by His glorious resurrection. Accordingly, Luke's Gospel is a summation of God's saving purpose accomplished in Jesus of Nazareth for the benefit of all who renounce their sin and rest upon His redemptive accomplishments, the inauguration of everything anticipated

---

New Testament. Rather (in keeping with the metaphor), the brick wall needs to be replaced with a picket fence.

8. The Greek verb here means: 'to know exactly, completely, through and through.' Walter Bauer, *A Greek-English Lexicon of the New Testament and Other Early Christian Literature* (rev. ed., Chicago: The University of Chicago Press, 2000), p. 369.

in Old Testament. Luke's conclusion, incorporating a post-resurrection appearance of Jesus, reinforces this:

> While they were still talking about this, Jesus himself stood among them and said to them, 'Peace be with you.'
> They were startled and frightened, thinking they saw a ghost. He said to them, 'Why are you troubled, and why do doubts rise in your minds? Look at my hands and my feet. It is I myself! Touch me and see; a ghost does not have flesh and bones, as you see I have.'
> When he had said this, he showed them his hands and feet. And while they still did not believe it because of joy and amazement, he asked them, 'Do you have anything here to eat?' They gave him a piece of broiled fish, and he took it and ate it in their presence.
> He said to them, 'This is what I told you while I was still with you: Everything must be fulfilled that is written about me in the Law of Moses, the Prophets and the Psalms.'
> Then he opened their minds so they could understand the Scriptures. He told them, 'This is what is written: The Messiah will suffer and rise from the dead on the third day, and repentance for the forgiveness of sins will be preached in his name to all nations, beginning at Jerusalem. You are witnesses of these things. I am going to send you what my Father has promised; but stay in the city until you have been clothed with power from on high.'
> When he had led them out to the vicinity of Bethany, he lifted up his hands and blessed them. While he was blessing them, he left them and was taken up into heaven. Then they worshiped him and returned to Jerusalem with great joy. And they stayed continually at the temple, praising God. (Luke 24:36-53)

It is nothing short of spellbinding, this appearance of Jesus to His disciples (including His earlier visitation on the Emmaus road). I find it to be one of the most exhilarating scenes in the entire Bible. Yet despite its climactic significance (including the Copernican shift in relationship to Old Testament interpretation), is it truly the final act of the Jesus story—the account of His resurrection from the dead and ascension into heaven? Are these the events that define the completion of Christianity? Candidly, as a reader of the narrative, I find myself wanting more, a sensation akin to that experienced by many moviegoers at the conclusion of *The Fellowship of the Ring*. As a stand-alone artistic production, few would deny its worthiness as a well-crafted and compelling film. Yet, simultaneously, neither could anyone deny that its conclusion leaves the viewer demanding another installment—a sequel. *This is precisely the function served by the book of Acts*, as made evident by *its* introduction:

> In my former book, Theophilus, I wrote about all that Jesus began to do and to teach until the day he was taken up to heaven, after giving instructions through the Holy Spirit to the apostles he had chosen. After his suffering, he presented himself to them and gave many convincing proofs that he was alive. He appeared to them over a period of forty days and spoke about the kingdom of God. On one occasion, while he was eating with them, he gave them this command: 'Do not leave Jerusalem, but wait for the gift my Father promised, which you have heard me speak about. For John baptized with water, but in a few days you will be baptized with the Holy Spirit.'
> Then they gathered around him and asked him, 'Lord, are you at this time going to restore the kingdom to Israel?'
> He said to them: 'It is not for you to know the times or dates the Father has set by his own authority. But you will receive power when the Holy Spirit comes on you; and you will be my witnesses in Jerusalem, and in all Judea and Samaria, and to the ends of the earth.'
> After he said this, he was taken up before their very eyes, and a cloud hid him from their sight. (Acts 1:1-9)

It seems impossible to miss. The Gospel of Luke is a *prequel* to the book of Acts; the book of Acts is a *sequel* to the Gospel of

Luke. Metaphorically, they function as two volumes set side by side in a single slipcover.[9] Though Luke's second volume has not infrequently been assigned such titles as, 'The Acts of the Apostles,' or 'The Acts of the Holy Spirit,' such labels, respectfully, miss the point. Luke's prequel is an account of the earthly activity of an earthly Jesus. His sequel is an account of the earthly activity of a heavenly Jesus.[10]

There does exist, however, a nuanced distinction between Luke's two volumes that exposes their respective emphases: the Gospel traces Jesus' movement *centripetally*, progressively moving *toward* Jerusalem (culminating in His death, burial, and resurrection)—while Acts traces Jesus' movement *centrifugally*, progressively moving *away from* Jerusalem (an outworking of the consequences of His death, burial, and resurrection).[11] It is this nuance that lures our attention toward the principal theme of Acts, a programmatic declaration of mission made by the resurrected Lord Himself that serves to encompass the entirety of Luke's writing:

> But you will receive power when the Holy Spirit comes
> on you; and you will be my witnesses in Jerusalem, and
> in all Judea and Samaria, and to the ends of the earth.
> (Acts 1:8)

The Christian mission begins in *'Jerusalem'* (chaps. 1–7). It spreads to *'Judea and Samaria'* (chaps. 8–12). And it finally extends, in principle, to *'the ends of the earth,'* ultimately to the very heart of the world's superpower, Rome (chaps. 13–28). Acts, then, is a book resolutely focused on the mission of Jesus Christ that He, in turn, mediates to the church. It also incorporates morsels of information about life in a local congregation. But

---

9. An image originally conveyed to me by Pastor Thomas N. Smith.

10. Hence the title of an outstanding work by Alan J. Thompson, *The Acts of the Risen Lord Jesus: Luke's Account of God's Unfolding Plan* (Downers Grove: InterVarsity Press, 2011).

11. Dennis E. Johnson, *The Message of Acts in the History of Redemption* (Phillipsburg: P & R Publishing, 1997), p 14.

certainly not, in most cases, to arrive at definitive prescriptions for church practice; and, in some cases, only enough to raise questions that will require the reader to look elsewhere for answers.[12] The early Christians cast lots to determine the individual appointed by Jesus to assume the apostolic position forsaken by Judas. Is this a practice to be emulated by Christians today? And this, of course, raises a corollary question: is the apostleship an office to be filled in this epoch of church history? The early Christians in Jerusalem became very communal with their material possessions. Should each of us follow this model—empty our bank accounts, sell our possessions, and live together in a kibbutz? Is it legitimate to assume that all church members will receive the Holy Spirit at a point subsequent to their conversion, as do the Samaritans (Acts 8:4-16)?[13]

Acts may prove frustrating for the reader who fails to appreciate Luke's agenda, which is something other than the provision of a descriptive manual to be meticulously followed by our contemporary congregations. It is, rather, to record the ongoing mission of the exalted Lord, a mission that moves forward in a community of people empowered by the means of a supernatural resource purchased for them by Jesus Christ in His death and resurrection, referred to by Him as, 'the gift my Father promised.' But to what is Jesus referring? Better yet, to whom is Jesus referring?

---

12. 'If you go to Acts to answer all of the later questions about infant baptism, church order, or apostles after the first generation, you will be frustrated because of a lack of complete, and sometimes any, answers. Luke's agenda was not ours.' Ben Witherington III, *The Acts of the Apostles: A Socio-Rhetorical Commentary* (Grand Rapids: William B. Eerdmans Publishing Company, 1998), p 1.

13. Acts should not be studied in a manner that seeks answers to questions it never intends to address definitively. A concise and helpful treatment of this interpretive dilemma is provided in Gordon D. Fee and Douglas Stuart, *How to Read the Bible for all its Worth: A Guide to Understanding the Bible* (Grand Rapids: Zondervan Publishing House, 1982). Particular attention should be given to the chapter bearing a title that identifies the specific challenge at hand, 'The Problem of Historical Precedent,' pp. 87-102.

> But you will receive power when the Holy Spirit comes
> on you; and you will be my witnesses in Jerusalem, and
> in all Judea and Samaria, and to the ends of the earth.
> (Acts 1:8)

Stated most simply, the principal theme of the book of Acts is
this: *Spirit empowered mission—the universal expansion of Christianity effected by the potency of the Holy Spirit under the direction of the resurrected Lord.* Moreover, to approach this book with any
other set of presuppositions runs the risk of obfuscating this
theme, a point forcefully made in 1917 by Roland Allen, the
High Church Anglican missionary in North China:

> We have been content to read 'Acts' as the external
> history of the Church: we have used it as happy hunting
> ground for arguments on behalf of different theories
> of Church government. For each of these theories we
> have sometimes claimed authority of the Holy Spirit
> on the strength of one or two isolated sentences or
> even of a single word introduced incidentally by
> St. Luke ... But in tithing the mint and rue of 'Acts' we
> have passed over mercy and the love of God. The great,
> fundamental, unmistakable teaching of the book has
> been lost ... it is in the revelation of the Holy Spirit
> as a missionary Spirit that the 'Acts' stands alone in
> the New Testament ... it is the one prominent feature.
> It is asserted, it is taken for granted, from the first
> page to the last. Directly and indirectly it is made all-
> important. To treat it as secondary destroys the whole
> character and purpose of the book.[14]

A Resolute Agenda

Interspersed throughout Acts are clues that serve to reinforce
Luke's grand theme, glimpses of progress in this Spirit
empowered mission:

> Those who accepted his message were baptized, and
> about three thousand were added to their number
> that day. (2:41)

---

14. Roland Allen, *Pentecost and the World* (London: Oxford University Press, 1917),
pp. 39-41.

> And the Lord added to their number daily those who were being saved. (2:47)

> But many who heard the message believed; so the number of men who believed grew to about five thousand. (4:4)

It is not unusual in certain evangelical circles to hear claims such as following: 'It's spiritual growth that we are pursuing. We're not into numbers.' Yet in keeping with the mission Jesus has assigned to the church the response should be, 'But why not? *Acts clearly is.*' *Empire building* should be eschewed as a contradiction to the gospel, of course, as well as any and all clamor to advance a ministerial reputation. But such things should never be confused with a holy aspiration to see the relentless movement forward of what unfolds steadily throughout the book of Acts:

> Nevertheless, *more and more men and women* believed in the Lord and were added to their number. (5:14)

> In those days when the number of disciples *was increasing* ... (6:1)

> So the word of God *spread.* The number of disciples in Jerusalem *increased rapidly,* and *a large number of priests* became obedient to the faith. (6:7)

> When the apostles in Jerusalem heard that *Samaria* had accepted the word of God ... (8:14)

> Then the church throughout Judea, Galilee and Samaria enjoyed a time of peace and was strengthened. Living in the fear of the Lord and encouraged by the Holy Spirit, it *increased in numbers.* (9:31)

> *All those* who lived in Lydda and Sharon saw him and turned to the Lord. (9:35)

> This became known all over Joppa, and *many people* believed in the Lord. (9:42)

> The Lord's hand was with them, and *a great number of people* believed and turned to the Lord. (11:21)

He [Barnabas] was a good man, full of the Holy Spirit and faith, and *a great number of people* were brought to the Lord. (11:24)

But the word of God continued to *spread and flourish.* (12:24)

When the Gentiles heard this, they were glad and honored the word of the Lord; and *all who were appointed for eternal life* believed. The word of the Lord spread through the whole region. (13:48-49)

At Iconium Paul and Barnabas went as usual into the Jewish synagogue. There they spoke so effectively that *a great number of Jews and Greeks* believed. (14:1)

They preached the gospel in that city and won *a large number of disciples.* (14:21)

So the churches were strengthened in the faith and *grew daily in numbers.* (16:5)

Some of the Jews were persuaded and joined Paul and Silas, as did *a large number of God-fearing Greeks* and *quite a few prominent women.* (17:4)

Now the Berean Jews were of more noble character than those in Thessalonica, for they received the message with great eagerness and examined the Scriptures every day to see if what Paul said was true. As a result, *many of them* believed, as did also *a number of prominent Greek women* and *many Greek men.* (17:11-12)

Some of the people became followers of Paul and believed. Among them was Dionysius, a member of the Areopagus, also a woman named Damaris, and *a number of others.* (17:34)

Crispus, the synagogue leader, and *his entire household* believed in the Lord; and *many of the Corinthians* who heard Paul believed and were baptized. (18:8)

Says missionary/theologian Harry Boer:

Acts is governed by one dominant, overriding and all-controlling motif. This motif is the expansion of the faith through missionary witness in the power of the

Spirit. So strong, so central, is this motif, so graphically is it portrayed, and so completely is the witness that it sets forth integrated with the life of the Church, that its very centrality obscures it for us ... One hardly knows where in Acts to look for a distinction between Church and missions. Restlessly the Spirit drives the Church to witness, and continually churches rise out of the witness. The Church is missionary Church. She is not missionary Church in the sense that she is 'very much interested' in missions, or that she 'does a great deal' for missions. In Acts missions is not a hobby of an 'evangelical section' of the Church. The Church as a whole is missionary in all her relationships. Johannes Durr has spoken a strong word here: 'The origin of missions coincides wholly with the founding of the Church. Therefore the New Testament does not know the word "missions," since the matter which it signifies is identical with what is understood by Church.'[15]

Luke's intention was not to compose a book of systematic theology. Nor was it his aim to provide a detailed historical record of each day in the life of the church.[16] On what basis, then, has he determined the actual content to be included in his sequel, over against the massive amount of material he intentionally omits? His criteria for inclusion (under the inspiration of the Holy Spirit) have been determined by a resolute fidelity to his agenda: to articulate and delineate the ongoing mission of Jesus Christ through the Spirit empowered church. Or as it might be popularly described, 'The Jesus Story, Part 2: The Movement Out.'

His distinctive manner of writing is stereotypical of a style that flourished between 300 B.C. and A.D. 200, Hellenistic historiography; a style of historical writing intended not merely to inform, but also to encourage, entertain, and persuade;[17]

---

15. Harry R. Boer, *Pentecost And Missions* (Grand Rapids: William B. Eerdmans Publishing Company, 1961), pp. 161-162.

16. Such a book would need to be significantly greater in size, given that Acts spans as much as forty years.

17. Fee and Stuart, *How to Read*, p. 89. James Dunn adds, 'Good history has never

an approach, it could be argued, analogous to Ken Burns' series for PBS, *The Civil War.* Acts is an apostolic docudrama[18], an accurate but selective history designed to educate and motivate in keeping with its essential theme. Its cast includes ninety-five people: men like Stephen, Philip, and Barnabas, and women like Mary, Dorcas, and Priscilla. Its two *primary* players are *Peter* (the leading figure in chaps. 1–12) and *Paul* (the leading figure in chaps. 13–28). Yet, even regarding them, no substantial biographical portrait is provided. Is this a *flaw* in Luke's writing? To the contrary, it is another manifestation of its *focus*—that all of his choices in this sequel have been determined by his burden to indelibly impress a concept upon the minds of his readers: that the primary mission of the church of Jesus Christ is our ever-expanding witness to Him. And nothing else, however noble or philanthropic, may be allowed to replace, compromise, or even compete with it.[19]

Accompanying the Primary Mission

Other emphases are inextricably woven into Luke's focus on Spirit empowered mission, one of which is the prominence of preaching. Though it is not uncommon for people to associate the book of Acts with miraculous signs of power, preaching is a subject that occupies a more substantial place. Indeed,

---

been simply a matter of pedantic communication of information.' *The Acts of the Apostles* (Valley Forge: Trinity Press International, 1996), p. xvi.

18. Carey C. Newman, 'Acts,' *A Complete Literary Guide to the Bible*, eds., Leland Ryken and Tremper Longman III (Grand Rapids: Zondervan Publishing House, 1993), pp. 436-438.

19. So by way of example, Donald Bloesch asks, 'Should the church as a church provide low income housing for the poor?' His answer reflects an appropriate tension, ' ... in an emergency situation, when the poor are being left homeless, and when the state cannot or will not act, then the church may direct its funds towards this purpose, though only in service of its primary mission. When benevolence money is diverted away from missions for such purposes, however, then the church may be guilty of a grave dereliction of its duty to fulfill the great commission ... Our motivation is compassion, but our goal is evangelism. The Christian must seek the greatest good of his neighbor, which is his eternal salvation.' *The Invaded Church* (Waco: Word Books, 1975), pp. 113-114, 110).

miracles frequently set the table *for* proclamation. For example, in thirteen verses Luke records the coming of the Spirit on the Day of Pentecost, while Peter's subsequent sermon explaining its implications takes twenty-three. The account of a lame man healed in the Temple is narrated in ten verses, which is then followed by two explanatory sermons of Peter totaling twenty-two. There are ten extended sermons in Acts, along with thirty preaching summaries. A reading of the entire book in a single setting will leave the reader with the sensation that Acts is little more than a collection of sermons tied together by threads of narrative. Furthermore, the telling feature of these sermons is their shared subject matter: not the call to cultural transformation by partnering with God to 'redeem' the world (redemption is what *Jesus* does on the cross), nor the invitation to join God in His 'kingdom-building' efforts in various forms of social justice.[20] Their theme is the redemptive work of Jesus, along with the corresponding summons to repent and believe. It is this relentless repetition, in fact, that reinforces the true nature of the church's mission: not that her people would become new 'incarnations' of Christ (a disturbing notion at best),[21] rather that they would serve as His 'ambassadors' offering eternal life through the gospel.

Another distinguishing accent in Acts is Luke's repeated mention of prayer, conspicuous in fourteen of the first fifteen chapters (and in later chapters as well); a fact not surprising

20. 'There is no language in Scripture about Christians building the kingdom. The New Testament, in talking about the kingdom, uses verbs like *enter, seek, announce, see, receive, look, come into,* and *inherit.* Do a word search and see for yourself. We are *given* the kingdom and *brought into* the kingdom. We testify about it, pray for it to come, and by faith it belongs to us. But in the New Testament, we are never the ones who bring the kingdom.' DeYoung and Kluck, *Why We Love,* p. 49.

21. Jesus *does* send his disciples into the world as He has been sent (John 17:18). Nonetheless, 'there is no necessary overtone of incarnation or of invasion from another world' ... (one must always recognize) ... 'the ontological gap that forever distances the origins of Jesus' mission from the origins of the disciples' missions.' D. A. Carson, *The Gospel According to John* (Grand Rapids: William B. Eerdmans Publishing Company, 1990), p. 566.

to those acquainted with Luke's Gospel in which prayer is mentioned more frequently than in the combined references to prayer in Matthew, Mark, and John's Gospels. Once again, its recurring manifestation in the Acts narrative is owing to a phenomenon that will repeatedly prove to be a consequence associated with the theme of Spirit empowered mission: the experience of opposition and hostility to the preaching of the gospel—persecution that will, on occasion, even culminate in the death of the one bearing witness to Jesus Christ. Nevertheless, Luke repeatedly displays the unstoppable saving sovereignty of God, who not only controls but exploits the evil agendas of Christ-haters to advance the very gospel they seek to destroy.

Furthermore, as this mission advances from Jerusalem into Judea and Samaria, and then into Asia Minor and Europe, the reader of Acts is confronted with the shattering of racial and ethnic barriers as the church incorporates human beings from every tribe, language, people, and nation. It is no indication that ethnicity is devalued or eliminated by the gospel. Rather, that ethnicity is *transcended* by the gospel. So that while Jews remain Jews and Gentiles remain Gentiles (and Hispanics remain Hispanic!), the curse of Babel is reversed and a new, integrated humanity is formed. The gift of the Spirit unites all Christians into one family of brothers and sisters who now share the same Father and Elder Brother.

A Third Installment

When Luke's narrative finally arrives at its concluding chapter, the gospel mission has reached Rome, the center of world power—in many ways regarded as 'the ends of the earth'—its reader cannot help but admire the church's fidelity to her appointed mission despite the manifold voices that have sought to dissuade her from it. The declaration of the risen Lord *has* been realized:

> But you will receive power when the Holy Spirit comes
> on you; and you will be my witnesses in Jerusalem,
> and in all Judea and Samaria, and to the ends of the
> earth (1:8).

Or has it?

Is Acts 28 the final destination envisioned by Jesus in Acts 1:8?
Are we to conclude that Luke's sequel encompasses both the
culmination and conclusion of the Christian mission? In
my own city of Portland, Oregon, there are more than half
a million people who have yet to hear a clear and compelling
declaration of the gospel. Is it legitimate to assume from Acts
that the primary mission Jesus assigned to the church should
have no compelling or constraining influence on me and our
congregation? While the inspired narrative closes with the
apostle Paul evangelizing in Rome, the reader is left with a
dialectical sensation all too familiar, one reminiscent of that
experienced at the conclusion of Luke's *first* installment:
simultaneous elation and dissatisfaction—a tension that begs
another sequel, a *third* installment, a final volume to set inside
the slipcover that contains the prior two. Acts itself demands
another narrative for the simple reason that the mission of
the church in its fullest extent, given to her by Jesus and
empowered by the Spirit, has yet to be achieved. A. T. Pierson
captured this stirringly in an earlier generation:

> Church of Christ! The records of these acts of the
> Holy Ghost have never reached completeness. This is
> the one book which has no proper close, because it
> waits for new chapters to be added so fast and so far as
> the people of God shall reinstate the blessed Spirit in
> his holy seat of control.[22]

After I had completed five years of pastoral ministry as an
associate staff member in a large California church, and just
prior to moving away to plant a new congregation some fifty

---

22. Arthur Tappan Pierson, *The Acts of the Holy Spirit* (London: Marshall, Morgan,
and Scott, 1895), pp. 141-142

miles up the interstate, a gracious reception was provided for
us so that well-wishers could express their warm and prayerful
blessings. When the evening concluded and we drove away
from the church building for the final time, I said to my wife,
'I am so glad, *finally*, to now be able to get beyond the gospel.' I suppose there were many factors that contributed to
that sentiment, some of which were external to me. But, retrospectively, the two most obvious were my own profound arrogance and ignorance. To be sure, I have since confessed this
arrogance and ignorance on many occasions. And God has
graciously granted me repentance, using a handful of strategic
people to open my eyes to the Bible's central message and mission. These, in turn, have become consuming passions in my
life and ministry for nearly twenty-five years. But why the self-
exposure? The reason is simple. It is to explain something of
the claim I made at the outset of this chapter—a claim made,
not merely as the result of a more insightful understanding
of the biblical text (I am no D. A. Carson!), not merely as
the consequence of a deeper appreciation of church history
(I am no Timothy George!), and not merely as the outcome of
a clearer awareness of the evangelical church in the Western
world (I am no David Wells!). It is owing, in no small part, to
the awareness of my past failures and present susceptibilities
that I can say with some measure of believability:

> At all times and in all places there is a frightening
> conspiracy to undermine the primary mission of the
> church of Jesus Christ.

Do not be deceived, my friend. Do not give ear to the siren
voices calling you to other preoccupations. Might it be
that many of the accusations of irrelevance leveled against
gospel-proclaiming congregations are, in fact, backhanded
affirmations of the very opposite, albeit from people indifferent
to the redeeming work of Jesus Christ? The central task of the
church is the promotion of the Christian gospel to the people

of this world, for by it the Spirit 'transmits to men the life that shall make possible the recognition of the lordship that is Christ's.'[23]

Will you be included in this sequel?

---

23. Boer, *Pentecost*, pp. 146-147.

2

THE FINAL WORDS OF FIRST IMPORTANCE

The church is the pilgrim people of God.
It is on the move—hastening to the ends of the earth
to beseech all people to be reconciled to God.
It cannot be understood rightly
except in a perspective that is missionary.
LESLIE NEWBIGIN

~~~~~~~~~~

The essential task of the church is mission.
For Acts mission means evangelism,
the proclamation of the good news of Jesus
and the challenge to repentance and faith.
I. HOWARD MARSHALL

~~~~~~~~~~

Whether lulled into complacency by universalism
or into indifference by viewing missions
as the specialty of certain persons,
the church will be awakened by Acts,
which declares that being on the move
with the gospel witness across cultural thresholds
is the church's number one job.
WILLIAM LARKIN

~~~~~~~~~~

[1]In my former book, Theophilus, I wrote about all that Jesus began to do and to teach [2]until the day he was taken up to heaven, after giving instructions through the Holy Spirit to the apostles he had chosen. [3]After his suffering, he presented himself to them and gave many convincing proofs that he was alive. He appeared to them over a period of forty days and spoke about the kingdom of God. [4]On one occasion, while he was eating with them, he gave them this command:

'Do not leave Jerusalem, but wait for the gift my Father promised, which you have heard me speak about. [5]For John baptized with water, but in a few days you will be baptized with the Holy Spirit.'

[6]Then they gathered round him and asked him, 'Lord, are you at this time going to restore the kingdom to Israel?'

[7]He said to them: 'It is not for you to know the times or dates the Father has set by his own authority. [8]But you will receive power when the Holy Spirit comes on you; and you will be my witnesses in Jerusalem, and in all Judea and Samaria, and to the ends of the earth.'

[9]After he said this, he was taken up before their very eyes, and a cloud hid him from their sight.

[10]They were looking intently up into the sky as he was going, when suddenly two men dressed in white stood beside them. [11]'Men of Galilee,' they said, 'why do you stand here looking into the sky? This same Jesus, who has been taken from you into heaven, will come back in the same way you have seen him go into heaven.'

(Acts 1:1-11)

A Mission without Ambiguity

Were it your aim to discover *the primary mission* of the church of Jesus Christ by exclusively observing the *practice* of professing Christian congregations in your community, would your findings be well defined and conclusive? Or would they be inconsistent and confused?

Before answering, consider carefully the constraint of this question. It is not one that asks you to broadly identify the legitimate ministries, activities, or agendas distinct to local churches—things like congregational worship, expressions of discipleship, the mutual exercise of spiritual gifts, or the care and benevolence displayed to needy church members. Nor does this question solicit you to summarize the various and diverse demonstrations of goodness and justice displayed by *individual Christians*. For a growing number of evangelicals, an indiscriminating use of various Bible proof texts, along with a confusion of categories regarding their application, has muddled the distinction between the calling of a congregation and that of an individual Christian. The result is that many congregations now find themselves awash in diverse concerns they correspondingly define as '*mission.*' This has occasioned a dilution and, in some cases, a virtual neglect of the *stated* mission of the church because, as Stephen Neill has put it so aptly, 'If *everything* is mission, *nothing* is mission.'[1] Kevin DeYoung fittingly asks,

> 'If I am commanded to do justice, does that mean *ipso facto* that it is the church's mission to do justice? By the same token, if I am commanded to love my wife as my own body, does that mean it is the church's mission to love my wife as it does its own body?'

He then elaborates:

> ... 'The mission of the church ... seems to be something narrower than the set of all commands given to individual Christians—it's proclamation, witness, and disciple making (which includes teaching everything Jesus commanded). This is simply another way of saying that bearing witness to Christ is the church's unique responsibility in a way that film making or auto repair or tree planting is not, though all of these may be examples of ways in which an individual Christian follows Jesus.'[2]

So I ask you again: Were it your aim to discover *the primary mission* of the church of Jesus Christ by exclusively observing the *practice* of professing Christian congregations in your community, would your findings be well defined and conclusive? Or would they be inconsistent and confused? However you may be inclined to answer, this much is self-evident in the book of Acts: the mission that Jesus Christ

---

1. Stephen Neill, *Creative Tension* (London: Edinburgh House Press, 1959), p. 81.

2. Kevin DeYoung and Greg Gilbert, *What is the Mission of the Church? Making Sense of Social Justice, Shalom, and the Great Commission* (Wheaton: Crossway, 2011), p. 233.

assigns to His church defies all accusations of ambiguity—a fact made apparent throughout the entirety of Luke's sequel,[3] but never more explicitly than in his opening paragraph, which can be divided into three sections. *Section #1* calls the reader's attention to *the initial coming of Jesus Christ,* culminating in His ascension (vv. 1-3). *Section #3* is preoccupied with *the ultimate coming of Jesus Christ,* precipitated by His ascension (vv. 9-11). Squeezed between these two paragraphs is *Section #2,* where Luke sets forth *the intervening commission of Jesus* Christ—one that defies all accusations of ambiguity.

Let us consider each of these sections in the sequence in which I have listed them.

Section #1: The Initial Coming of Jesus Christ

> In my former book, Theolophilus, I wrote about all that Jesus began to do and to teach until the day he was taken up to heaven ... (vv. 1-2a)

As mentioned in the prior chapter, this is a reference to Luke's Gospel, his carefully investigated record of the life and ministry of Jesus, the one in whom the Old Testament expectations have found their fulfillment. Accordingly, his first installment is absorbed with the *deeds* of Jesus, including a detailed account of His supernatural conception, baptism, filling with the Holy Spirit, and temptations by the devil. It also comprises a record of His miracles, healings, and displays of

---

3. The same may be said of the mission of the church as set forth by Jesus in the Gospels, though each account bears its own unique emphasis. Matthew calls attention to the *sovereignty* of the one who assigns the mission: 'All authority in heaven and on earth has been given to me. Therefore go and make disciples of all nations' (Matt. 28:18-19); Mark highlights the *consequences of responses* to the mission: 'Go into all the world and preach the gospel to all creation. Whoever believes and is baptized will be saved, but whoever does not believe will be condemned' (Mark 16:15-16); Luke defines the Christian mission in terms of its *Old Testament fulfillment:* 'This is what is written: the Messiah will suffer and rise from the dead on the third day, and repentance for the forgiveness of sins will be preached in his name to all nations' (Luke 24:46-47); and John stresses the *continuity of mission* the disciples share with Jesus: 'As the Father has sent me, I am sending you' (John 20:21).

power over the forces of darkness. Its climax incorporates His arrest, trials, scourging, crucifixion, burial, and resurrection. Luke displays a similar concern to record various expressions of the *teaching* of Jesus, including the foreshadowing scene of a twelve-year-old boy who astonishingly engages the rabbinic teachers at the Jerusalem Temple. When the public ministry of Jesus commences, Luke cites His teaching in the Galilean synagogues, as well as in the homes of both the religious elite and socially despised. He includes Jesus' parables, the Sermon on the Plain, the Olivet discourse, and selected portions of His intimate instruction during the Passover meal just prior to His arrest in the garden of Gethsemane. Luke indicates that great numbers of people travel significant distances to listen to the teaching of Jesus. Thus, His deeds and teaching are the foci of content in Luke's *'former book.'*[4]

Here, in this introductory statement to Theophilus,[5] Luke qualifies the infinitives *'to do and to teach'* with the verb *'began'*—suggesting an obvious implication: his Gospel is a compilation of only the *beginning* of what Jesus did and taught up to the point of His ascension. This *second* volume, Acts, is a record of what Jesus *continues* to do and teach.[6] The peculiarity between these two volumes, then, is not that of *Jesus'* work and the *church's* work, but between the two stages of the work of Jesus Christ. Acts is a record of His *ongoing work*, a principal feature that distinguishes Christianity from other religious

---

4. The term *proton logon* indicates that it was the first volume in the series.

5. *Theophilus*, a common Greek name meaning 'loved by God,' is most likely a reference to an individual as the recipient of this work. Yet, Luke 'presumably also hoped that Theophilus would act as a patron or sponsor in bringing his work to a wider audience.' David G. Peterson, *The Acts of the Apostles*, PNTC (Grand Rapids: William Eerdmans Publishing Company, 2009), p. 102.

6. The opening of v. 1 actually includes the particle *men* which is not translated in the NIV or ESV It is equivalent to 'on the one hand' (here describing Luke's Gospel account), which leads the reader to expect the corresponding contrast 'on the other hand' (in relationship to Acts). Luke does not include this, but the context implies it. Johannes P. Louw and Eugene A. Nida, *Greek-English Lexicon of the New Testament Based on Semantic Domains* (New York: United Bible Societies, 1989), vol. 1, p, 795.

expressions that regard the work of their respective founders
as confined to the boundaries of their lifetimes. Contrarily,
the earthly accomplishments of Jesus only represent the
beginnings of His incarnational ministry, the implication of
which becomes palpable by virtue of His resurrection from the
dead. So Luke summarizes:

> After his suffering, he presented himself to them and
> gave many convincing proofs[7] that he was alive. He
> appeared to them over a period of forty days and spoke
> about the kingdom of God (v. 3).[8]

Luke will not allow the religion of Jesus to be grounded in
phenomena that are purely subjective and mystical. Instead,
Christianity is to be regarded as the product of concrete,
objective, historical realities: most specifically, a resurrected
and living Jesus who could be seen, heard, and touched–a
glorified man who ate food with His friends. Indeed, it is this
that legitimizes the gospel mission in a postmodern culture
that prizes inclusivity as the supreme virtue. Christians dare
to announce that eternal life is found in one, exclusive source.
But on what basis do we herald this exclusivity? The same was
appealed to by Paul as he declared the gospel to the pluralists
of Athens: the resurrection of Jesus Christ, which is the
ultimate verification of the truth of Christianity.

To summarize, the Jesus of history *began* His ministry
on earth; the Christ of glory *continues* His ministry on
earth. The ascension functions as the hinge in between; an
event that, far from implying Jesus' absence or inactivity,
calls attention to the location from where He rules as the
universal sovereign (*cf.* Acts 2:33-36). Yet this ascension
occurs only:

---

7. In using *tekmerion*, its only use in the NT, 'Luke could not have chosen a stronger
term to convey the sense of proof beyond doubt.' Peterson, *The Acts*, p. 104.

8. Mention of it at the opening and closing of Acts (1:3; 28:31) reveals its function as an *inclusio*. God's reign is the subtext of the narrative sandwiched in
between.

> ... after giving instructions through the Holy Spirit to
> the apostles he had chosen. (v. 2b)

Jesus is still the Spirit-filled man *par* excellence, even subsequent to His resurrection. As such, He provides His apostles with *'instructions.'* But this softens the meaning of the original word which actually speaks of an official sanction: 'To give definite orders, implying authority ... to command,'[9] 'to commission.'[10] The ESV gets closer to the original–*'after he had given them commands'*–yet clutters the issue by translating the Greek singular into a plural form, likely regarding it as a general reference to the entirety of Jesus' teaching during His post-resurrection period. But the participle means most literally, 'having given *commandment.*' That its singular emphasis should be preserved here in v. 3 is reinforced by the use of the singular synonym in the following verse, 'he gave them this *command*: "Do not leave Jerusalem, but wait for the gift my Father promised,"' which quite possibly serves as an elaboration of v. 3. Luke's point is this: 'Jesus was taken up to heaven after he had given a commandment through the Holy Spirit to the apostles he had chosen.'

The emphasis is obvious: this was Jesus' *last* command–His *concluding* command. Would it not seem logical to regard it as among His *ultimate* commands? Is it an overstatement to propose that the *final* words of the resurrected Lord are to be regarded as those of *first* importance, defying all accusations of ambiguity?

This is the emphasis of Luke's initial paragraph; that his first volume, the Gospel, is a record of the life and ministry of Jesus, climaxing in His verifiable resurrection from the dead and subsequent ascension–*but not before giving a specific command to His chosen sent ones.*

---

9. Louw and Nida, *Greek-English Lexicon*, vol. 1, p. 426.

10. Gottlob Schrenk, 'εντελλομαι,' *Theological Dictionary of the New Testament*, ed. Gerhard Kittel (Grand Rapids: William B. Eerdmans Publishing Company, 1965), vol. II, p. 544.

Section #3: The Ultimate Coming of Jesus Christ

> After he said this, he was taken up before their very
> eyes, and a cloud hid him from their sight. (v. 9)

To highlight that the apostles witness the ascension of Jesus,
Luke's account employs three different Greek verbs in vv. 9-11,
here translated: 'before their very eyes' (v. 9), 'looking intently'
(v. 10), and 'you have seen him go' (v. 11). But what *do* they see?
That Jesus is *'taken up'* portrays the ascension as a supernatural
act of God (indicated by the passive voice of the verb). Yet is
this 'vertical' movement to be regarded as the presupposition
of a location in space that can be pinpointed on an astrological
map? When a Christian from Bangkok and a Christian from
Miami look 'upward' to heaven as their anticipated home, they
both envision the same reality—an existential certainty assured
to them by the Scriptures. At the same time, owing to the influence of Pythagoras, they understand this home to be something separate from the direction of their gaze. In other words,
while this 'up-above-ness' encompasses reality, it is a reality that
transcends our own; therefore the movement *'up'* must be regarded metaphorically. Helpfully, Barth explains:

> Heaven ... is the sum of the inaccessible and incompre-
> hensible side of the created world, so that although it is
> not God Himself, it is the throne of God, the creaturely
> correspondence to His glory, which is veiled from man,
> and cannot be disclosed except on His initiative ... The
> point of the story (the ascension) is not that when Jesus
> left His disciples He visibly embarked upon a wonderful
> journey into space, but that when He left them He en-
> tered the side of the created world which was provision-
> ally inaccessible and incomprehensible ... the God-ward
> side of the universe, sharing His throne, existing and
> acting in the mode of God, and therefore to be remem-
> bered as such, to be known once for all as this exalted
> creature, this exalted man, and henceforth to be accept-
> ed as the One who exists in this form to all eternity ...[11]

---

11. Karl Barth, *Church Dogmatics*, 4 vols. (Edinburgh: T & T Clark, 1960), III/2,
pp. 453-454.

> He went to the place where no man can go, to the
> sphere within the created world which is hidden from
> that which is earthly, to the cosmic holy of holies.[12]

Adding to the supernatural aura of the ascension is the hiddenness of Jesus in a cloud. Peter, James, and John would never forget a prior, terrifying moment when, on the Mount of Transfiguration, Jesus was suddenly illuminated as bright as lightning itself (Luke 9:28-36). The cause of their fear, however, was not due solely to the remarkable nature of the experience, but owing to their acquaintance with the significance of such a cloud in the Hebrew Scriptures. The 'cloud' frequently served as a theophany, a visible manifestation of God's immediate presence, thus usually associated with His glory. It was the means by which God led the children of Israel out of Egypt through the wilderness during the day (Exod. 13:21; cf. 40:36-38). Moses encountered it more immediately at the tent of meeting where the Lord spoke to him 'face to face' (Exod. 33:9-11), and also on Mount Sinai at the replacing of the Ten Commandments where the Lord 'proclaimed his name' (Exod. 34:4-7). It was this cloud that engulfed the Tabernacle entirely at its completion (Exod. 40:34-35).[13] Here, at the ascension, it indicates Jesus' 'total envelopment in God's presence and glory.'[14] The apostles may have assumed initially that the cloud would dissipate, leaving Jesus alone with them as had occurred at the transfiguration site. But such would not be the case. His manner of being with them will no longer occur as it had in His initial coming.

> They were looking intently up into the sky as he was
> going, when suddenly two men dressed in white stood
> beside them. (v. 10)

---

12. *Ibid.*, IV/2, p. 153.

13. See also Exod. 16:10; 19:9; 24:15-18; 1 Kings 8:10-12; Ezek. 10:3-4.

14. Peterson, *Acts*, p. 115.

They are angels, most likely, a conclusion enhanced by the whiteness of their clothes.[15] As such, their presence reveals the heavenly character of this event. That there are 'two' is even more revealing, particularly when one recalls this as a fact similarly documented in Luke's account of the empty tomb (Luke 24:4). Why, at both the scene of the resurrection and the ascension, is attention given to the appearance of *two* supernatural beings? According to Old Testament legislation, *two* was the minimum number of witnesses required to establish a matter in court (Deut. 19:15). Their presence here is to function as trustworthy interpreters of the ascension, which they do by *posing a question* and *providing an explanation*, both of which presuppose a strong exhortation:

> 'Men of Galilee,' they said, 'why do you stand here looking into the sky?' (v. 11a)

It is a question of incredulity: 'What's the point of this? Sky-scanning will only lead to indolence,' an earthly immobilization by virtue of celestial obsession—a phenomenon not unlike that which, in recent years, resulted from the ministry of the late Harold Camping.[16] The angels then add an explanation to their question:

> 'This same Jesus, who has been taken from you into heaven, will come back in the same way you have seen him go into heaven.' (v. 11b)

Their inference? 'You will not bring Jesus back by gazing into the sky. He will return in His own good time.' More explicitly, they indicate that this will occur 'in the same way' the apostles have seen Him depart. But does this suggest that the return

---

15. And perhaps also by the prompter of attention *idou*—left untranslated in the NIV but rendered 'behold!' in the ESV.

16. Camping was a radio broadcaster and the president of *Family Radio*. Though best known for his predictions published in a book entitled *1994*, he had made both prior and subsequent predictions. His most recent were May 21, 2011 (the occasion of the rapture) and Oct. 21, 2011 (the end of the world).

of Jesus is little more than a movie of the ascension played in reverse? What, in fact, constitutes this 'sameness?'

The one to return is, literally, 'This Jesus,' which is modified by the participial phrase, 'the one having been taken up from you.' Hence the NIV rendering, *'This same Jesus.'* The event to which the angels refer, then, is not a mere 'return of the Jesus spirit,' or the 'eschatological advent of the Jesus life force,' or the 'final execution of the Jesus program.' This return is decidedly *personal:* the Son of God in His glorified human nature and body. Yet this 'sameness' is not just determined by the *person* returning. It is defined by the *manner* of His return: *'in the same way,'* the angels explain, signifying that the coming back of Jesus will be *visible* and *glorious* as His ascension has been[17]—a reality to which Jesus Himself had testified elsewhere, that people will 'see the Son of Man coming in a cloud with power and great glory' (Luke 21:27).[18]

This does not, however, deny distinguishable differences between the ascension and the Parousia. Though Jesus' return will be personal, it will not be private. Presently, eleven apostles witness His ascension. At His return 'every eye will see him' (Rev. 1:7; *cf.* Luke 17:24-25). Furthermore, though His ascension is a solitary experience, millions of holy ones (both angelic and human) will accompany Him as His entourage at His return:

> Whoever is ashamed of me and my words, the Son of Man will be ashamed of them when he comes in his glory and in the glory of the Father and of the holy angels. (Luke 9:26; *cf.* 2 Thess. 1:7)

---

17. Most literally, 'so will he come in the manner that you saw him going into heaven.'

18. 'Clouds serve as God's war chariot in the imagination of the OT poets and prophets ... Jesus, like God in the OT, rides on a cloud (Acts 1:9). One of the most pervasive images of Christ's return is as one who rides His cloud chariot into battle (Matt. 24:30; Mark 13:26; 14:62; Luke 21:27; Rev. 1:7; *cf.* Dan. 7:13).' Leland Ryken, James C. Wilhoit, Temper Longman, gen. eds., 'Cloud,' *Dictionary of Biblical Imagery* (Downers Grove: InterVarsity Press, 1998), p. 157. See also Ps. 18:9; 68:4; Isa. 19:1-2; Dan. 7:13; Nah. 1:3.

> For we believe that Jesus died and rose again, and so we
> believe that God will bring with Jesus those who have
> fallen asleep in him. According to the Lord's word, we
> tell you that we who are still alive, who are left until the
> coming of the Lord will not precede those who have
> fallen asleep. For the Lord himself will come down
> from heaven, with a loud command, with the voice of
> the archangel and with the trumpet call of God, and
> the dead in Christ will rise first. After that, we who are
> still alive and left will be caught up together with them
> in the clouds to meet the Lord in the air. And so we
> will be with the Lord forever. (1 Thess. 4:14-17)

In summary, the angelic testimony regarding the ascension
poses a question and *provides an explanation.* Considered together,
they *presuppose an exhortation—the* exhortation given by Jesus in
the immediately preceding paragraph. To be sure, the apostles
have seen Jesus depart. Similarly He will return. But in between
His *going and coming* there must be a corresponding *coming and
going:* the *Spirit* must come and *they* must go. The exhortation
presupposed by the angelic testimony to Jesus' ascension is
His unambiguous articulation of the mission of the church.

Section #2: The Intervening Commission of Jesus Christ

> On one occasion,[19] while he was eating with them,[20]
> he gave them this command: 'Do not leave Jerusalem,
> but wait for the gift my Father promised, which you
> have heard me speak about. For John baptized with
> water, but in a few days you will be baptized with the
> Holy Spirit.' (vv. 4-5)

Jesus urges the apostles to remain in the holy city. But for
what reason is He insistent? Given that this waiting is tied

---

19. It should be noted that v. 4 begins with *kai.* Though not translated by the NIV,
it does suggest a continuation from v. 3, over against the introduction of a new line
of thought disassociated from the immediate context.

20. The ESV translates this, 'And while staying with them.' But the precise translation of *synalizomai* is 'eating salt with' and is here used in the more extended sense
of sharing a meal (cf. Luke 24:36-48; Acts 10:41). Louw and Nida, *Greek-English
Lexicon,* p. 250.

to '*the gift my Father promised,*' it is safe to assume that His command is connected to the fulfillment of prophecy. Indeed, the Old Testament Scriptures anticipate a coming day of great restoration within Israel, one that would commence in the city of David. 'According to Luke's narrative map, all roads leading into God's salvation are to or from Jerusalem. It is a city built with the bricks of prophecy, and the fate of all creation depends on what happens there.'[21] Not only is Jerusalem associated with God's promise to rule His people through the Davidic kings (*e.g.*, 2 Sam. 7:4-17; Pss. 2, 110), and the epicenter of predictions regarding the nation as a whole (*e.g.*, Isa. 40:1-2; Jer. 30-33; Zech. 8),[22] it is the last days' location *to which* many people will be drawn and *from which* the word of the Lord will be sent forth (*e.g.*, Isa. 2:2-3; Micah 4:2). To inaugurate such a restoration, however, will necessitate a power external to God's people themselves; hence, according to Jesus, the promised gift for which the apostles must wait— elsewhere explained as being 'clothed with power from on high' (Luke 24:49). Both are references to the eschatological gift of the Holy Spirit, for which Acts 2 will supply an obvious example of Old Testament anticipation: Joel 2:28-32, which in its original setting concludes with a reference to deliverance in Jerusalem. And this is not a remote Old Testament notion supported by a solitary text. There are other references as well:

> ... till the Spirit is poured on us from on high ... (Isa. 32:15)

> I will pour out my Spirit on your offspring, and my blessing on your descendants. (Isa. 44:3)

---

21. Robert Wall, 'The Acts of the Apostles,' *The New Interpreter's Bible*, vol. 10 (Nashville: Abingdon Press, 2002), p. 41.

22. Hence, Luke's Gospel opens with godly Jews waiting for 'the consolation of Israel' (2:25) and 'the redemption of Jerusalem' (2:38). Some of the prophecies related to a renewed Jerusalem/Israel are tied to expectations of a Messiah: a new branch from David's line (Jer. 33:15-16), whose coming will be cause of rejoicing in Jerusalem (Zech. 9:9), and at which time her Temple is visited and her people cleansed (Mal. 3:1-4).

> I will give them an undivided heart and put a new
> spirit in them. (Ezek. 11:19)

> I will give you a new heart and put a new spirit in you
> ... And I will put my Spirit in you. (Ezek. 36:26-27)

> I will no longer hide my face from them, for I will
> pour out my Spirit on the people of Israel, declares the
> Sovereign LORD. (Ezek. 39:29)

These are prophetic anticipations of a great last days' gift: the indwelling Holy Spirit, the initial reception of whom Jesus here likens typologically to the experience of immersion. Just as John the Baptist overwhelmed people with water, so too the people of the new covenant will be deluged with the Holy Spirit.[23]

The men to whom Jesus speaks are not unfamiliar with the Old Testament Scriptures. It would not be unusual for them to associate the end times' gift of the Spirit with the advent of the Messiah and the restoration of Israel. It is, in fact, the Spirit of God who will make the rule of God 'a living and present reality to his people.'[24] Beyond this, it is important to remember that for the prior forty days Jesus has been speaking to the apostles about the kingdom of God. Admittedly, they had never before proven to be exceptional students. But Jesus is the ultimate teacher who, on at least one prior occasion, had opened their minds to understand the Scriptures (Luke 24:45). It would be careless to assume, then, that the question they direct to Jesus in v. 6 is a *non sequitur*—a fact reinforced by the inferential conjunction connecting v. 6 to v 5, more appropriately translated 'therefore,' or 'so,' as in the ESV:

> So when they had come together they asked him,
> 'Lord, will you at this time restore the kingdom to
> Israel?' (v. 6)

---

23. The one who baptizes 'with the Spirit' is here unidentified, though elsewhere his identity is made explicit (Matt. 3:11; Mark 1:8; Luke 3:16; John 1:33).

24. Stott, *The Message*, p. 40.

Two schools of interpretation have frequently set forth their respective understandings of this verse, both of which have resulted in a subsequent inability to appreciate the relationship between v. 6 and vv. 7-8. This has left the reader with the sense that Jesus' response to the apostles' seemingly irrelevant question is little more than a firm rebuke of their dimwittedness (v. 7), followed by a disconnected summary of the missionary program to which he is appointing them (v. 8). The classic dispensational interpretation, for example, regards the reply of Jesus as an implicit affirmation of a kingdom distinguished by God's unique blessing upon national Israel—which, nevertheless, has been postponed for a distant future that has been determined solely by the secret and sovereign purpose of God. The apostles, therefore, are urged to redirect their attention to more appropriate and immediate endeavors.[25] The interpretation commonly advanced by traditional reformed scholarship is to regard Jesus' response, not as a *postponement* of a nationalistic kingdom, but an unequivocal corrective to this gross distortion. Calvin himself comments, 'There are as many errors in this question as words.'[26] The kingdom of God is not to be regarded as a body politic, but as a universal and spiritual reign inaugurated and advanced by the means of the advent and empowerment of the Holy Spirit.[27]

The chief problem with each of these interpretations is found in their shared characteristic: both infer that Jesus avoids a direct answer to the apostles' question about the restoration

---

25. See J. D. Pentecost, *New Wine: A Study of Transition in the Book of Acts* (Grand Rapids: Kregel Publications, 2010), pp. 31-34.

26. John Calvin, *Commentary upon the Acts of the Apostles* (repr. ed., Grand Rapids: Baker Book House, 2003), p. 43.

27. As a representative of this view, Stott writes: 'Their question must have filled Jesus with dismay ... The verb, the noun and the adverb of their sentence all betray doctrinal confusion about the kingdom. For the verb *restore* shows that they were expecting a political and territorial kingdom; the noun *Israel* that they were expecting a national kingdom; and the adverbial clause *at this time* that they were expecting its immediate establishment. In his reply (7-8) Jesus corrected their mistaken notions of the kingdom's nature, extent and arrival.' Stott, *The Message*, p. 41.

of the kingdom and Israel (whether by implicit postponement
or outright rejection); more emphatically, the answer He
does supply changes the subject entirely! But Jesus' answer
neither relegates the kingdom to a distant future, nor does He
radically redefine their understanding of its essence, both of
which would assume the apostles' failure to comprehend the
emphasis and implications of His teaching for the prior forty
days. Look carefully at His initial reply:

> He said to them, 'It is not for you to know the times
> or dates the Father has set by his own authority.' (v. 7)

Jesus' answer does not fault the *fact* of Israel's restoration,
only the apostles' inquiry into the *timing* of it. Absent is any
denial of the expectation of restoration. Contrarily, Jesus en-
dorses this expectation by means of articulating the climactic
event that will inaugurate it: the coming of the Holy Spirit.
The question posed by the apostles, then, *is* the *logical* question. It demonstrates their appreciation of the connection
being made by Jesus, that the Spirit's outpouring *does* signal
the season of Israel's restoration. Their *misunderstanding* is
a failure to apprehend the dynamic of an inaugurated eschatology—their assumption that the kingdom of God would
erupt onto the scene of human history in the twinkling of
an eye, in one great cataclysmic moment. Few would debate
that the age to come has invaded this present age with the
initial advent of King Jesus and His saving accomplishments.
The reality long awaited through the centuries of biblical history has now been introduced. But it is only at His second
advent that the age to come supersedes entirely this present
age, with the result that the kingdom inaugurated becomes
the kingdom consummated. At present, then—during the
time between these two comings of Jesus—the ages overlap;
which means that the kingdom of God is simultaneously *already* and *not yet*.

Having yet to grasp this, it is no surprise that the apostles are concerned about the *timing* of the kingdom's con-

summation. Jesus, appropriately, redirects their attention to the *terms of its fulfillment*. Their burden is to know *when*. He wants them to know *how*.

> While Jesus thereby agrees with the theological subtext of the apostles' query—the Spirit's outpouring does indeed signal the season of Israel's restoration—he applies it to their vocation: God's reign will be reestablished among God's people not by some apocalypse from heaven but by a mission on earth.[28]

This means that v. 8 is not a detached response that bears an implicit rebuke. Rather, it is Jesus' answer to the question of the apostles in v. 6. It heralds the beginning of the process of the restoration of God's rule in Israel;[29] a fact that becomes even more obvious when one considers the Old Testament underpinnings to the following words of Jesus:

> But you will receive power when the Holy Spirit comes on you; and you will be my witnesses in Jerusalem, and in all Judea and Samaria, and to the ends of the earth. (v. 8)

We have already acknowledged that this verse provides the programmatic structure for the Acts narrative. It is now essential to recognize Jesus' words as a composite of phrases taken from the prophecy of Isaiah that anticipate a coming salvation brought about by God and His suffering Servant.[30] This can be easily displayed in three sets, each comprised of an Isaianic antecedent, followed by Jesus' corresponding allusion to it in Acts 1:8.

---

28. Wall, 'Acts,' p. 42.

29. 'While it must not be denied that the futuristic aspect is present in the Lukan conception of the restoration of Israel, the beginning of the process in Acts has to be acknowledged.' David W. Pao, *Acts and the Isaianic New Exodus* (Grand Rapids: Baker Academic, 2002), p. 96.

30. These ideas have been developed by others upon whom I am significantly dependent: Johnson, *The Message of Acts*, pp. 34-52, Pao, *Acts*, pp. 91-96, and Thompson, *Acts of the Risen Lord*, pp. 106-108.

Set #1

Isa. 32:15, *'till the Spirit is poured on us from on high'*[31]– *(an event that marks an end to the desolation of Judah and the inauguration of the new age).*

Acts 1:8, *'when the Holy Spirit comes on you.'*

Set #2

Isa. 43:10, *'You are my witnesses'*—(the people of God will become witnesses to the salvation that is uniquely God's when the new age appears). (*Cf.* Isa. 43:12; 44:8.)

Acts 1:8, *'you will be my witnesses.'*

Set #3

Isa. 49:6, *'It is too small a thing for you to be my servant to restore the tribes of Jacob and bring back those of Israel I have kept. I will also make you a light for the Gentiles, that my salvation may reach to the ends of the earth'*—(The ultimate servant of the Lord, Jesus, will not only restore the corporate servant of the Lord, Israel, this restoration will also include Gentiles.)

Acts 1:8, *'to the ends of the earth.'* (The ministry of the servant is extended to the servant community, which now functions as a witness that will be the means by which God's salvation reaches the ends of the earth.) (*Cf.* Acts 13:47.)

This brief comparison again confirms that Jesus' reply to the apostles' question is not a radical reinterpretation of the common expectations of Israel's restoration. His is not the language of postponement or negation. It is the affirmation that God's promises are to be fulfilled imminently. It is the language of promise and fulfillment set on the plane of redemptive history. But having established the *essence* of this commission—the restoration of Israel—what is the actual *substance* of it?

Note, firstly, the commission's promise:

... you will be my witnesses ... (v. 8b).

---

31. Though not reproduced in the Acts text, 'on high' is found in the parallel passage, Luke 24:49.

It is a recurring designation in Acts, a label applied almost exclusively to the Twelve; those who were 'witnesses of the life, suffering, and death of Jesus (which has taken place according to Scripture), of his resurrection, and of the message of forgiveness that they will proclaim.'[32] For example:

> ... it is necessary to choose one of the men who have been with us the whole time the Lord Jesus was living among us, beginning from John's baptism to the time when Jesus was taken up from us. For one of these must become a *witness* with us of his resurrection. (1:21, 22)

> God has raised this Jesus to life, and we are all *witnesses* of it. (2:32)

> You killed the author of life, but God raised him from the dead. We are *witnesses* of this. (3:15)

> God exalted him to his own right hand as Prince and Savior that he might bring Israel to repentance and forgive their sins. We are *witnesses* of these things. (5:31-32)

> We are *witnesses* of everything he did in the country of the Jews and in Jerusalem. They killed him by hanging him on a cross, but God raised him from the dead on the third day and caused him to be seen. He was not seen by all the people, but by *witnesses* whom God had already chosen—by us who ate and drank with him after he rose from the dead. (10:39-41)

> When they had carried out all that was written about him, they took him down from the cross and laid him in a tomb. But God raised him from the dead, and for many days he was seen by those who had traveled with him from Galilee to Jerusalem. They are now his *witnesses* to our people (13:29-31).

And here is this commission, '... *you will be my witnesses.*' It is a *promise* that announces what will occur in the future. It

---

32. J. Beutler, 'μαρτυς,' *Exegetical Dictionary of the New Testament*, eds. H. Balz and G. Schneider, (Grand Rapids: William B. Eerdmans Publishing Company, 1993), vol. 2, pp. 394-395.

may also be a *command* mandating something that must occur in the future.[33] Hence, Larkin refers to this as 'a command-promise.'[34] Furthermore, when Jesus says, 'you will be *my* witnesses,' He is not merely assuring the apostles that they will *belong to Him* (a possessive genitive); rather, more principally, that *the witness they bear must be of Him* (an objective genitive) (*cf.* Luke 24:48). Christian witness is not to be mistaken for the promotion of a political agenda, nor reinterpreted as the advocacy for a compelling expression of social justice. The crucified and resurrected Lord is the object of witness in Acts 1:8, a command-promise given to His apostles, free of any haziness or ambiguity.

Secondly, consider *the commission's extent:*

> ... in Jerusalem, and in all Judea and Samaria, and to the ends of the earth (v. 8c).

Motivated by a well-intended desire to establish the relevance of this commission, many utilize it as a transferable paradigm, substituting the geographical references announced by Jesus for those respective to their own unique contexts. Some, for example, might apply it follows: '... you will be my witnesses in San Francisco, and in all Silicon Valley and Santa Cruz, and to the ends of the earth.' Others would employ it to their setting: '... you will be my witnesses in London, and in all Essex and Suffolk, and to the ends of the earth.' Doing this uncritically, however, fails to give adequate appreciation to the biblical/theological significance of the locations stipulated by Jesus. Thus it undermines one's capacity to identify this declaration as the heralding of the inaugural fulfillment of Israel's restoration—which, in turn, adds to the mistaken notion that the words of Jesus in v. 8 have no meaningful relationship to the question asked by the apostles in v. 6.

---

33. Daniel Wallace, *Greek Grammar Beyond the Basics* (Grand Rapids: Zondervan Publishing House, 1996), pp. 568-569.

34. William J. Larkin, Jr., *Acts*, IVPNTC (Downers Grove: InterVarsity Press, 1995), p. 41.

But as has already been seen, Acts 1:8 is a promise of the *way* in which God's plan for the restoration of Israel will unfold: by the means of apostolic witness which is to commence '*in Jerusalem,*' the epicenter of Israel's religious life. It will then extend to '*all Judea and Samaria,*' representing the southern and northern kingdoms respectively—the two portions into which, following the death of Solomon, the kingdom divided. Any expectation of Israel's restoration would necessarily assume a reunited kingdom, a subject of emphatic Old Testament prophecy (Ezek. 37). Finally, its restless advance will spread to '*the ends of the earth.*' Recalling the Isaianic antecedent to which Jesus alludes in Acts 1:8, '*I will also make you a light for the Gentiles, that my salvation may reach to the ends of the earth*' (Isa. 49:6), it is plain that the phrase He uses here, '*the ends of the earth,*' is both 'geographic and ethnic in scope, inclusive of all people and all locales.'[35] Surely James Dunn is right when he says, 'Paul's success in bringing the gospel to Rome was the most significant step on the way to that goal, but not the goal itself'[36]—a conclusion reinforced by the parallel declaration, '*repentance for the forgiveness of sins will be preached in his name to all nations*' (Luke 24:47). Jointly, these geographic/ethnic references are three stages in the outworking of the restoration of Israel: 1) the dawn of salvation in Jerusalem ['*you will be my witnesses in Jerusalem*']; 2) the reconstitution and reunification of Israel ['*and in all Judea and Samaria*']; and, 3) the inclusion of Gentiles within the people of God ['*and to the ends of the earth*'].[37]

Practically, it is safe to assume that the mere mention of each geographic/ethnic reference was fraught with its own corresponding anxiety for the apostles. '*Jerusalem?* You're kidding. It was the site of the Lord's crucifixion.' '*Judea?*

---

35. Darrell L. Bock, *Acts*, ECNT (Grand Rapids: Baker Academic, 2007), p. 65.

36. James Dunn, *The Acts of the Apostles* (Valley Forge: Trinity Press International, 1996), p. 11.

37. Pao, *Acts*, p. 95.

But we were rejected there.' 'Samaria? Witness to those half-breeds?' 'The ends of the earth? The Gentiles hate us as much as we hate them!' And beyond these apprehensions, there was the dawning realization of the mission's magnitude: 'All people in all places? The scope of the task is infinitely beyond us. On what basis can Jesus expect us to achieve this?'

It is the recognition of the promise and extent of this commission that directs us, thirdly, to the commission's resource:

> But you will receive power when the Holy Spirit comes
> on you ... (v. 8a)

Jesus speaks of a coming event that hearkens back to an Old Testament prototype: the departure into heaven of Elijah the prophet (2 Kings 2). On that occasion, prior to his leaving, Elisha asks his mentor to bequeath a 'double portion' of his prophetic spirit. Elijah acknowledges that his apprentice has asked for a 'difficult thing,' but that if Elisha sees him when he departs, he will receive the desired empowerment. Elijah is subsequently met by a chariot of fire and taken to heaven in a whirlwind, an event that Elisha does see. Thus he is granted an abundant endowment of the Spirit for the sake of his prophetic work.

Similarly, the apostles are granted the privilege of witnessing the glorious departure of Jesus. As a result, they will become the recipients of the Spirit and His abundant empowerment in a few days hence (Acts 2:1-4). Like Elisha, they too were not unacquainted with the Spirit's ministry, but had witnessed firsthand the effects of His power in the ministry of their master who, before them, was anointed with the Spirit as God's chosen Servant for the purpose of prophetic proclamation:

> The Spirit of the Lord is on me, because he has
> anointed me to proclaim good news to the poor.
> He has sent me to proclaim freedom to the prison-
> ers and recovery of sight for the blind, to set the
> oppressed free, to proclaim the year of the Lord's
> favor. (Luke 4:18-19)

It is the anticipation of an analogous experience that Jesus promises to His apostolic witnesses in Acts 1:8, a unique resourcing they will receive for the herculean task of a universal witness that is now set before them: the indwelling Holy Spirit with His attending power.[38] It is the dynamic means by which the commission's promise and extent will be realized, here set forth by Jesus as an unpretentious case of cause and effect:

> But you will receive power when the Holy Spirit comes on you; and you will be my witnesses in Jerusalem, and in all Judea and Samaria, and to the ends of the earth.

Thus God's promise regarding the restoration of Israel will be fulfilled.

The Primary Task of All Christians

Does Acts 1:1-11 have any ongoing relevance for contemporary Christians? Examining this passage carefully may leave you feeling initially as if it has no applicability to you. It is true that Christians today cannot be witnesses in the same *foundational* sense that the apostles were. But this does not mean that those who are not direct observers of the death and resurrection of Jesus have no responsibility to declare these events. As the narrative of Acts unfolds, Luke makes it very clear that all who repent and believe in Jesus Christ are given the indwelling Holy Spirit and can be empowered to speak the word of God boldly (Acts 4:31). When he records the initial outward advancement of the Christian mission, he highlights the fact that those who take the gospel into the regions of Judea and Samaria are not apostles but ordinary Christians driven from Jerusalem by persecution (Acts 8:1)—and that they 'preached the word wherever they went' (8:4). In the same way, Luke indicates that Christians (other than the apostles) take the gospel to Phoenicia, Cyprus, and Antioch (11:19-21). Luke's implicit

---

38. The circumstantial participle, here translated, '*when the Holy Spirit comes on you,*' specifies the moment in time when the apostles receive power.

assumption is that all who appropriate the apostles' testimony qualify as witnesses. Indeed, this is the mission of the entire Christian church, the holy commission of every person who has embraced the resurrected Christ and been given the gift of the empowering Holy Spirit. We are thus less than Christian when we fail to embrace the direct responsibility of taking the life-giving message of the gospel to the ends of the earth, which most certainly includes the diverse and unreached cultural groups embedded within our own neighborhoods.

Let me ask you once again: Were it your aim to discover *the primary mission* of the church of Jesus Christ by observing exclusively the *practice* of professing Christian congregations in your community, would your findings be well-defined and conclusive? Or would they be inconsistent and confused?

> The fact that the Great Commission is the last instruction of the risen, now ascended and imminently returning Lord gives it great weight. He is not mentioning an optional ministry activity for individuals with cross-cultural interests and churches with surplus funds. The Great Commission is the primary task the Lord left his church. The church must always be a missionary church; the Christian must always be a world Christian.[39]

Nothing, however noble, can ever be an adequate substitute for it.

Are you mindful of this mission? It is one that simultaneously stretches backward to encompass the ancient promises of God, and forward to their ultimate consummation. It is a mission so simply defined that it defies any accusation of ambiguity. It is a mission that requires your role as a witness to the world of the saving death, burial, and resurrection of Jesus Christ.

Are you acquainted with this power for witness? If you are a Christian you have been given an indwelling resource related

---

39. Larkin, *Acts*, p. 43.

specifically to this task: the Spirit of the living God. These two, in fact, are experientially intertwined: the power of the Spirit and the work of witness. So much so that the work of witness is entirely ineffective apart from the power of the Spirit, and the power of the Spirit is nearly insensible apart from the work of witness.

Are you a Christian? These, for you, are the final words of first importance:

> But you will receive power when the Holy Spirit comes on you; and you will be my witnesses in Jerusalem, and in all Judea and Samaria, and to the ends of the earth. (v. 8)

3

WAITING

It is striking that at almost every important turning point
in the narrative of God's redemptive action in Acts
we find a mention of prayer.
DAVID G. PETERSON

The spiritual history of a mission or church
is written in its prayer life.
ARTHUR MATTHEWS

The church does not perform anything
by means of angelic intervention, or by invocations,
or by any other wicked or curious art;
but by calling on the name of our Lord Jesus Christ,
she has been accustomed to work miracles
for the advantage of mankind.
IRENAEUS

[12]Then the apostles returned to Jerusalem from the hill called the
Mount of Olives, a Sabbath day's walk from the city. [13]When they
arrived, they went upstairs to the room where they were staying. Those
present were Peter, John, James and Andrew; Philip and Thomas,
Bartholomew and Matthew; James son of Alphaeus and Simon the
Zealot, and Judas son of James. [14]They all joined together constantly
in prayer, along with the women and Mary the mother of Jesus, and
with his brothers.

[15]In those days Peter stood up among the believers (a group numbering
about a hundred and twenty) [16]and said, 'Brothers and sisters, the
Scripture had to be fulfilled in which the Holy Spirit spoke long ago
through David concerning Judas, who served as guide for those who
arrested Jesus. [17]He was one of our number and shared in our ministry.'

[18](With the payment he received for his wickedness, Judas bought a field; there he fell headlong, his body burst open and all his intestines spilled out. [19]Everyone in Jerusalem heard about this, so they called that field in their language Akeldama, that is, Field of Blood.)

[20]'For,' said Peter, 'it is written in the Book of Psalms:

"May his place be deserted;
> let there be no one to dwell in it,"

and,

"May another take his place of leadership."

[21]Therefore it is necessary to choose one of the men who have been with us the whole time the Lord Jesus was living among us, [22]beginning from John's baptism to the time when Jesus was taken up from us. For one of these must become a witness with us of his resurrection.'

[23]So they nominated two men: Joseph called Barsabbas (also known as Justus) and Matthias. [24]Then they prayed, 'Lord, you know everyone's heart. Show us which of these two you have chosen [25]to take over this apostolic ministry, which Judas left to go where he belongs.' [26]Then they cast lots, and the lot fell to Matthias; so he was added to the eleven apostles.

(Acts 1:12-26)

Hoist the Sails

I have never been very good at waiting, at least not that I can remember. I *will* wait ... if I am *forced* to wait. But waiting is at cross-purposes with everything natural to me. It can make me difficult to live with, and difficult to work with—because, for all of the wrong reasons, I am just not very good at it.

Waiting.

Sometimes God makes us wait. Sometimes He is the author of our waiting. Why? It is a provocative question—and one for which the Bible supplies distinct answers, if not comprehensive ones. Nevertheless, it is the extraneous question given the specific passage before us—Acts 1:12-26—where the essential question with relationship to waiting is not 'Why?' but 'How?'

As we have discovered, the resurrected Lord has defined the mission of His church: '... *you will be my witnesses.*' Furthermore, He has unambiguously articulated the extent of this mission: '... *in Jerusalem, and in all Judea and Samaria, and to the ends of the earth.*' But clarity notwithstanding, are the capacities to achieve this work restricted to the energies, abilities, and potencies of those called to it? Thankfully not, in that Jesus additionally promises an ample resource of supernatural proportions: '*But you will receive power ...*' An access of power, however, which is specifically dependent upon a historical event prophetically anticipated: '... *when the Holy Spirit comes on you.*' It is a *time-based* pledge, a fact established more emphatically in Jesus' earlier command: '*Do not leave Jerusalem, but wait for the gift my Father promised.*' It is an echo of His exhortation in Luke's Gospel: '*I am going to send you what my Father has promised; but stay in the city until you have been clothed with power from on high*' (Luke 24:49). Jesus is unequivocal: the apostles are not to commence the mission until they are resourced for it. Though the inauguration of God's kingdom is on the verge of realization—the restoration of Israel that will spread to the ends of the earth—such will remain unrealized until the Holy Spirit descends to indwell and empower the followers of Jesus. So what do they do during the intervening time, the period between the ascent of Jesus '*into heaven*' (1:11) and the descent of a sound like the blowing of a violent wind '*from heaven*' (2:1)? They wait.

But for how long do they wait? Consider the chronological markers. It was during the *Passover* season that Jesus was crucified and subsequently resurrected on the third day. It is on Pentecost, fifty days later, that the Spirit will descend upon these Christians. Meanwhile, Luke's narrative indicates that Jesus has already engaged in a post-resurrection teaching ministry that has spanned forty days, concluding with His ascension. Therefore, the period of time the apostles are required to wait for the advent of the Spirit is *ten days*. You say, 'But this isn't a too terribly long time to wait. Even *you* could manage this.' You may be right ... especially if I was aware of the waiting boundary. But what of the apostles? Are they cognizant of this time frame? Is there anything in the text to suggest an awareness of the limitations to their waiting; that the inauguration of the long-awaited last days will burst upon them in just a week and a half? All they have, apparently, is the promise of Jesus: 'But you will receive power when the Holy Spirit comes on you; and you will be my witnesses in Jerusalem, and in all Judea and Samaria, and to the ends of the earth.' This raises a question of practicality that is worthy of consideration:

How do they wait, as they wait, for the fulfillment of God's promise?

And what about you? How do you wait for the yet-to-be-fulfilled promises God has made on the pages of His word? What about the promise of complete freedom from sin and its effects? What about the promise of perfect intimacy with other human beings? What about the promise of joy at being in the unshielded presence of the glory of God? What about the promise of reunion with our family members who have died and preceded us to heaven? What about the promise of never-ending life in the new creation? These, along with so many others, are promises God has made to all Christians. Are you waiting well? How do you wait for the fulfillment of God's great redemptive promises?

A young boy, who for weeks had been eager with anticipation, went on a sailboat outing with his grandfather. To his disappointment, however, there was very little breeze, which resulted in the boat not moving through the water as quickly as he would have liked. So he asked: 'Grandpa, will the wind come?' 'Yes,' the old man warmly replied, 'the wind will come, though I can't say when. In the meantime, let's hoist the sails.'[1]

It is an image that wonderfully captures the essence of the ten-day waiting period here in Acts 1:12-26. The

---

1. This is a fictional story developed from an idea found in R. Kent Hughes, *Acts: The Church Afire* (Wheaton: Crossway Books, 1996), p. 24.

apostles 'hoist the sails'—that is, they ready themselves until the wind of the promised Holy Spirit blows upon them in fulfillment.

An Active Waiting

> Then the apostles returned to Jerusalem from the hill called the Mount of Olives, a Sabbath day's walk from the city. (v. 12)

This is not to infer that the ascension occurred on a Sabbath day (highly unlikely if this takes place precisely forty days from resurrection Sunday). It is a reference to a traditional Jewish means of measuring the distance traveled by the apostles in their return to Jerusalem: approximately two-thirds of a mile. Mention of it here underscores their immediate faithfulness to Jesus' instructions (1:4).

> When they arrived, they went upstairs to the room where they were staying. (v. 13a)

The use of the definite article in the original text adds an emphasis not conveyed by our English translations: 'they went up to *the* upper room'—that is, a room apparently well known to the early Christian community. It may be a reference to the location where Jesus gathered with these same apostles prior to His crucifixion; and, perhaps, the room where He appeared to them on the evening of His resurrection—both occasions distinguished by His promise of the coming Holy Spirit.[2] At this gathering, however, it is not only the apostles who are present. Others are among them:

> Those present were Peter, John, James and Andrew; Philip and Thomas, Bartholomew and Matthew;

---

2. Admittedly, it is not possible be certain about which room Luke is referring. He does use a different word here (*hyperoon*) than that used of the last supper location (*anagaion*). Other suggestions have included: their gathering place on the day of Pentecost (2:1), and the home of Mary the mother of John Mark (12:12). In any case, it must be a room of significant size given the number of people it accommodates, though it appears only the apostles were residing there.

> James the son of Alphaeus and Simon the Zealot, and
> Judas son of James. They all joined together constantly
> in prayer, along with the women and Mary the mother
> of Jesus, and with his brothers. (vv. 13b-14)

Notice that specific mention is made of the family of Jesus
(*cf.* Mark 6:3); in particular, that '*his brothers*' are among this
gathering—a fact that is nothing short of astounding, given
their open antagonism to Jesus in the earlier Gospel accounts.
'He is out of his mind,' they once said of Him (Mark 3:21).
At another point they taunted Him openly, a contemptuous
display interpreted by the Gospel writer as follows: 'For even his
own brothers did not believe in him' (John 7:5). The incarnate
Lord was no stranger to a divided family. Living as man in a
fallen world necessarily included the experience of a home-
life marked by profound sibling hostility.[3] Consequently, to
now read that His brothers are among this gathering of His
followers is nothing short of astounding. It reveals something
transformational. What accounts for it? Jesus' resurrection
from the dead; more particularly, His personal resurrection
appearance to James, His brother (1 Cor. 15:7)—who not only
appears with this initial group of believers, but will eventually
become the leader of the Jerusalem church and the author of
an inspired New Testament letter. Mary, the mother of Jesus,
is also among these disciples. This will prove to be her final
appearance on the pages of the New Testament; and fittingly
so, in that she who was formerly overshadowed by the Spirit in
the conception of her Savior-son will be present at the advent
of the Spirit who will give birth to the church.

In addition to the family of Jesus, Luke calls attention
to '*the women*' who are assembled in this upper room. It is
unlikely that these are the wives of the apostles (who played no
role in Luke's first volume), but rather the women to whom
he has previously called attention: those who traveled with

---

3. This is a fact that qualifies him as a sympathetic high priest able to resonate with
the domestic heartbreak experienced by nearly all people.

Jesus and supported Him financially out of their own means (Luke 8:1-3), who were at Calvary when He was crucified (Luke 23:49, 55-56), and who were the first witnesses of the resurrection (Luke 24:1-10, 22-24). This is a prominent feature of Luke's writing—the unique attention he gives to women.[4] In many ways it foreshadows the theological declaration that will explicitly be made in the not-too-distant future: 'There is neither Jew nor Gentile, neither slave nor free, nor is there male or female, for you are all one in Christ Jesus' (Gal. 3:28). As with ethnic and economic barriers, gender barriers are being abolished by the gospel, here made evident by the indication that women are gathered with the men for prayer.[5] Throughout Acts, female followers of Jesus continue to factor prominently in the mission of the church (*e.g.*, Acts 2:17-18; 12:12; 18:18-26; 21:8-9).

This gathering, then, includes the family of Jesus and His prominent female disciples. His chosen apostles are now among them as well, having obediently returned to Jerusalem from the Mount of Olives. But not *all* are present and accounted for. The apostolic band, frequently identified throughout the New Testament as *'the Twelve,'* is minus one. *Eleven* names appear on this list, rendering it conspicuously *unfinished*. As David Peterson pithily states: 'The circle of the

---

4. In Luke's infancy narrative, five persons speak by the power of the Holy Spirit to proclaim Jesus' place in salvation history, supplying theological understanding and perspective to the event of His birth. Of these five, three are women (Elizabeth, Mary, and Anna). Luke indicates that Jesus heals a woman subject to bleeding for twelve years and whom He addresses affectionately as 'Daughter' (Luke 8:43-48). He heals the woman crippled for eighteen-years to whom Jesus refers as 'a daughter of Abraham,' a significant status marker for a woman (Luke 13:11-17). Jesus raises the son of the widow of Nain (Luke 7:11-17). Luke cites Jesus as referring to women as positive examples of faith: the persistent widow (Luke 18:1-8) and the woman (perhaps a prostitute?) who anointed His feet (Luke 7:36-50). He commends Mary for sitting at His feet and listening to His teaching (Luke 10:38-42).

5. 'Given the culture's usual downplaying of women's public roles, the equal participation of women is noteworthy, especially their apparent mixing with the men.' Craig Keener, *The IVP Bible Background Commentary* (Downer's Grove: InterVarsity Press, 1993), p. 325.

Twelve has been broken.'[6] Missing from it is the one name that, for obvious reasons, always appears last in every other listing of the apostles: Judas Iscariot. Is this of any significance for the apostolic Christians who 'hoist the sails' and wait for the sacred wind?

Having identified all parties present, Luke then writes:

> They all joined together constantly in prayer ... (v. 14a)

Waiting for God was not indolence or passive inactivity on the part of these Christians. Nor was it the abandonment of effort. Waiting for God was an aggressive activity under His command. Moreover, it proves to be a *community project* as these disparate Christians 'joined together' with one mind and passion.[7] It is the first of several occasions in Acts when the followers of Jesus pray as a display of their active waiting upon God. For example, at the appointment of an apostolic replacement:

> *Then they prayed,* 'Lord, you know everyone's heart. Show us which of these two you have chosen to take over this apostolic ministry, which Judas left to go where he belongs.' (1:24-25)

After their first experience of persecution:

> ... Peter and John went back to their own people and reported all that the chief priests and the elders had said to them. When they heard this, *they raised their voices together in prayer to God ... After they prayed,* the place where they were meeting was shaken. And they were all filled with the Holy Spirit and spoke the word of God boldly. (Acts 4:23-31)

When it became necessary to appoint official servants to serve the needs of the congregation:

> They chose Stephen, a man full of faith and of the Holy Spirit; also Philip, Procorus, Nicanor, Timon,

---

6. Peterson, *The Acts*, p. 119.

7. One of Luke's favorite words, *homothymadon*, means more than sharing a location. It conveys the notion of common consent, mutual agreement, unanimity. Louw and Nida, *Greek English Lexicon*, vol. 1, p. 368.

Parmenas, and Nicolas from Antioch ... They
presented these men to the apostles, *who prayed and
laid their hands on them.* (6:5-6)

When the full inclusion of the Samaritans needed to be
confirmed:

... *they prayed* for the new believers there that they
might receive the Holy Spirit. (8:15)

When Peter had been delivered from imprisonment and
execution:

... he went to the house of Mary the mother of John,
also called Mark, where *many people had gathered and
were praying.* (12:12)

As church leaders were seeking insight for the first missionary
journey:

... they were worshipping the Lord and fasting, the
Holy Spirit said, 'Set apart for me Barnabas and Saul
for the work to which I have called them.' So after *they
had fasted and prayed,* they placed their hands on them
and sent them off. (13:2-3)

When newly planted congregations were in need of pastoral
leadership:

Paul and Barnabas appointed elders for them in each
church and, *with prayer and fasting,* committed them to
the Lord, in whom they had put their trust. (14:23)

At the conclusion of Paul's sermon to the Ephesian elders:

... he *knelt down with all of them and prayed.* (20:36)

'Every great decision in the apostolic period, and in the whole
life of early Christianity, is sustained by persistent prayer.'[8]
Certainly the narrative of Acts sustains this assertion. And
here, at the very outset of the Christian movement in Acts 1:14,
Luke indicates that these pre-Pentecost believers were in

---

8. Walter Grundmann, 'καρτερεω, προσκαρτερεω, προσκαρτερησις,' *TDNT*,
vol. III, p. 618.

prayer 'constantly,' a verbal idea that means to be resolute and persistent, if not obstinate.[9] It is the exact description used by Luke to describe the post-Pentecost Christians: 'They *devoted themselves* to the apostles' teaching and to fellowship, to the breaking of bread and to *prayer*' (2:42). It was this kind of praying that was not only modeled by Jesus (Luke 6:12), it was urged strongly upon the apostles by Him—that they should 'always pray and never give up' (Luke 18:1).[10]

Of course, one might legitimately respond: 'But there is nothing in the immediate text to indicate that Jesus commanded the apostles to pray; they were merely to wait.' This is true. So the obvious question follows: 'Why *are* they so tenacious in prayer?' Once again, they do have the example of Jesus' life—that *He* prayed at His baptism in anticipation of the Holy Spirit coming upon Him (Luke 3:21-22). And they also have His definitive instruction: 'If you then, though you are evil, know how to give good gifts to your children, how much more will your Father in heaven give the Holy Spirit to those who ask him!' (Luke 11:13). The apostles, then, are 'hoisting the sails' and preparing for the wind. But given the uniqueness of this situation, someone could reply: 'What is the purpose of fervently praying for something that God has already promised to give? Doesn't this make prayer gratuitous and irrelevant?' But this logical appeal must be answered by a clearer logic: 'How may a person pray expectantly for anything that has not been promised?' The promises of God provide His people with the *warrant* to pray, along with the assurance that He will listen. William Willimon captures this perfectly:

> It is up to the risen Christ to make good on his promise to bestow the Spirit and to restore the kingdom to Israel. In a sense this is what prayer is—the bold, even

---

9. The periphrastic participle *proskarterountes* used with the imperfect *esan* stresses the continuous nature of their prayers. Bauer, *A Greek-English Lexicon*, p. 881.

10. Prayer is a pervasive theme in both of Luke's volumes (Luke 1:10; 3:21; 5:16; 6:12; 9:18, 28-29; 11:1-4; 18:1; 22:41-44, 46; Acts 1:24-25; 2:42; 4:24-30; 6:6; 8:15; 9:11, 40; 10:2, 9, 30; 12:5, 12; 13:3; 14:23; 16:25; 20:36; 21:5; 28:8).

arrogant effort on the part of the community to hold God to his promises. In praying, 'Thy kingdom come, thy will be done,' we pray that God will be true to himself and give us what has been promised. Prayer is thus boldness born out of confidence in the faithfulness of God to the promises he makes, confidence that God will be true to himself. What may appear as prayerful insolence by the church in praying that we shall receive the Spirit, the kingdom, the power, and restoration is in fact the deepest humility, the church's humble realization that only God can give what the church most desperately needs.[11]

Therefore, the call to wait is not an invitation to dormancy. It is a divinely ordained opportunity to 'hoist the sails.' Hence, the apostolic Christians pray constantly. *It is how they wait, as they wait, for the fulfillment of God's promise.* Is this of true of you as you wait for the fulfillment of God's promises? Are you waiting actively and aggressively ... by praying persistently?

The Apostasy of the Apostle

In those days Peter stood up among the believers[12] (a group numbering about a hundred and twenty) and said, 'Brothers and sisters, the Scriptures had to be fulfilled in which the Holy Spirit spoke long ago through David concerning Judas, who served as a guide for those who arrested Jesus. He was one of our number and shared in our ministry.' (vv. 15-17)

As mentioned earlier, the name of Judas Iscariot consistently appears at the last position in every recorded list of the apostles. Also true is the repeated appearance of a name at the

---

11. William H. Willimon, *Acts* (Atlanta: John Knox Press, 1988), p. 27.

12. The NIV appropriately translates *adelphon* as 'believers' so as to contrast the Christian application of the term with its familial use at the conclusion of v. 14. *Adelphos* is regularly used to include females when a group of believers is in view (1:15, 16; 6:3; 9:30; 10: 23; 11:1, 12, 29; 12:17; 14:2; 15:3, 22, 32, 33, 40; 17:6, 10, 14; 18:18, 27; 21:7, 17, 20; 28:14, 15). In 1:16 *andres* might be regarded as more explicitly masculine, but the context suggests otherwise. The phrase *andres adelphoi* refers to males and females together.

first position in such lists: Peter. This, too, is not coincidental, but indicative of Jesus' appointment of Peter to a position of first among equals, an idea conveyed openly by Jesus even as He anticipates Peter's scandalous fall:

> 'Simon, Simon, Satan has asked to sift all of you as wheat. But I have prayed for you, Simon, that your faith may not fail. And when you have turned back, strengthen your brothers.' (Luke 22:31-32)

It is the very thing Peter now begins to do in this upper room: strengthen his brothers and sisters. How? By functioning as an interpreter of the Scripture (here defined as the words of the Holy Spirit spoken through human instrumentality, *i.e.*, David). For what reason? That these Christians might do whatever is necessary to prepare themselves for Pentecost. Not only, then, are they relentlessly engaged in prayer. Their waiting has also included a fresh examination of the Old Testament Scriptures, now seen through the interpretive lens that has been recently supplied for them by Jesus (Luke 24:25-27, 32, 44-47). But what has Peter discovered in the process of appropriating this 'Christian' hermeneutic? Two 'necessities' from the Psalms that are immediately relevant to the challenge presently facing them.

Despite the feverish schemes and manipulations of Jesus' enemies, they could never effectively silence Him until Judas approached them with insider access—he who '*served as a guide for those who arrested Jesus.*' Luke's Gospel states it chillingly:

> Then Satan entered into Judas called Iscariot, who was of the number of the twelve. He went away and conferred with the chief priests and officers how he might betray him to them. And they were glad, and agreed to give him money. So he consented and sought an opportunity to betray him to them in the absence of a crowd. (Luke 22:3-6, esv)

That Luke is conspicuous about the treacherous nature of this act is made evident by his reference to Judas as '*of the number of*

the Twelve'—a label he later reiterates when identifying the Gethsemane betrayer, 'one of the Twelve' (Luke 22:47). Yet might this
repeated designation expose something more, a sense of humiliation unique to the apostolic band? Sin has insidiously reached
into the innermost circle of Jesus' followers and left them with
an open wound. The resonance of this is overheard again in the
similar language Peter uses here as he recollects of Judas:

> He was one of our number and shared in our ministry.
> (v. 17)

Peter has been deeply grieved by this betrayal; perhaps, even
ashamed by it. No doubt, such is the case for all in this small
band of Christ-followers. But Peter is now convinced that
Judas' deception must not become a cause for disheartenment
or despair. The budding Christian community is to set this
betrayal within the context of the revealed purpose of God.
This 'apparent tragedy' is to be understood by the means of
its typological antecedent—namely, that the ancient psalmist's
laments over the treachery of his own close associates reach
their climax in the Messiah by one intimate to Him. Before
doing this, Luke adds a brief parenthetical digression for
those who (like Theophilus?) are unacquainted with the
circumstances of Judas' demise.[13]

> (With the payment he received for his wickedness,
> Judas bought a field; there he fell headlong, his body
> burst open and all his intestines spilled out. Everyone
> in Jerusalem heard about this, so they called that field
> in their language Akeldama, that is, Field of Blood.)
> (vv. 18-19)

Though Christians throughout the years have made various
attempts to rehabilitate Judas, the New Testament describes or

---

13. There is no need to explain this to those present in the upper room. Luke
indicates in v. 19 that everyone in Jerusalem was well acquainted with these details. Moreover, he translates Akeldama as 'Field of Blood' for the benefit of those
unfamiliar with Aramaic, an unnecessary step for the Aramaic speakers gathered
with Peter.

portrays him as a traitor (Luke 6:16), a hypocrite (Luke 22:47), a betrayer (Luke 22:48; Matt. 26:25), a person in whom Satan entered (Luke 22:3; John 13:2), and the treasurer of the apostolic company who would frequently pilfer from their accumulated resources (John 12:6; 13:29). Ultimately, as a rank lover of money, he initiated the process of handing over Jesus to the religious leaders, perhaps hoping that the wages earned for his treachery would secure a more comfortable economic position and higher social status.[14] But the end result is a gory suicide for the apostle who becomes an apostate,[15] a fate not entirely dissimilar to that of a later couple who, like Judas, seek financial profit through the exploitation of things spiritual (Acts 5:1-10).[16]

The betrayal of Jesus Christ was the foulest crime ever committed. Nevertheless, the thoughtful critic of Christianity (and even a Christian insider) might be inclined to raise the obvious and poignant questions:

> You say Jesus is the Son of God, Israel's Messiah, Saviour and Restorer, come to right our wrongs and to expose the priests' corrupt abuse of their sacred office for money? How then did He not know any better than to choose a man like Judas to be one of His chief companions, representatives and, if you please,

---

14. The word *chorion* may be better understood as a parcel of land, a property, or even possibly 'a term for a small estate.' Bock, *Acts*, p. 83.

15. Matthew's account of the events leading up to and culminating in the death of Judas includes details that are different from those in Acts. These are not contradictory narratives however, but complementary, each reflecting their respective author's unique perspective of the same events. Several commentators have tackled this challenge (See Peterson, *The Acts*, pp. 124-125 and Longenecker, 'Acts,' pp. 263-264). Marshall's summary is among the most succinct: '1) Judas hanged himself (Matt.), but the rope broke and his body was ruptured by the fall (possibly after he was already dead and beginning to decompose) (Acts); 2) What the priests bought with Judas's money (Matt.) could be regarded as his purchase by their agency (Acts); 3) The field bought by the priests (Matt.) was the one where Judas died (Acts).' I. Howard Marshall, *The Acts of the Apostles*, TNTC (Grand Rapids: William B. Eerdmans, 1980), p. 65.

16. 'Luke shapes his story after familiar Jewish death stories of the wicked in which the more wicked the deed the more graphic and inopportune the death (Acts 12:20-23; Josh. 7; 2 Sam. 20:4-13).' Wall, 'Acts,' p. 50.

treasurer of His group? He paid dearly for it in the end by his betrayal and death. But if He really was the Son of God, He ought to have known what Judas was like and not have chosen him. After all, if He didn't know how to choose better officials than that, what hope would He have of restoring Israel and of bringing in the kingdom of God?[17]

Peter's agenda is to correct this misperception, to make clear that Judas' betrayal and apostasy were neither unexpected nor unfortunate. To the contrary, they were foretold on the prophetic pages of Scripture and, therefore, could not have not happened. The forcefulness of his language is emphatic as he introduces Judas' treachery: *'Brothers and sisters, the Scripture had to be fulfilled ...'* It is Peter's *first* use of an imperfect verb that means, 'it was necessary, it had to be so.' Appearing twenty-eight times cumulatively in Luke's two volumes, it is a word that expresses the predetermined sovereignty of the divine will (Luke 9:22; 17:25; 24:7; Acts 3:21; 9:16; 14:22), particularly in passages that speak of the fulfillment of Scripture (Luke 22:37; 24:26, 44; Acts 1:21; 17:3). It is a theme to which the apostles repeatedly appeal when heralding the suffering and death of the Messiah—a suffering and death, they would have their hearers understand, that are not solely consequences of a meticulous providence, but actualizations of the inexorable purpose of God set forth in Scripture. For example:

> This man was handed over to you by *God's deliberate plan and foreknowledge.* (2:23)

> But this is how *God fulfilled what he had foretold through all the prophets,* saying that his Messiah would suffer. (3:18)

> Indeed Herod and Pontius Pilate met together with the Gentiles and the people of Israel in this city to conspire against your holy servant Jesus, whom you anointed. They did what *your power and will had decided beforehand should happen.* (4:27-28)

17. David Gooding, *True to the Faith* (Coleraine: Myrtlefield House, 2013), p. 54.

This is the passage of Scripture the eunuch was reading: 'He was led like a sheep to the slaughter, and as a lamb before its shearer is silent, so he did not open his mouth. In his humiliation he was deprived of justice. Who can speak of his descendants? For his life was taken from the earth.'

The eunuch asked Philip, 'Tell me, please, who is the prophet talking about, himself or someone else?' *Then Philip began with that very passage of Scripture and told him the good news about Jesus.* (8:32-35)

The people of Jerusalem and their rulers did not recognize Jesus, yet in condemning him *they fulfilled the words of the prophets* that are read every Sabbath. (13:27)

When they carried out *all that was written about him,* they took him down from the cross and laid him in a tomb. (13:29)

Each of these makes clear that the sufferings of Jesus are not symptomatic of a plan tragically derailed, but in keeping with a predetermined purpose perfectly fulfilled. In the present case, they are paradigmatic of the point Peter is seeking to establish in Acts 1—that the betrayal of the Messiah by a close friend who would subsequently forfeit his leadership has been foreordained by God and announced in the Scripture. This is not a shameful embarrassment from which Christians should hide, but a foreordained intention that Christians should proclaim.[18]

Reading the Old Testament As Christian Scripture

At the conclusion of Luke's digression, Peter resumes his address by seeking to substantiate his claim—'*the Scriptures had to be fulfilled*'—in connection to the defection of Judas.

---

18. This in no way exonerates Judas from his culpability. His actions are defined as '*his wickedness.*' It is an illustration of the mystery of divine sovereignty: what God immovably decrees in eternity, man of his own volition will demand in time. 'The Son of Man will go as it has been decreed. But woe to that man who betrays him!' (Luke 22:22).

Peter does this by citing two specific texts from the Psalms. Yet it is essential to bear in mind that the Christocentric hermeneutic Peter applies to the Psalms–*a Davidic typology*– does not originate with the apostles, but with Jesus, who subsequently taught it to them, beginning on the evening of the resurrection: '... everything must be fulfilled that is written about me in the Law of Moses, the Prophets and the *Psalms*. Then he opened their minds so they could understand the Scriptures' (Luke 24:44-45). It is in the light of this interpretive watershed, that Peter proceeds,

> 'For ... it is written in the Book of Psalms:
> "May his place be deserted;
> let there be no one to dwell in it,"
>
> and,
>
> "May another take his place of leadership."' (v. 20)

Peter's first citation is taken from Psalm 69, a psalm associated with Jesus six times in the New Testament, five of which are directly preceded by an appeal to their inscripturated tradition:

> His disciples remembered that *it is written*: 'Zeal for your house will consume me.' (John 2:17; *cf.* Ps. 69:9)

> But this is to fulfill *what is written in their Law*: 'They hated me without reason.' (John 15:25; *cf.* Ps. 69:4)

> There they offered Jesus wine to drink, mixed with gall. (Matt. 27:34; *cf.* Ps. 69:21)

> *And David says*: 'May their table become a snare and a trap, a stumbling block and a retribution for them. May their eyes be darkened so they cannot see, and their backs be bent forever.' (Rom. 11:9-10; *cf.* Ps. 69:22-23)

> For even Christ did not please himself but, *as it is written*: 'The insults of those who insult you have fallen on me.' (Rom. 15:3; *cf.* Ps. 69:9)

Hence, Peter's present reference, '... *it is written in the Book of Psalms: "May his place be deserted; let there be no one to dwell in it"*' (*cf.* Ps. 69:25), is not a display of irresponsible eisegesis, but part of a New Testament interpretive tradition: a messianic typology. As originally composed, this psalm refers to actual events in the life of David, God's anointed king. It expresses his deep suffering, his prayers for deliverance, and his call for God to exercise judgment against his enemies. Peter's second citation is taken from Psalm 109, '*May another take his place of leadership*' (cf. Ps. 109:8). Here, too, David describes adversaries who hate and slander him—then calls attention to one foe in particular, ostensibly the ringleader, upon whom he seeks God's severe judgment. As Peter appeals to these texts, he does so not in a manner that proves indifferent to their original contexts. His implication is that their respective contexts serve a typological function; that they find their consummate expression in the one David prophetically anticipates: the eschatological Son of David, *the* Anointed One: Jesus.[19]

Similarly, the enemies of David can now be seen as those who foreshadow the enemies of Jesus.[20] As such, Judas purchases a parcel of land with the wages he receives for his disloyalty. Because his guilty blood was spilt upon it—'*there he fell headlong, his body burst open and all his intestines spilled out*'—the parcel became known as the '*Field of Blood.*' Perhaps contributing to this appellation is the fact that Jesus' innocent blood was sacrificed to buy this property—that it was acquired by '*blood money*' (Matt. 27:6). Finally, Matthew's Gospel indicates that the land was allocated to be a cemetery

---

19. 'This method of using the OT is not so culturally bound that it is invalid for Christians today. If the apostolic principles of interpretation are carefully noted, and proper regard is paid to OT texts in their original context before a Christian application is attempted, the inspired preachers and authors of the NT will not lead us astray by their example.' Peterson, *Acts*, pp. 125-126. A fitting word indeed!

20. Some suggest that Peter uses the Jewish exegetical principle *qal wahomer* ('the light to the heavy'), 'allowing Peter to assert that what has been said of false companions and wicked men generally applies, *a minore ad majorem*, specifically to Judas, the one who proved himself uniquely false and evil.' R. N. Longenecker, *Biblical Exegesis in the Apostolic Period* (Grand Rapids: William B. Eerdmans Publishing Company, 1975), p. 97.

for the ceremonially unclean, thereby fulfilling the psalmist's imprecation: '*May his place be deserted; let there be no one to dwell in it*' (cf. Ps. 69:25).

But not only is the demise of Judas a necessary piece of God's plan of salvation, so, too, is the election of one to assume his position: '*May another take his place of leadership*' (Ps. 109:8). David has prayed that his arch-betrayer would die before his time, with the result that someone else would replace his leadership position within the community. How much more should this be so for someone who has betrayed God's Messiah? Consequently, for the *second* time, Peter draws upon a word that embraces God's predetermined plan:

> Therefore it is necessary to choose one of the men who have been with us the whole time the Lord Jesus was living among us, beginning from John's baptism to the time when Jesus was taken up from us. For one of these must become a witness with us of his resurrection. (vv. 21-22)

This is no mere suggestion on the part of Peter: 'Given the nature and extent of the assigned task, my calculations would suggest that we seriously consider adding another man to the team.' This is a prophetically warranted obligation: 'It is *God's purpose* that we have a twelfth man'—an action shown to be compulsory by virtue of the conjunction '*therefore*' that links the present paragraph (vv. 22-23) to the preceding paragraph (vv. 15-17). In other words, it is the death of Judas that creates the need for a replacement. But why is this so seemingly important—enough to be regarded as a divine mandate? And why is it necessary to choose just '*one*'? Is there something inherently significant about the number *twelve*? Why not thirteen apostles? In fact, why not jettison the notion of any number at all and simply appoint as many who meet the compulsory requirements?

Before answering, consider the distinct requirements for this '*twelfth*' apostle. Firstly, this replacement must be a man.[21]

---

21. This is the 'default understanding' of the noun *aner*. Carson argues: '... one

While it is true that *gender barriers* are being obliterated by the gospel, *gender distinctions* related to divisions of labor within God's kingdom is another matter. Secondly, this *'twelfth man'* must be an individual qualified to bear witness[22] to the entire gospel tradition, the boundaries of which are defined by the ministry of John the Baptist (the inception point for the kingdom work of Jesus) and the ascension of Jesus.[23] The *'twelfth man'* needs to be able to say: 'I *saw* the Spirit descend upon Jesus at the Jordan River and *heard* God's audible voice speak of Him. I *observed* as Jesus transformed water into wine and fed thousands. I *witnessed* His healings of diseased people, His exorcisms of the demonically tormented, the displays of His power in resurrecting the dead. I *looked on* as Jesus was arrested in the garden, scourged by the soldiers, mocked by the hostile crowds. I *witnessed* His crucifixion, the surrender of His life, the piercing of His side, His lifeless corpse detached from the cross. I *observed* the tomb in which Jesus was buried, the giant millstone rolled across its opening, Pilate's seal placed upon it, the Roman guard positioned in front of it, and Jesus' people devastated by it. But then, on the third day, I *saw* the stone rolled away and the tomb emptied. I *watched* as the women rejoiced, the disciples pondered, and the priests schemed. And then, finally, *I saw Him.* Not a ghost or a phantom, but Him; a resurrected man, *the man,* who talked with us, ate with us, and breathed upon us. I am an *eyewitness* of the life, burial, death, resurrection, and exaltation of Jesus Christ—which means that I can now *attest* that this Jesus whose ascension into heaven I have also *observed* is no fraudulent replacement, but the same person subsequent to His resurrection as He who existed prior to His crucifixion.'

---

should assume the reference is to male human beings unless there is convincing counter-evidence.' Carson, *Inclusive Language,* p. 153, 158. Such is the case in v. 16.

22. A witness is not merely one who observes, but who proceeds to bear witness about what is seen. Bauer, *A Greek-English Lexicon,* p. 619-620.

23. It is for this reason that James (the brother of Jesus) and Saul of Tarsus (even subsequent to his conversion) could not qualify to be one of the Twelve.

Of course, *all* Christians, by definition, believe this body of truth about Jesus. Moreover, it is their stated mission to openly and unashamedly proclaim it; even to the point of being willing, when necessary, to sacrifice greatly for the sake of its advancement. Equally true, however, is the uniqueness of the apostles' witness. They are to bear a singular and foundational role in the establishment of Christianity that transcends the testimony of all other Christians. It can be said that all followers of Jesus must witness *to* Him; but the apostles *witnessed Him.* Consequently, the testimony of every other Christian is altogether dependent upon theirs. But at present, how many apostles are enlisted for the mission that will commence when the promised Holy Spirit is given? Eleven. Divine necessity will not allow this, Peter asserts. There must be *twelve.*

After the definition of the credentials necessary to fill the office left vacant by Judas, the field of potential candidates is narrowed to two men. How do the eleven move forward to identify the *twelfth?*

> So they nominated two men: Joseph called Barsabbas (also known as Justus) and Matthias. Then they prayed, 'Lord, you know everyone's heart. Show us which of these two you have chosen to take over this apostolic ministry, which Judas left to go where he belongs.' Then they cast lots ... (vv. 23-26a)

At first glance this looks to be an unusual decision-making technique, but a fuller appreciation of all that contributes to it may cause it to become more comprehensible. First of all, it is essential to remember who had *'chosen'* the other eleven apostles, a fact about which Luke has been explicit at the opening of this chapter: 'I wrote about all that Jesus began to do and teach until the day he was taken up to heaven, after giving instructions through the Holy Spirit to the apostles *he had chosen'* (1:1-2). Now, at the closing of this chapter, the identical language is used. This, along with the prior reference to 'the Lord Jesus' (v. 21), contributes to the conclusion that the 'Lord' who has 'chosen' is indeed Jesus—the great knower of human hearts, a fact Luke repeatedly makes clear in his Gospel (cf. Luke 5:22; 6:8; 9:46-47; 22:21-22).[24] The implications are astounding: not only is Jesus to be regarded as one to whom prayers can be offered (cf. 7:59-60; 9:10-16), He is the one who continues to direct the affairs of His community though ascended into heaven. This is a point more emphatically implied by the verb tense used to speak of Jesus' choosing—a perfective aorist, which indicates that this choice of a twelfth apostle *has already been made*. Properly speaking, then, the apostles do not cast lots to make the decision, but to reveal the decision that has already been made by the ascended Lord.

Secondly, this casting of lots does not occur haphazardly or in a vacuum, but is set in the context of a disciplined piety: a) the entire Christian community has been engaged in incessant prayer (v. 14), as well the specific prayer mentioned here on the part of the apostles (v. 24); b) they have submitted themselves to the diligent study of Scripture which has exposed the need for an apostolic replacement (vv. 16, 20); and, c) they have thoughtfully determined the necessary qualifications appropriate to this unique office (vv. 21-22).

Finally, then, 'they cast lots'—a practice clearly sanctioned in the Old Testament (e.g., Lev. 16:8; Num. 26:55; 1 Chron. 26:13-14), but summarized most succinctly by the wisdom writer: 'The lot is cast into the lap, but its every decision is from the LORD' (Prov. 16:33). It was a process used, in particular, 'to reveal God's selection of someone or something out of several possibilities where he kept people in the dark and desired their impartiality in the selection.'[25] In all likelihood,

---

24. This implies Jesus' deity, given that this is a commonly attested attribute of God (cf. 1 Sam. 16:7; 1 Kings 8:39; Ps. 7:9; 44:21; 139:2, 23; Acts 15:8).

25. Bruce K. Waltke, *The Book of Proverbs*, NICOT (Grand Rapids: William B. Eerdmans Publishing Company, 2004/2005), vol. 2, p. 37.

stones were marked in a way that distinguished each from the other. They were placed in a container that was shaken until one of the stones came out. Interestingly, this proves to be the Bible's final mention of casting lots. It may be that this practice, heretofore referred to with some frequency in the Old Testament, was intended to belong uniquely to the old epoch. Given its placement in Acts—just prior to the event that will signal a new age and a new kind of relationship between God and His people—it is quite possible that Luke is highlighting the casting of lots as 'a symbol of the end—the signing off, as it were—of the old era.'[26]

And Then There Were Twelve

'But I am still perplexed by all of this—all of the *drama* associated with this scene. It's not quite over-the-top. But its apparent emphasis certainly seems exaggerated. Luke's reason for including it escapes me.' Is this your sentiment? The resolution to your dilemma may be found in the clue that appears in the final phrase of this chapter:

> ... and the lot fell to Matthias; so he was added to the eleven apostles. (v. 26b)

The Lord's choice for the apostleship had been revealed: Matthias is to fill the post abandoned by Judas. Interestingly, no reference to Matthias is ever again made in the New Testament. Yet this, in itself, may be revealing. Luke is not preoccupied with the man himself (other than making reference to his qualifications for this ministry), nor is he concerned with his particular accomplishments as an apostle. What *is* important to Luke? The specific number inferred in his arithmetical calculation: *Matthias makes twelve*. But again you say: 'This emphasis to which you keep referring—this business of "*twelve*"—it's precisely what I seem to be missing.'

---

26. Ajith Fernando, *Acts*, NIVAC (Grand Rapids: Zondervan Publishing House, 1998), p. 79.

One of my principal intentions in the prior chapter was to demonstrate that God's kingdom on earth is to be inaugurated by the outpouring of the Holy Spirit on the people of God, thereby fulfilling God's promise of a restored Israel in a now/not yet sense; moreover, that this restored Israel would expand inexorably to the ends of the earth. But this begs a question: as originally conceived, how was the nation of Israel constituted? It was a composite of tribes that originated with the sons of Jacob ... *twelve* tribes to be exact. If the coming kingdom of God is to be inaugurated by the new covenant gift of the Spirit that subsequently gives birth to a restored Israel—not merely Israel as a remnant, but Israel in its ideal—what does this *necessitate* for the apostolic community awaiting Pentecost? Can there truly be a witness to the 'ends of the earth' *before* the Messiah's claim on the whole house of Israel has been reiterated?

It is no mere coincidence that Jesus chose *twelve* apostles from very nearly the inception of His ministry (Luke 6:12-13). Doing so served to represent a renewed and reunited people of God by means of the ideal number—all of which means that in the betrayal Judas represented something more significant than the mere failure of an individual. It fractured the typological integrity of the group that was to constitute the inception of the restored people of God. *This is why there must be a twelfth man.* And also why no effort is made to supplement the *Twelve* as each one meets their respective deaths (*e.g.*, Acts 12:2). Acts 1:15-26 is not a precedent for how to replace church leaders who have resigned, died, or disqualified themselves. It is a one-time event bearing a unique historical-redemptive significance. Once the *Twelve* has been reconstituted at the heart of the community and the Spirit subsequently poured out, faithful Israel will have come into existence and the promise of God inaugurated.

Of course, the biblical and theological consequences of this now seem impossible to miss: the locus of true Israel is the apostolic community.[27] For this reason, designations formerly unique to ethnic Israel are now applied to Christians (either individually or collectively). We are the 'children of Abraham' (Gal. 3:7), the '[true] circumcision' (Phil. 3:3, NASB), 'a holy temple' (Eph. 2:21), the 'chosen people' (Col. 3:12), 'a kingdom and priests' (Rev. 1:6), the 'holy nation' (1 Peter 2:9), and God's 'very own' (Titus 2:14). Each of these is laden with its own redemptive meaning. Yet they all seemingly converge at their zenith when, in an inspired preview of the consummation, the church of Jesus Christ (comprised of the total company of God's redeemed people from every epoch) is referred to as the 'New Jerusalem' (Rev. 21:2, 9-10).

The entire storyline of the Scriptures has brought us to this strategic moment in the book of Acts—the very moment in salvation history when the beginning of the new creation explodes into existence. But such will not take place until Pentecost. Why? Though Matthias has filled the place left vacant by Judas, the Spirit has not yet filled the place left vacant by Jesus. In the meantime, what is preoccupation of the apostolic Christians?

> How do they wait, as they wait, for the fulfillment of God's promise?

They hoist the sails. How? 1) By praying constantly; and, 2) By responding obediently—preparing themselves by the means of the Christ-centered Scriptures for the moment when the sacred wind will begin to blow.

---

27. Should the title 'Israel' always be identified with the entire Jewish people? Two observations can be made from this text: 1) There is nothing in the New Testament to indicate that the Twelve are physically related to the twelve different tribes. This, by itself, should give pause to someone who is quick to deny a certain symbolic value to the designation 'Israel'; and, 2) The qualifications required of potential candidates who may complete the circle of the Twelve reveals that true Israel is now to be defined in terms of a certain kind of relationship to Jesus. Therefore, a Jewish person who rejects Jesus as Messiah is not a member of Israel, but an apostate from Israel (e.g., Rev. 2:9).

Do *you* wait well—particularly as you wait for the fulfillment of God's promised blessings? As I admitted earlier, it is certainly not a skill I have mastered. But a significant reason for this has been my slowness to recognize that waiting, for a Christian, is not synonymous with passive inactivity or fatalistic surrender. It is an act that is made effectual by holy busyness: praying constantly and responding obediently. And as you do this, dear friend, keep in mind God's wonderful promise to those who wait:

> Have you not known? Have you not heard?
> The LORD is the everlasting God,
>   the Creator of the ends of the earth.
> He does not faint or grow weary;
>   his understanding is unsearchable.
> He gives power to the faint,
>   and to him who has no might he increases strength.
>
> Even youths shall faint and be weary,
>   and young men shall fall exhausted;
> but they who wait for the LORD shall renew their strength;
>   they shall mount up with wings like eagles;
> they shall run and not be weary;
>   they shall walk and not faint. (Isa. 40:28-31, ESV)

The *twelve* apostles of the ascended Lord Jesus experience this sacred invigoration after only ten days of waiting. Who knows? Perhaps it will only be ten days for you. In the meantime ... *hoist the sails.*

4

WHAT IS PENTECOST?

Things are coming loose, breaking open.
Can it be the same wind
which on the very first morning of all mornings
swept across dark waters,
the wind of creation?
The wind is once again bringing something to life.
WILLIAM H. WILLIMON

As a body without breath is a corpse,
so the church without the Spirit is dead.
JOHN R. W. STOTT

The Holy Spirit alone
can reveal to the Church her missionary character ...
only He can teach the hearts of men that
every Christian has a call to missionary service.
HARRY R. BOER

When the day of Pentecost came, they were all together in one place. ²Suddenly a sound like the blowing of a violent wind came from heaven and filled the whole house where they were sitting. ³They saw what seemed to be tongues of fire that separated and came to rest on each of them. ⁴All of them were filled with the Holy Spirit and began to speak in other tongues as the Spirit enabled them.

⁵Now there were staying in Jerusalem God-fearing Jews from every nation under heaven. ⁶When they heard this sound, a crowd came together in bewilderment, because each one heard their own language being spoken. ⁷Utterly amazed, they asked: 'Aren't all these who are speaking Galileans? ⁸Then how is it that each of us hears them in our native language? ⁹Parthians, Medes and Elamites;

residents of Mesopotamia, Judea and Cappadocia, Pontus and Asia, [10]*Phrygia and Pamphylia, Egypt and the parts of Libya near Cyrene; visitors from Rome* [11]*(both Jews and converts to Judaism); Cretans and Arabs—we hear them declaring the wonders of God in our own tongues!'* [12]*Amazed and perplexed, they asked one another, 'What does this mean?'*

[13]*Some, however, made fun of them and said, 'They have had too much wine.'*

(Acts 2:1-13)

An Unfortunate Obscurity

Renovation. Rejuvenation. Revitalization. Resurgence. Restoration. Renewal. Reanimation. Reawakening.

Or better yet ... *Revival.*

But what notions rise to the surface of your mind when you hear mention of this term—*revival?* Some, owing to a kind of ecclesiastical muscle memory, invariably think of a series of scheduled evangelistic meetings conducted at a church building: 'Make sure you don't forget to attend our annual *"revival"* on the Monday, Tuesday, and Friday of the third week in March.' Others imagine something much more bizarre: a religious happening in a backwater location, organized in a portable building with sawdust floors, distinguished by emotional excesses, and led by an Elmer Gantry le charlatan. All of this is quite distorted and unfortunate. The English verb *'to revive'* appears several times in the Scripture (almost exclusively in the Old Testament). Used with reference to *material* existence, it speaks of a person who has been restored to life from a former condition of weakness or death (*e.g.,* 1 Sam. 30:12; 1 Kings 17:22; 2 Kings 13:21, ESV). But the term is also employed in contexts that are *spiritual* in orientation. Thus, to be *'revived'* describes the experience of a person who is moved, by divine impetus, from a slumbering indifference into a state of refreshed enthusiasm and vitality. It is the rekindling of spiritual affections—the reanimation of spiritual fervor; a reawakening to God that is not exclusive to individuals, but can be pertinent to entire communities:

> Restore us again, God our Savior,
>   and put away your displeasure toward us.
> Will you be angry with us forever?
>   Will you prolong your anger through all generations?
> *Will you not revive us again,*
>   *that your people may rejoice in you?*
> Show us your unfailing love, LORD,
>   and grant us your salvation. (Ps. 85:4-7)

Obvious here is not only the Psalmist's impassioned plea for revival, but his cognizance of and dependence upon the one in whom authentic revival is sourced: the divine Savior and covenant Lord. Revival is neither a religious experience engineered by human ingenuity, nor is it sustained by human agency. Revival is *God-sent*. As one describes it:

> To speak of 'holding a revival' is a misnomer. No human being can kindle the interest, quicken the conscience of a people, or generate that intensity of spiritual hunger that signifies revival ... No man can schedule a revival, for God alone is the giver of life. But when darkness deepens, when moral declension reaches its lowest ebb, when the church becomes cold, lukewarm, dead; when the fullness of time has come and prayer ascends from a few earnest hearts ... then history teaches that it is time for the tide of revival to sweep in once more.[1]

Pentecost is just this: a revival—not given for the sake of what God's people would experience mystically, but for the purpose Jesus intends His people to achieve missionally. More precisely, Pentecost signals the revival of Israel for the purpose of taking God's salvation to the entire human race. It is a redemptive event simultaneously distinguished by: 1) its historical

---

1. F. Carlton Booth, 'Revival,' *Baker's Dictionary of Theology*, ed. Everett F. Harrison (Grand Rapids: Baker Book House, 1987), p. 420.

uniqueness. The day of Pentecost marks the fulfillment of events that are the subjects of Old Testament prophesy (akin to Christmas, Good Friday, and Easter Sunday); and, 2) its enduring benefits. Though never to be repeated, Pentecost has never been retracted. It is the fulfillment of God's great last days' promise: the establishment of a new age and kingdom, conceived and birthed within Israel, that would steadily extend from Israel to encompass the entire world.

The reality that must be acknowledged, however, is that mere mention of the name–*Pentecost*–frequently stimulates an anxiety among God's people that manifests itself in diverse expressions: confusion (for many), embarrassment (for some), and divisiveness (for others). In fact, an accurate understanding of Pentecost should produce the opposite dispositions within all Christians: clarity (in the nature and purpose of our mission), dignity (because of the potency provided to accomplish it), and unity (owing to our common life in the gospel). Therefore, it will be the aim of this chapter, along with the two subsequent chapters, to answer the following three questions respectively: 1) *What Is Pentecost?* (vv. 1-13); 2) *What Does Pentecost Mean?* (vv. 14-36); and, 3) *What Response Does Pentecost Demand?* (vv. 37-41).

The Providential Occasion

> When the day of Pentecost came, they were all together in one place. (v. 1)

This is a reference to the one hundred and twenty Christians to whom Luke referred earlier—a group of people for whom being '*all together*' had become a temporary pattern, rather than dispersing into Jerusalem and beyond. There is a decisive difference between *pre*-Pentecost and *post*-Pentecost Christianity. It is legitimate to assume that these followers of Jesus are relentlessly at prayer still, mindful that their mission will not commence until the Holy Spirit is given. But it is now appropriate to ask: What is Luke's purpose in drawing attention to Pentecost in particular? Is there significance to this? Or is it merely fortuitous? Might the meaning of this day have some relationship to the great redemptive event that will come to distinguish it?

Pentecost was the second of three great annual feasts celebrated by the Jewish people, Passover being the first and the Feast of Tabernacles the third. In particular, Jewish *men* from the entire Mediterranean world would stream into the Holy City for the purpose of presenting gifts and offerings to the Lord (*e.g.*, Exod. 23:14-17; 34:22-23). Specifically, Pentecost was an agricultural festival, a day consecrated to express thanks to God for His goodness in providing the harvest that had already been gathered; and to seek God's blessing on the remainder of the crop yet to be gleaned, which accounts for the fact that Pentecost had been referred to originally as the Festival of the Harvest and the Festival of the Firstfruits. It eventually absorbed the designation '*Pentecost*' (derived from the Greek term meaning '*fifty*') as a result of following the Passover festival that occurred fifty days prior. Since Passover was scheduled in mid-April, this placed the occurrence of Pentecost at the beginning of June, during which time traveling conditions were at their best. This ensured that the greatest number of pilgrims attended the Festival of Pentecost;[2] Jerusalem was never more cosmopolitan than during this occasion.

But Pentecost was not just a celebration of the harvest's firstfruits. Like all the Jewish festivals, Pentecost was designed to awaken echoes of the great redemption story that had come to define the Jewish people: the Exodus from Egypt. On the evening that eventually came to be regarded as Passover, the blood of sacrificial lambs was applied to the lintel and doorposts of Jewish homes so that the avenging angel would 'pass over' those inside, only to slaughter the firstborn of the Egyptians. As a result, the Israelites left their captors that very night, were delivered through the Red Sea miraculously, and

---

2. David J. Williams, *Acts*, NIBC (Peabody: Hendrickson Publishers, 1990), p. 39.

journeyed into the desert. Fifty days subsequent to Passover, they arrived at Mount Sinai where Moses ascended the mountain and received the covenant. Pentecost, then, was not concerned exclusively with agricultural blessings. It was an event that recalled the occasion when God provided His unique way of life to those He had redeemed.

At the very least, a brief appreciation of Pentecost's historical context should cause some hesitation before dismissing any notion of relevance in connection with the events of Acts 2. It is just a happenstance that they occur on this day? Not likely. In point of fact, though the NIV translates v. 1, 'When the day of Pentecost arrived,' the original reads, 'When the day of Pentecost was being fulfilled.' The difference highlighted in the Greek text more clearly underscores that Pentecost is to be regarded within the framework of God's fulfilled promises, that a significant event predicted by God has indeed arrived;[3] in this case, the eschatological prophecies regarding the advent of the Spirit (cf. Isa. 32:15; 44:3-5; Joel 2; Ezek. 36-37; Luke 24:49; Acts 1:4-5, 8). Hence, one has most helpfully translated this: 'When the promised day of Pentecost had come.'[4] Furthermore, a Christocentric hermeneutic, grounded in kosher sensitivity, would recognize the typological implications of the Pentecost events. Jesus has recently asserted that the apostolic Christians will soon bear powerful witness to Him and His redemptive achievements. What will be the initial result of this? Firstfruits— the harvest of three thousand people, accompanied by the expectation of an even greater yield to follow. To what is this harvest attributed? Just as Moses ascended Mount Sinai and then descended with the Law, so, too, Jesus has ascended into heaven and is also descending—not with a written law carved on tablets of stone, but with the dynamic energy of the Holy

---

3. The present tense of *symplerousthai* actually means: 'in the very process of being fulfilled.'

4. Eduard Lohse, 'πεντηκοστε,' *TDNT*, vol. VI, p. 50.

Spirit[5] who will write His law on human hearts. Is the advent of the Spirit *'on the day of Pentecost'* a random occurrence? *God is not random.* The convergence of both day and event is the providential realization of God's design.

The Spectacular Manifestations

> Suddenly a sound like the blowing of a violent wind came from heaven and filled the whole house where they were sitting. They saw what seemed to be tongues of fire that separated and came to rest on each of them. (vv. 2-3)

Luke's initial description of the events of Pentecost is nearly palpable, a scene dramatized with spectacular special effects that rival those produced by *Industrial Light and Magic*—sensory phenomena that are audible and visible. Presently, these Christians *hear* a sound so overpoweringly loud it bears a violent quality; furthermore, they *see* something remarkable. Yet Luke's description of these 'special effects' employs the language of analogy. The sound[6] is *'like'* the blowing of a violent wind, but is not a violent wind. The vision of something that *'seemed'* to be fiery tongues is not actual fire.[7] Rather, they are theophanic phenomena that accompany the presence of the divine.

One can recall the terrifying *'sound'* associated with the revelation of God on Mount Sinai:

> On the morning of the third day there was thunder and lightning, with a thick cloud over the mountain, and a very loud trumpet blast. Everyone in the camp

---

5. As Peter will soon make explicit in his sermon, the sending of the Holy Spirit is a distinct work of the ascended Christ (2:33)—a reality that may be hinted at linguistically in chapters 1 and 2. Acts 1:10-11 mentions four times that Jesus ascends' *into heaven.'* Acts 2:1 then records the sound of violent wind *'from heaven.'* This verbal association may imply a cause and effect—that Jesus is behind the events of Pentecost; a fact affirmed in other New Testament texts.

6. Properly speaking, it is the sound that fills the house, not the wind. Nevertheless, wind and breath are common emblems of the Spirit (*e.g.*, Ps. 33:6; Ezek. 37:9-10; John 3:8)..

7. Both of these, *hosper* and *hosei* respectively, are markers of comparison.

> trembled. Then Moses led the people out of the
> camp to meet with God, and they stood at the foot
> of the mountain ... As the sound of the trumpet grew
> louder and louder, Moses spoke and the voice of God
> answered him.
>
> When the people saw the thunder and lightning and
> heard the trumpet ... they trembled with fear. They
> stayed at a distance and said to Moses, 'Speak to us
> yourself and we will listen. But do not let God speak to
> us or we will die.' (Exod. 19:16-17, 19; 20:18-19)

Likewise, *'fire'* appears as a frequent feature of biblical
theophanies. God's initial self-revelation to Moses occurred at a
bush that burned 'in flames of fire' (Exod. 3:2-6). His presence
with Israel through the wilderness wanderings displayed itself
at night 'in a pillar of fire' (Exod. 13:21-22). And not only was
God's presence on Mount Sinai attended by traumatizing
sound, it was also distinguished by consuming *fire:*

> Mount Sinai was covered with smoke, because the
> LORD descended on it in fire. The smoke billowed
> up from it like smoke from a furnace, and the whole
> mountain trembled violently. (Exod. 19:18)

That Luke identifies the *'sound like the blowing of a violent
wind'* as coming–*'from heaven'*–ensures that these phenomena
are not to be regarded as natural, but supernatural, as a
display of the in-breaking of heaven itself. Violent wind and
fire are forces beyond all powers of human domestication,
simultaneously terrifying and exhilarating. But why are they
conscripted here to signify the presence of the divine? Is there
something significant to these manifestations beyond the
pyrotechnics of this theophany? Dennis Johnson suggests that
these signs, 'echoes of new beginnings in the Old Testament,'
are employed to display 'the new creation, the new exodus,
the new revelation, and the new resurrection that the Spirit
initiates at his coming.'[8] He is certainly right. To sharpen the

---

8. Johnson, *The Message of Acts*, p. 57.

focus even further, it should be asked: Is there any specific import to the idiosyncratic shape of this symbol that has come to rest upon each Christian? Given the primary theme of Acts, is it possible that it bears a correspondence to the mission Jesus has assigned to His followers?

The Telescoping Explanation

When astronomers closely examine a star through a telescope, everything else in their field of vision is compressed and condensed. Similarly, Luke's account of this transition into the next stage of God's saving program is now telescoped into a single sentence of explanation:

> All of them were filled with the Holy Spirit. (v. 4a)

It is no exaggeration to define this modest statement as an epoch-changing event in the storyline of God's dealings with human beings. During the old covenant era, the indwelling of the Lord's Spirit was a selective indwelling not experienced by all within the covenant community. The Spirit came to rest upon certain individuals in keeping with the uniqueness of their callings: a king (1 Sam. 16:13), a priest (Ezek. 2:2), a craftsman (Exod. 31:2-5). Additionally, this indwelling could be intermittent, withdrawn from one who had been previously endowed with the Spirit's presence (1 Sam. 16:14; cf. Ps. 51:11). Finally, it should be acknowledged that Old Testament revelation regarding the Spirit is limited, leaving the reader with very little to suggest that the Spirit is anything more than a sub-personal power.

These observations are not an effort to demean the old covenant. To the contrary, it stands as a display of God's sovereign grace to Israel: Yahweh would be her God, she would be His unique people, and the law (the covenant document) would be the basis of their relationship. Inherent to this covenant arrangement, however, were two inescapable weaknesses: 1) the Israelites possessed an organic propensity

to resist the law of God; and, 2) the covenant itself made
no provision to empower the Israelites to keep its demands.
Yet, embedded into the old covenant itself are hints of its
own predetermined obsolescence, not the least of which are
statements that promise a coming day when God will make
a *new* covenant with His people, a covenant superior to the
former in that it will address the very weaknesses the old
covenant could only expose: it will purge people of their sin
and furnish them with the necessary empowerment to be
faithful to God (Jer. 31:31-34; Ezek. 36:24-27).

It is this epochal fulfillment that has now come to the
forefront in Acts 2, telescoped in the simple explanation
provided by Luke: *'All of them were filled with the Holy Spirit.'*[9] It
is the realization of the promises made long ago by the prophets
and recently reiterated by Jesus (Acts 1:5, 8): *the inauguration
of the new covenant.* As such, the discontinuities between the
covenants are pronounced here, specifically in relationship
to humanity's experience with the Spirit: 1) the Holy Spirit
comes to rests upon *'all'* who embrace the covenant Lord
(Acts 2:38; 15:8); 2) He will never be withdrawn, but forever
remain with the people of Jesus (John 14:16-17); and, 3) He
is revealed to be far more than a force or a power, but is a
divine presence (Acts 5:3) distinguished by the characteristics
of Jesus Himself (Acts 16:7).

For what purpose is the Holy Spirit given in this new
manner? Peter's sermon will subsequently explain what Luke

---

9. While Acts 2:4 is the fulfillment of being 'baptized with the Holy Spirit' (Acts 1:5),
Luke here uses a more emphatic term, *eplesthesan*, that is especially appropriate when
emphasizing relatively short events or immediate effects (Luke 1:15, 41, 67; Acts 2:4;
4:8, 31; 9:17; 13:9). It designates 'short outbursts of spiritual power/inspiration,
rather than the inception of long-term endowment of the Spirit,' a fact that explains
why a person might be 'filled with Holy Spirit' on many occasions while at the
same time remaining 'full' of the Spirit. Max Turner, *Power from on High: The Spirit
in Israel's Restoration and Witness in Luke-Acts* (Eugene: Wipf & Stock Publishers,
2000), pp. 167-168. Its use here does not deny this event as the inception of the
apostles' permanent reception of the Holy Spirit. For a fuller treatment, see my *Spirit
Empowered Preaching* (Ross-shire: Christian Focus Publications, 1998), pp. 102-112.

presently describes: the Spirit is given for the purpose of verbal proclamation. The eschatological gift is the Spirit of prophecy.[10] Consequently, *all of these Christians*, not only the apostles—

> ... began to speak in other tongues as the Spirit enabled them. (v. 4b)

This is reminiscent of Numbers 11. At a point when Moses finds himself exhausted and depressed by the demands of leadership, he is instructed by God to assemble seventy of Israel's elders at the tent of meeting *outside the camp* of Israel. In turn, God will grant these men the empowerment of the Spirit so they might share the burden of governing with Moses. When the Spirit does come to rest upon them, this holy bestowal displays itself openly: they prophesy, thus displaying their similarity to Moses. Though this occurs only once, it nevertheless furnishes them with credibility to serve as Moses' assistants. Two of the elders, for reasons not disclosed, are not present with those gathered at the tent of meeting. Yet the Spirit rests upon them as well, with the result that they also prophesy. Given that this occurs *inside the camp*, it becomes known to the other Israelites. Jealous for Moses' unique role among God's people, Joshua calls this to his attention and insists these two elders be stopped immediately. Yet Moses responds to Joshua in a manner that, at the time, must have seemed astonishing:

> Are you jealous for my sake? I wish that all the LORD's people were prophets and that the LORD would put his Spirit on them! (Num. 11:29)

It is on the day of Pentecost that Moses' yearning is finally realized: all of God's people are given the Holy Spirit, which, in turn, results in verbal proclamation—an echo of Jesus' own experience, who, prior to the outset of His public ministry,

---

10. Prophesying was the common manifestation of a person possessed by the Spirit during the Old Testament epoch as well (*e.g.*, Num. 11:26-29; 1 Sam. 10:9-10; 2 Sam. 23:2), though such people were considerably few by comparison.

requires the anointing of the Holy Spirit for the express purpose
of proclamation (Luke 4:16-21). Accordingly, in Luke's playful
ambiguity, what was originally *seen* is now *heard*: the '*tongues
of fire*' give way to '*other tongues.*' This is an empowerment
to speak in intelligible languages,[11] supernaturally imparted
by the Spirit, of which these Christians have no command
in ordinary circumstances. What purpose is served by this
unusual experience? Is the point of this to provide a mystical
boon for these Christians and to ensure their affections for
Jesus remain fervent? Or might this bear some connection to
the mission Jesus has assigned to His followers?

The Trenchant Reactions

> Now there were staying in Jerusalem God-fearing Jews
> from every nation under heaven. (v. 5)

This narrative statement, though seemingly inconsequential at
first glance, establishes the ideal context for the significance of
the unfolding events. It makes clear, firstly, that this gathering
of people about to be encountered by the Spirit of prophecy is
exclusively *Jewish*; even more definitively, that it is comprised
of '*God-fearing Jews.*' This specific adjective is never applied to a
Gentile—whether a near-convert to Judaism like Lydia (referred
to as 'a worshiper of God,' Acts 16:14), or a pious Gentile

---

11. There is a slight difference between the tongues mentioned here and those explained in 1 Cor. 14. Paul establishes a two-step process in the Corinthian setting:
step 1) the actual speaking of the tongue; and, step 2) the subsequent interpretation of the tongue for the benefit of the entire congregation and the conviction of
outsiders. See Bock, *Acts*, p. 97. Given that Paul makes no attempt to explain these
tongues as anything different from what occurred at Pentecost—namely, intelligible
foreign languages (the same Greek term is used, *glossa*)—it is most likely that the same
phenomenon is being addressed here rather than an ecstatic or celestial language
designed to effect spiritual devotion. '... it seems more reasonable to interpret the un-
explained in the light of the explained.' Stott, *Acts*, p. 68. Hence, there is a one-step
form involving an intelligible foreign language and immediate understanding (Acts),
and a two-step form involving an intelligible foreign language requiring an interpretation (Corinth). The latter is necessitated by the fact that the majority of the Corinthians were probably Greek-speaking exclusively. The alteration, then, appears to be
an accommodation in keeping with the uniqueness of each setting and audience.

like Cornelius (designated as 'devout,' Acts 10:2). Rather, it describes a devotion that 'consists in watchful vigilance against transgressing the Law.'[12] Hence, it is applied solely to Jews, stressing their zeal for covenantal faithfulness (*cf.* Luke 2:25; Acts 8:2; 22:12). Secondly, this multitude of God-fearers is *centralized*. They are staying '*in Jerusalem.*' Thirdly, Luke's statement reveals that this group of Jews is *representative*; that it consists of Jews '*from every nation under heaven.*' It includes Jews born in Jerusalem. But it especially calls attention to those who have migrated from other lands and established residence in Jerusalem, referred to as 'Diaspora Jews.' Nor is it to be forgotten that among these God-fearers is a vast number of pilgrims who have traveled from various locations throughout the ancient world to celebrate the Festival of Pentecost. While anticipating the events that are to unfold, this is Luke's way of underscoring 'the universality of the Jewish foundation of the church.'[13]

> When they heard this sound, a crowd came together in bewilderment, because each one heard their own language being spoken. Utterly amazed, they asked: 'Aren't all these who are speaking Galileans?' (vv. 6-7)

When the Holy Spirit descends upon the followers of Jesus, thus empowering their prophetic speaking, they apparently move outside from their prior assembly inside; perhaps, by design. As a result, this spectacular phenomenon is noticed by other people who, in turn, rush to the source of the noise. Their reaction to what they observe is strong and visceral, captured by a complex of terms that describe their profound sense of alarm:

> '*bewilderment*' (v. 6): 'to cause such astonishment as to dismay—to cause consternation, to confound.'[14]

---

12. Rudolf Bultmann, 'ευλαβης,' *TDNT*, vol. II, p. 754.

13. Peterson, *The Acts*, p. 135.

14. Louw and Nida, *Greek-English Lexicon*, vol. 1, p. 313.

'amazed' (v. 7, 12): 'to cause someone to be so astound-
ed as to be practically overwhelmed ... to astound
completely.'[15]

'astonished' (v. 7, ESV The NIV has translated this
hendiadys as, *'utterly amazed'*): 'to be extraordinarily
impressed or disturbed by something.'[16]

'perplexed' (v. 12): 'to not know what to do, to be very
confused.'[17]

But what, properly speaking, is the basis of their fierce
dismay? It is grounded in their ethnic stereotypes. The
question–*'Aren't all these who are speaking Galileans?'*–should
be understood pejoratively. In the minds of these God-
fearers, the vast range of linguistic expertise being displayed
by these provincial Galileans should be impossible. They
were regarded as country bumpkins from the backwater
country in the north (*cf.* John 1:46; 7:52)–'boorish dolts in
the eyes of sophisticated Jerusalemites.'[18] In part, this was the
consequence of the Galilean manner of speaking, which was
notorious for swallowing syllables (recall the cockney accent of
Eliza Doolittle in *My Fair Lady*).[19] It served to make Galileans
conspicuous, a fact painfully discovered by Peter on the night
he vociferously attempted to deny any attachment to Jesus. In
rebuttal, people said to him: 'Surely you are one of them; your
accent gives you away' (Matt. 26:73). In this case, these tongues-
speaking Galileans, empowered by the Spirit, are not granted
a heavenly diction that furnishes them with the vocal clarity of
James Earl Jones. Their speech still bears the timbre of their

---

15. *Ibid.*, vol. 1, p. 313.Bauer, *A Greek-English Lexicon*, p. 444.

16. Bauer, *A Greek-English Lexicon, p. 444.*

17. Louw and Nida, *Greek-English Lexicon*, vol. 1, p. 381.

18. B. J. Malina and J. H. Neyrey, 'Conflict in Luke-Acts: Labeling and Deviance
Theory,' in J. H. Neyrey, ed., *The Social World of Luke-Acts: Models for Interpretation*
(Peabody: Hendrickson Publishers, 1991), p. 104.

19. 'Galilean speech was distinguished by its confusion or loss of laryngeals
and aspirates.' F. F. Bruce, *The Book of Acts* NICNT (Grand Rapids: William B.
Eerdmans Publishing Company, 1988), p. 54.

syllable-swallowing humanity, as evidenced by the continued confusion on the part of this multitude of God-fearers:

> 'Then how is it that each of us hears them in our native language? Parthians, Medes and Elamites; residents of Mesopotamia, Judea and Cappadocia, Pontus and Asia, Phrygia and Pamphylia, Egypt and the parts of Libya near Cyrene; visitors from Rome (both Jews and converts to Judaism); Cretans and Arabs—we hear them declaring the wonders of God in our own tongues!' Amazed and perplexed, they asked one another, 'What does this mean?' (vv. 8-12)

Who is posing these questions of bewilderment (here conveyed by Luke in choral form, a way of indicating that *many* are asking the same questions)? Devout, law-keeping Jews—people who, as an expression of their faithfulness to Yahweh, have come to Jerusalem for the purpose of celebrating Pentecost. Indeed, many of these people live in Jerusalem. Hence the logical inference: the vast majority of this multitude—*if not all of it*—understand Aramaic, an inference that will soon be proven true beyond doubt when the multitude evidences its comprehension of Peter's sermon. So why bother with these foreign languages? Why not speak to these God-fearers in Aramaic? And if Aramaic is not preferable, why not speak to these people in the *lingua franca*—Greek—the language commonly employed at this time as a means of communication among speakers of other languages? Either of these languages could be utilized, yet neither is employed. Instead, these various groupings of Jewish people are given to hear *their* native language or local dialect.[20] Why? It is to ensure that the message reaches each person in a form they can most readily understand and embrace. Moreover, says David Peterson, these Pentecostal experiences of linguistic phenomenon mean that:

---

20. The Greek term *dialektos* can have either meaning. Bauer, *A Greek-English Lexicon*, p. 232.

> [f]or one brief moment of time the divisions in
> humanity expressed through language difference
> (*cf.* Gen. 11:1-9) were overcome. These divisions are
> presented in Genesis as the judgment of God. What
> happened on the day of Pentecost suggests that God's
> curse had been removed ... God was expressing his
> ultimate intention to unite people 'from every tribe
> and language and people and nation' (Rev. 5:9-10; 7:9)
> under the rule of his Son (Eph. 1:9-10) ...[21]

Babel is being reversed; a fact Luke may be hinting at in his
choice of the Greek word that is here translated *'bewilderment'*—
the same term used in the Septuagint account of Babel to
speak of the confusion of languages (Gen. 11:7). Yet, despite
the shared similarity between Babel and Pentecost (the display
of diverse languages), there are two telling differences: 1) the
confusion at Babel was the consequence of the unintelligibility
factor created by so many languages, while on Pentecost
the confusion was the consequence of understanding the
numerous languages; and, 2) the diversity of languages on
Pentecost does not prove to be a means of division as at Babel,
but the beginnings of unification as Peterson suggests. Indeed,
this is a feat God intends to achieve, but not by homogenizing
the various peoples of this world. Were this the case, the Spirit
of prophecy might have supplied a universal language for
these Christians to speak and, in turn, equipped the various
groups gathered in Jerusalem with the power to comprehend—
in truth, an unnecessary hypothetical notion given that they
already possess a shared faculty in Aramaic and Greek. But
the Spirit opts for none of these alternatives. Why? The aim of
Christianity is to bridge cultures without eroding the diversity
they represent. At Pentecost this is achieved as the Spirit
furnishes the people of Jesus with an empowered proclamation
that proves pertinent to each group of listeners.[22]

---

21. Peterson, *The Acts*, p. 136.

22. Hence, the astonishment of Pentecost is not that people, otherwise unable,
could now understand the apostolic Christians. Rather, that as a gracious display

More specifically, what is the content of this unique proclamation empowered by the Holy Spirit? The apostolic Christians declare '*the wonders of God.*' Though appearing nowhere else in the Greek New Testament, the word translated '*wonders*' ('mighty works,' ESV) is used in the Septuagint to speak of God's mighty interventions in Israel's history, including the exodus and the wilderness events (*cf.* Deut. 11:2). Here, these '*wonders*' refer to the mighty deeds of God 'which relate to, and consist in, the story of Christ, and which form the content of NT proclamation;'[23] specifically, that God's salvation plan prophesied in the Old Testament has now arrived as its fulfillment in the life, death, resurrection, and ascension of Jesus Christ.

This is the Pentecostal gift: the advent of the Spirit, who subsequently rests upon all the followers of Jesus, that results in empowered verbal proclamation, so that they would fulfill their mandated mission of bearing witness to Him. This is not to infer that Luke's appreciation of the Spirit's coming is entirely confined to missionary empowerment. This would be an overstatement, especially in the light of subsequent texts that imply the Spirit's reproduction of Christian character (*cf.* Acts 6:3, 5; 7:55; 11:24; 13:52). Nevertheless, for a contemporary evangelicalism that is unhealthily curved inward–('*What can I expect the Holy Spirit to do for me?*')– Luke's emphasis is a necessary corrective. His attention, as defined by Pentecost, is tenaciously turned outward, strongly concentrated on the Spirit's empowerment for the fulfillment of the Christian mission to the ends of the earth. So William Willimon says:

> To those in the church today who regard the Spirit as an exotic phenomenon of mainly interior and purely personal significance, the story of the Spirit's descent

---

of power, God causes the Christians to speak in the 'heart language' of the listeners.

23. W. Grundmann, 'μεγαλεια,' *TDNT*, vol. IV, p. 541.

at Pentecost offers a rebuke. Luke goes to great pains
to insist that this outpouring of the Spirit is anything
but interior. Everything is by wind and fire, loud talk,
buzzing confusion, and public debate. The Spirit is
the power which enables us to 'go public' with its
good news, to attract a crowd and, as we shall see
in the next section, to have something to say worth
hearing. A new wind is set loose upon the earth,
provoking a storm of wrath and confusion for some,
a fresh breath of hope and empowerment for others.
Pentecost is a phenomenon of mainly evangelistic
significance ...[24]

Yet it is precisely at this point that prudence requires a
measure of patience. To be sure, God desires the salvation
of the entire world. But the reversal of the Babel motif must
not be pressed too quickly. While the catalog of nations listed
here by Luke (vv. 9-11) may imply the universal extent of the
Christian mission, an extent definitively articulated in 1:8, it
is necessary to recognize that the representatives from each of
these of designated nations are Jews, a fact Luke emphasized
earlier: '... God-fearing Jews from every nation under heaven' (v. 5).[25]
Alan Thompson captures this succinctly: 'It is as if everyone
associated with Israel from the four corners of the earth is
here,'[26] a fact made obvious by a brief observation of the map
provided.[27]

---

24. Willimon, Acts, p. 33.

25. Stott's explanation is to be appreciated: '... we must not press Luke's 'every nation' literally ... He was speaking, as the biblical writers normally did, from his own
horizon not ours, and was referring to the Graeco-Roman world situated round
the Mediterranean basin, indeed to every nation in which there were Jews.' Stott,
The Message, p. 63.

26. Thompson, Acts of the Risen Lord, p. 110.

27. This is taken from The NIV Study Bible.**<<permission needed?>>**

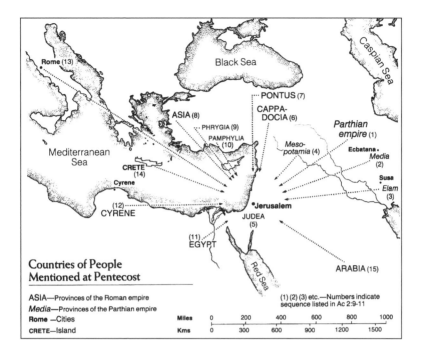

Countries of People Mentioned at Pentecost

ASIA—Provinces of the Roman empire
Media—Provinces of the Parthian empire
Rome—Cities
CRETE—Island

(1) (2) (3) etc.—Numbers indicate sequence listed in Ac 2:9-11

Hence, Jews from the east, west, north, and south have converged on Jerusalem, thus calling attention to one of the great prophetic expectations of the last days: the return of the exiles to Israel (*e.g.*, Isa. 49:5; Ezek. 20:40). Consequently, not only do these verses serve to reinforce the significance associated with the appointment of the twelfth apostle (1:12-26), they build upon the foundational structure it established: God is reconstituting Israel. In fulfillment of His promise, God is reviving the nation. It is the prophet Ezekiel who provides a graphic portrayal of this. He cites the declaration of the Sovereign Lord as follows:

> For I will take you out of the nations; I will gather you from all the countries and bring you back into your own land. (Ezek. 36:24)

But why is this even necessary? Yahweh explains:

> Son of man, when the people of Israel were living in their own land, they defiled it by their conduct

and their actions. Their conduct was like a woman's monthly uncleanness in my sight. So I poured out my wrath on them because they had shed blood in the land and because they had defiled it with their idols. I dispersed them among the nations, and they were scattered through the countries; I judged them according to their conduct and their actions. And wherever they went among the nations they profaned my holy name, for it was said of them, 'These are the LORD's people, and yet they had to leave his land.' (36:17-20)

The next chapter, accordingly, depicts Israel as a graveyard full of bones that are bereft of any sign of vitality. Death and decay have had their full effects on this landscape that reflects the aftermath of judgment. A suggestive question is asked of Ezekiel, but it is one for which only Yahweh Himself can supply an answer:

'Son of man, can these bones live?'
I said, 'Sovereign LORD, you alone know.'
Then he said to me, 'Prophesy to these bones and say to them, "Dry bones, hear the word of the Lord! This is what the Sovereign LORD says to these bones: I will make breath enter you, and you will come to life. I will attach tendons to you and make flesh come upon you and cover you with skin; I will put breath in you, and you will come to life. Then you will know that I am the LORD."'

So I prophesied as I was commanded. And as I was prophesying, there was a noise, a rattling sound, and the bones came together, bone to bone. I looked, and tendons and flesh appeared on them and skin covered them, but there was no breath in them.

Then he said to me, 'Prophesy to the breath; prophesy, son of man, and say to it, "This is what the Sovereign LORD says: Come, breath, from the four winds and breathe into these slain, that they may live."' So I prophesied as he commanded me, and breath entered them; they came to life and stood up on their feet—a vast army.

Then he said to me: 'Son of man, these bones are the people of Israel. They say, "Our bones are dried

up and our hope is gone; we are cut off." Therefore
prophesy and say to them: "This is what the Sovereign
LORD says: My people, I am going to open your graves
and bring you up from them; I will bring you back to
the land of Israel. Then you, my people, will know that
I am the LORD, when I open your graves and bring you
up from them. I will put my Spirit in you and you will
live ...'" (37:3-14).

It is the promise of the resurrection of Israel, a prophetic
anticipation of a new creation of the people of God, achieved
by the means of the Holy Spirit. Pentecost is the moment in
history when the fulfillment of the promise is inaugurated.

But for what reason does God effect such a reawakening
among His people? He has an ordained mission for them—a
mission stated in bits and pieces throughout the book of
Isaiah that eventually coalesce in the laconic statement of
Jesus Himself:

> But you will receive power when the Holy Spirit comes
> on you; and you will be my witnesses in Jerusalem,
> and in all Judea and Samaria, and to the ends of the
> earth. (1:8)

How, then, is Pentecost to be understood? It is the revival of
Israel, by the Spirit of God, for the purpose of fulfilling her
prophetic ministry to the world.

> ... Pentecost was a staging post on a much grander
> vista of biblical history. It signaled that something had
> been done (the atoning work of Messiah) and that
> something had not yet been fully accomplished (the
> gathering of the people of God into the visible church
> of Jesus Christ). The coming of the Holy Spirit was a
> result of the former and for enabling of the latter.[28]

What are the reactions to this Spirit empowered witness?
Some of the immediate reactions have already been noted:
'*bewilderment ... utterly amazed ... perplexed.*' Yet, some of these
God-fearers do seek greater understanding: '*What does this*

---

28. Thomas, *Acts*, p. 28

mean?' This serves to prepare the way for Peter's subsequent sermon. A different reaction also occurs, one that clearly desires no understanding:

> Some, however, made fun of them and said, 'They have had too much wine.' (v. 13)

Their accusation employs a term for *'wine'* that refers to a vintage still in the process of fermentation, and thus a quick stimulus to drunkenness since more of it would be consumed owing its sweet taste.[29] But this expression should not be taken as a literal assessment. It is a statement of mockery and scorn— an attempt to humiliate the Christians, as made evident by the modifying phrase: *'Some ... made fun of them.'*

These are the trenchant reactions to the Spirit empowered proclamation that occurs on the day of Pentecost. Yet none of them should be surprising to the contemporary Christian (particularly the reaction of mockery), given the transcendent message proclaimed, as well as the fallen nature of those who hear it. But some might reply that this venture into relevance is inappropriate. 'After all, isn't Pentecost about the revival of Israel and the fulfillment of her mission as the prophetic people of God? Isn't Pentecost to be understood as a unique event in redemptive history and, thus, unrepeatable? This has no relevance to any present expression of Christianity.'

Or does it?

On the one hand, a careful consideration of this text reveals that it is not a passage in which Luke is attempting to set forth a detailed description of individual Christian experience. This is the beginning of the new creation and the birth of God's eschatological people: the restored Israel who will carry the gospel to the nations of the world. Consequently, Christians will not necessarily experience the features of Pentecost that marked the inauguration of the Spirit's presence among the people of God (the dramatic

---

29. Louw and Nida, *Greek-English Lexicon*, vol. 1, p. 77.

sights and sounds). Of course, every person must be baptized with the Holy Spirit in order to become a Christian and to function as a gospel witness. But this, properly speaking, is not the burden of this passage.

On the other hand, the newness that defines the new covenant is rooted in the reality that all of God's people are given the gift of the indwelling Holy Spirit; moreover, that the Spirit who indwells them is, indeed, the Spirit of prophecy. As such, not only are contemporary Christians responsible to fulfill the apostolic mandate (a reality repeatedly recorded in Acts, and also prescribed in the remainder of the New Testament), they have been granted the enablement to do so.

Consider the command given to Adam and Eve—the paradigmatic couple of the original creation, recently brought to life by the breath of God:

> Be fruitful and increase in number; fill the earth and subdue it. Rule over the fish in the sea and the birds in the sky and over every living creature that moves on the ground. (Gen. 1:28)

Following the great deluge this same command is reiterated to Noah:

> Be fruitful and increase in number and fill the earth. The fear and dread of you will fall on all the beasts of the earth, and on all the birds in the sky, on every creature that moves along the ground, and on all the fish in the sea; they are given into your hands. (Gen. 9:1-2)

This is immediately recognized as the creation mandate. But it is more than a mandate. It is organic law fixed into the very constitution of human beings. For this reason, it is the *nature* of human beings to be reproductive, evidenced by the fact that they *are* reproductive whether or not they have any cognizance of this command. Likewise, it can be said that even those who are mindful of this mandate keep it instinctively and spontaneously, rather than consciously.

Now consider the command assigned to the apostolic Christians—the paradigmatic community of the new creation, brought into existence by the Breath of God:

> ... you will be my witnesses in Jerusalem, and in all Judea and Samaria, and to the ends of the earth (Acts 1:8).

This, too, is reiterated:

> ... go and make disciples of all nations (Matt. 28:19).

> Go into all the world and preach the gospel to all creation (Mark 16:15).

Known as the Great Commission, it is the new creation counterpart to the original creation mandate. It is the new creation mandate. But like the original, it is more than a mandate. To be missionary is organic to the life of the church, a reality embedded within her nature. Therefore, unless something is profoundly amiss, she cannot not witness. But why is this the case? Because on the day of Pentecost the missionary Spirit came to rest upon the church forever and, as such, implanted the missionary impulse within her— the impulse to witness to Jesus Christ—which is one of the certain proofs of the Spirit's indwelling presence. As such, Pentecost bears an influence that transcends its historical/ redemptive significance. It reminds the church of God's ancient promises and fulfillments, her unique mission in long-standing continuity with God's intention for Israel, and of the provision of the Holy Spirit by whose potency she is equipped to engage it successfully.

5

WHAT DOES PENTECOST MEAN?

The sign of the age to come
is the presence of the Spirit.
F. F. BRUCE

~~~~~~~~~~~~~~~~~~~~~~~~~~~

The departure of Jesus
has made witness to him necessary,
while the Pentecostal baptism with the Spirit
has made it possible.
ROBERT W. WALL

~~~~~~~~~~~~~~~~~~~~~~~~~~~

In these last days,
the Messiah has taken the throne at the Father's right hand,
and he is extending his dominion on earth
through the power of the Spirit.
DENNIS E. JOHNSON

~~~~~~~~~~~~~~~~~~~~~~~~~~~

14Then Peter stood up with the Eleven, raised his voice and addressed the crowd: 'Fellow Jews and all of you who live in Jerusalem, let me explain this to you; listen carefully to what I say. 15These people are not drunk, as you suppose. It's only nine in the morning! 16No, this is what was spoken by the prophet Joel:

> *17"In the last days, God says,*
> > *I will pour out my Spirit on all people.*
> *Your sons and daughters will prophesy,*
> > *your young men will see visions,*
> > *your old men will dream dreams.*
> *18Even on my servants, both men and women,*
> > *I will pour out my Spirit in those days,*

and they will prophesy.
¹⁹I will show wonders in the heavens above
and signs on the earth below,
blood and fire and billows of smoke.
²⁰The sun will be turned to darkness
and the moon to blood
before the coming of the great and glorious day
of the Lord.
²¹And everyone who calls
on the name of the Lord will be saved."

²²'Fellow Israelites, listen to this: Jesus of Nazareth was a man accredited by God to you by miracles, wonders and signs, which God did among you through him, as you yourselves know. ²³This man was handed over to you by God's deliberate plan and foreknowledge; and you, with the help of wicked men, put him to death by nailing him to the cross. ²⁴But God raised him from the dead, freeing him from the agony of death, because it was impossible for death to keep its hold on him. ²⁵David said about him:

"I saw the Lord always before me.
Because he is at my right hand,
I will not be shaken.
²⁶Therefore my heart is glad and my tongue rejoices;
my body also will rest in hope,
²⁷because you will not abandon me to the realm of the dead,
you will not let your holy one see decay.
²⁸You have made known to me the paths of life;
you will fill me with joy in your presence."

²⁹'Fellow Israelites, I can tell you confidently that the patriarch David died and was buried, and his tomb is here to this day. ³⁰But he was a prophet and knew that God had promised him on oath that he would place one of his descendants on his throne. ³¹Seeing what was to come, he spoke of the resurrection of the Messiah, that he was not abandoned to the realm of the dead, nor did his body see decay. ³²God has raised this Jesus to life, and we are all witnesses of it. ³³Exalted to

the right hand of God, he has received from the Father the promised
Holy Spirit and has poured out what you now see and hear. [34]*For*
David did not ascend to heaven, and yet he said,

> *"The Lord said to my Lord:*
>   *'Sit at my right hand*
> [35]*until I make your enemies*
>   *a footstool for your feet.'"*

[36]*'Therefore let all Israel be assured of this: God has made this Jesus,*
whom you crucified, both Lord and Messiah.'
(Acts 2:14-36)

Never To Be Forgotten

Has there ever been a preacher who has outlived the memory
of his *first* sermon? I highly doubt it, though many of us have
tried. It seems that *first* sermons are indelibly imprinted on
the hard drive of our memories, somehow untouched–*and*
untouchable–by every effort at deletion.

I was twenty-one when the opportunity to preach to
a group of high school students was first presented to me.
Though I had only been a Christian for about seven months,
I took up the task wholeheartedly, knowing immediately that
I would concentrate my efforts on Proverbs 3. How I actually *prepared* to preach remains a bit of a mystery. But I am
certain of this: I lacked any method of studying the Bible,
let alone a framework for constructing a sermon. So for next
several weeks I prayed, read and reread the text dozens of
times, jotted down everything that came to mind, and finally
composed a manuscript from which to 'preach.'

When the Wednesday evening arrived, and I was introduced to the students by the youth pastor, I stepped forward,
placed my Bible and notes on a music stand that I summarily
lowered, sat down on a stool and proceeded to preach. After all, even then, everyone knew that the distinguishing feature of Spirit-filled preaching is the aura of being casual and

conversational, spontaneous—even to the point of appearing unprepared. (Do the emergent Christians *really* believe they invented this image?) After I finished, the youth pastor concluded the meeting with prayer and dismissed the group. But this was not the evening's conclusion for me. Several of the students stepped forward with expressions of encouragement: 'Nice talk, Art.' 'It was really cool to see you up there.' 'Are you going to do it again?' 'I thought the story about the firefighter was hilarious.' It *surprised* me … it really did. Yet by the time all of the students had left for home, my surprise had morphed into something like … *expectancy*. In a matter of a few brief moments, their compliments had transformed me from a humble novice into a gifted expert: 'OK. I think I've got this business down.'

A bit later, one of the staff members, a wonderfully warm woman in her early fifties, walked over to me and said:

> 'That was terrific tonight, especially for your very first time preaching. I think you should keep at it.'
>
> 'Thanks,' I replied in well-feigned humility.
> After a brief pause, she spoke up again—this time, however, a bit more gingerly:
> 'Um … may I offer a suggestion?'
> 'Sure. Fire away!' I responded confidently, still basking in the stirring approval I had just received from the discerning *fifteen-year-olds* in the youth group.
>
> She said:
> 'Maybe next time, *before you begin to preach*, you should spit out your gum.'

At that very moment, I *swallowed* my gum … and realized that she was not wrong. I immediately evaporated into nothing … at least internally. My text had been—'Trust in the LORD with all your heart and lean not on your own understanding; in all your ways submit to him, and he will make your paths straight' (Prov. 3:5-6)—and for the entire thirty minutes I preached it, I simultaneously masticated a huge chunk of pink, juicy, *Hubba Bubba Bubble Gum*.

Take my word for it: preachers do not forget their *first* sermons. Their only refuge resides in the hope that everyone else will.

I expect that the apostle Peter never forgot his first sermon either, even long after he preached it. But, then again, how could he? It may be the greatest Christian sermon ever preached, its greatness being defined by: 1) the unique position it occupies at the most crucial turning point in redemptive history; 2) the immediate, radical, and overwhelming responses that result from it; and, 3) the model it supplies for all preachers seeking to preach sermons that are truly Christian. *It is an extraordinary sermon*—a feature made evident by the fact that the one proclaiming it, just fifty days prior, had committed the most infamous denial of Jesus Christ the world has ever known. Yet the resurrected Lord addresses Peter's egregious failure with restorative grace. Subsequently, he emerges as the principal preacher of the apostolic community, his own experience serving as a platform from which to herald the forgiveness that is to be found through the one who becomes the relentless subject of his sermon.

It is a scripturally-saturated sermon. In his introduction (vv. 14-21), Peter appeals to *Joel 2* to provide a clarifying explanation for the recent display of tongues-speaking. In his middle and longest section (vv. 22-32), Peter cites *Psalm 16* to establish a prophetic justification for the resurrection of the Messiah. And then, arriving at the sermon's apex (vv. 33-36), Peter quotes *Psalm 110* to defend the lordship of Jesus and, therefore, His authority to pour out the Holy Spirit, as has just been witnessed. Furthermore, it should be kept in mind that this inspired record of Peter's sermon is merely a cameo (it can be recited in about three minutes!), a point on which commentators universally agree,[1] but

---

1. See Bock, *Acts*, p. 111; Peterson, *The Acts*, pp. 156-157; Thompson, *Acts of the Risen Lord*, pp. 89-90; Witherington, *The Acts*, pp. 116-118; *et al.* A helpful summary of themes that distinguish the sermons in Acts can be found in Johnson, *The Message*, pp. 143-154.

also the clear implication of v. 40: 'With many other words he warned them ...' It seems reasonable to assume that other Old Testament references were highlighted by Peter as well.

It is a Christ-centered sermon. Though brief mention is made of the Holy Spirit at the outset of Peter's sermon, and also in recapitulation near the sermon's conclusion, the central theme of his sermon is decidedly *not* the Holy Spirit. The unmistakable subject of this address is Jesus. It includes mention of His life and ministry (v. 22), His crucifixion, (v. 23), His resurrection (vv. 24-32), and His ascension-exaltation (33-36). This is not surprising, given Jesus' earlier instructions to His disciples concerning the advent and ministry of the Spirit: 'When the Advocate comes, whom I will send to you from the Father—the Spirit of truth who goes out from the Father—he will testify about me ... He will glorify me' (John 15:26; 16:14). Here, the Spirit bears witness via the witness of Peter who employs Old Testament Scripture as the apologetic basis to validate his claims about Jesus (a consistent pattern in Peter's preaching).[2]

It is a convicting sermon. There is not the slightest hint of self-righteousness, contempt, or anger in Peter's sermon. Yet, he addresses the full culpability of his hearers without ambiguity: '*you* ... put him to death by nailing him to the cross ... God made this Jesus, whom *you* crucified ...' (v. 23, 36). Their personal responsibility is set before them, which does effect a reaction: 'they were cut to the heart' (v. 37a). But this reaction, in turn, gives birth to a corresponding reply: 'Brothers, what shall we do?' (v. 37). A student who was displeased with a lecture I was giving on the subject of evangelism interrupted me. Though

---

2. The apostolic use of the Old Testament has not uncommonly been regarded as 'skeletons in the closet' of diligent interpreters. However, if the entire Bible is *Christian* Scripture, then Christian expositors must take their interpretive cues from the apostles who learned their hermeneutic from Jesus. Their understanding and application of Old Testament texts provide the 'skeleton key' that opens the door for all those who follow them in the work of interpretation and exposition. See Dan G. McCartney, 'The New Testament's Use of the Old Testament,' *Inerrancy and Hermeneutic*, ed. Harvie M. Conn (Grand Rapids: Baker Book House, 1998).

she was being careful to maintain her self-control, she asserted strongly: 'You *can't* tell people they are sinners. You *mustn't*.' I responded: 'Then I can't tell people the gospel either because these are mutually interpreting.' Peter unabashedly (though not unkindly) names the glaring guilt of his audience.

Finally, *it is a relevant sermon*. When the God-fearers are confronted with a display that fills them with bewilderment— 'we hear them declaring the wonders of God in our own tongues' (v. 11)—a question is precipitated: 'What does this mean?' (v. 12). Peter's ensuing sermon is the germane response. It is not a 'one-size-fits all' sermon with no consideration given to the unique audience being addressed. Nor is it a theological lecture filled with irrelevant data cobbled together from the latest Bible software. This is a fresh word for real people; a Spirit empowered proclamation of the sacred text in direct reply to the question posed by the congregation presently gathered before Peter.

Of approximately one thousand verses in Acts, at least three hundred and sixty five are found in major and minor speeches and dialogues.[3] As such, it is likely that some readers will be faced with the need to overcome a predisposed bias against sermons which, to them, may seem to be a methodology that bespeaks a dogmatism that is no longer appropriate for a contemporary culture in which dialogue is regarded as more democratic. Willimon reacts strongly to this, urging his readers to remember that in relatively recent (American) history—

> ... Lincoln's Gettysburg Address did more than open a cemetery—it gave meaning and substance to a national cataclysm. Martin Luther King, Jr.'s 'I Have a Dream' speech reinterpreted our history and constitution and mobilized a people into action for justice. A good speech can turn us inside out.[4]

3. Thompson, *Acts of the Risen Lord*, p. 89.

4. Willimon, *Acts*, p. 34.

Yes. But here–*in this sermon that should inform all other Christian sermons*–the hearers are not merely turned inside out, they are brought from death to life. It is a sermon that answers the question: *What does Pentecost mean?*

The End Has Been Inaugurated

> Then Peter stood up with the Eleven, raised his voice
> and addressed the crowd: 'Fellow Jews and all of you
> who live in Jerusalem, let me explain this to you: listen
> carefully to what I say. These people are not drunk, as
> you suppose. It's only nine in the morning!' (vv. 14-15)

The tight relationship between the advent of the Holy Spirit and the subsequent declaration of the prophetic word continues to display itself. In keeping with the commission assigned to them by Jesus (1:8), the apostles–now for the first time empowered by the Spirit–serve as witnesses to Him. Luke indicates that they stand, no doubt to be seen and heard by this large group that now comprises several thousand people. Peter, as he had done earlier in Acts 1, assumes the role of primary spokesman and accordingly elevates the volume of his voice. His speaking here, however, is not in a language unknown to himself–the miracle in the earlier portion of this chapter. His communication is in Aramaic most likely, though Greek may have been used in keeping with the cosmopolitan background of these Jews. In either case, the implied point is clear: these people will not be persuaded that Jesus is the resurrected Lord by means of ecstatic events, but by intelligible preaching that is empowered by the Holy Spirit.

Upon acknowledging both the festival pilgrims and the resident Jews–*'Fellow Jews and all of you who live in Jerusalem'*– Peter begins his address by countering their earlier accusation of inebriation and its perceived irrationality: 'Everyone knows that Christians don't start drinking until noon!' Is this Peter's rejoinder? Not quite, though a wry humor is to be detected.[5]

---

5. Peterson, *The Acts*, p. 131.

For this reason, English translations supply the adverb *'only'* so as to exaggerate the point that *'nine in the morning'* is clearly too early for any reasonably-minded person to be drinking. Peter is deflating the tension of the moment by removing the mockery's sting: 'What you have just observed is not the effect of early morning binge drinking. It is nothing less than the next installment in the storyline of salvation.'

> No, this is what was spoken by the prophet Joel: "In the last days, God says, I will pour out my Spirit on all people." (vv. 16-17a)

Two implications are immediately apparent: 1) Peter has continued to study the Scriptures. Drawing upon the interpretive insights given to him by Jesus, it is his reading of the *Psalms* that lead to the appointment of the twelfth apostle in the prior chapter. But Jesus' instruction included more than the *Psalms*; it encompassed the *Prophets* as well: 'And beginning with Moses *and all the Prophets,* he explained to them what was said in all the Scriptures concerning himself' (Luke 24:27; *cf.* v. 44). Now, it is Peter's 'Christian' understanding of the prophecy of Joel that is brought to the forefront; and, 2) Peter continues to exhibit a high view of Scripture. Though the prophet Joel has penned these words (or, more properly, *'spoken'* them), he is only to be regarded as the intermediate agent through whom God speaks.[6] Joel says what God says.

What is the historical situation that originally occasions these words? Judah has endured an unprecedented national disaster as an expression of God's judgment for her sin: an invasion of locusts that has decimated the resources of the land (Joel 1:4-12). In response to thoroughgoing repentance, however, God promises to extend mercy to His people by restoring the land to its former prosperity. Yet Israel must take heed: this judgment is a harbinger (an anticipatory type) of a far more severe judgment that Joel refers to as 'the day of the

---

6. Wallace, *Greek Grammar*, pp. 433-434.

LORD' (Joel 1:15; 2:1-2, 11, 31; 3:14). Leading up this final day, Joel adds, will be a set of distinguishing events that occur over an undefined period of time; including the outpouring of the Spirit on all people (Israel), wonders in the heavens and on the earth, and the promise of salvation for all who call on the name of the Lord.

In his reference to this text Peter could not be any clearer. He matches the prophetic word to its eschatological fulfillment: *'this is what was spoken by the prophet Joel.'* Yet even a cursory glance at these two passages reveals that Peter makes a clarifying enhancement. He modifies the introduction of Joel's prophesy from—

> 'And *afterwards*, I will pour out my Spirit on all people'

to—

> 'In *the last days*,' God says, 'I will pour out my Spirit on all people.'

This can hardly be regarded as the imposition of a *different* meaning on Joel's original intent ('afterward' does refer generally to a future time). Rather, Peter sharpens the focus to alert his listeners to the eschatological significance of what they have just witnessed; that they are now seeing 'part of God's final act of redemption.'[7] The substituted refinement, *'In the last days,'* is taken from Isaiah 2:2 where it speaks of the time when all the world's nations will stream to the Lord's temple and the word of the Lord will extend out from Jerusalem. It is a theologically charged expression, referring to the final days of salvation's history. Peter's point here, staggeringly, is that this prophesied period of time—*'the last days'* (which will conclude with the last day, 'the day of the LORD')—has now been inaugurated. On what basis is Peter certain of this? Keeping in stride with the prophecy of Joel, he explains that the definitive event signaling the inception of *'the last days'* has just taken place: the Spirit of prophecy has been poured out.[8]

---

7. Peterson, *The Acts*, p. 141.

8. Bruce's comment adds perspective: "In another place Peter tells how the

What does this mean? To *'pour out'* the Spirit is a metaphorical expression. As mentioned in the prior chapter, the Holy Spirit is *like* a wind and fire, but is literally neither. Nor should it be inferred here that the Holy Spirit is a fluid. He is the living presence of God, bearing the full qualities of personhood and deity. Thus, when God says—*'I will pour out my Spirit'*—He is not defining the Spirit's essence, but the manner of the Spirit's coming—a manner that will prove altogether unique to *'the last days.'* It will not resemble a mist or a light rain (as in the old epoch), but a veritable deluge. It will be distinguished by liberality and universality. The Spirit will come to indwell *'all people'* regardless of gender (*'sons and daughters,'* v. 17—*'men and women,'* v. 18), age (*'young men ... old men,'* v. 17), and social status (*'Even on my servants,'* v. 18). Yet this universality is not without discrimination. *'All people'* is further defined by specific qualifying phrases: *'your sons and daughters,'* v. 17—*'your young men,'* v. 17—*'your old men,'* v. 17—and then, particularly, *'my servants,'* v. 18. This promise, it must be understood, does not encompass 'everybody irrespective of their inward readiness to receive the gift, but everybody irrespective of their outward status.'[9] More specifically, when the original setting of this prophecy is recalled—God speaking to Judah—it is patently clear that this gift of the Spirit is for all those *in Israel* who belong to God; now, in the wake of the gospel, Jewish people who have embraced Jesus as the Messiah.

This is in keeping with God's promise to restore Israel. However, as has been previously explained, this restoration

---

prophets who foretold about the coming manifestation of God's grace 'searched and inquired about this salvation; they inquired what person or time was indicated by the Spirit of Christ within them when predicting the sufferings of Christ and the subsequent glories" (1 Pet. 1:10-11). But now that Christ has been "made manifest at the end of the times" (1 Pet. 1:20), his followers have no further need to search and inquire (as the prophets did) what person or time the prophetic Spirit pointed to, for they *know*: the person is Jesus; the time is now.' Bruce, *Acts*, p. 61.

9. Stott, *The Message*, p. 74.

is for the purpose of fulfilling her mission to the nations. As such, God's generosity in this gift of the Spirit will express itself in a manifestation uniquely essential to this mission:

> Your sons and your daughters will prophesy, your young men will see visions, your old men will dream dreams. Even on my servants, both men and women, I will pour out my Spirit in those days, and they will prophesy (17b-18).

Other portions of the New Testament refer to prophecy as an endowment of the Spirit granted to Christians for the sake of strengthening congregational life (Rom. 12:4-7; 1 Cor. 12-14). As such, this gift may express itself in the following forms: 1) the proclamation of an inspired revelation (*e.g.*, 1 Cor. 14:3); 2) the telling of something that is hidden from view (*e.g.*, Matt. 26:68); or, 3) the foretelling of something that lies in the future (*e.g.*, Acts 11:27-28).[10] This is not a gift given to all, but only to a unique subset of Christians—an obvious deduction via Paul's question to the Corinthians: 'Not all are prophets, are they?' (1 Cor. 12:29, NET). The question assumes a 'no' answer.

Clearly, this is not the gift to which Joel referred. Nor is it the gift to which Peter presently refers, a fact anticipated earlier in the chapter when the 'tongues of fire' come to rest on *'each'* of the Christians (v. 3). Luke's subsequent comment reinforces this: '*All of them* were filled with the Holy Spirit,' (v. 4). Finally, and convincingly, Peter states in v. 16 that this is *precisely* what Joel envisioned: God pouring out His Spirit on *all* people that results in universal prophesying. How is this to be reconciled with the aforementioned limitations on prophecy? Are Peter and Paul at odds on this subject?

Before providing an answer to this question, it essential to note that Peter again alters Joel's words; not, on this occasion, by mere enhancement, but by actual addition. This becomes obvious when a close comparison is made of the two passages:

---

10. Bauer, *A Greek-English Lexicon*, p. 890.

Joel 2:28-29
Your sons and daughters will prophesy,
your old men will dream dreams,
your young men will see visions.
Even on my servants, both men and women,
I will pour out my Spirit in those days.

Acts 2:17-18
Your sons and daughters will prophesy,
your young men will see visions,
your old men will dream dreams.
Even on my servants, both men and women,
I will pour out my Spirit in those days,
and they will prophesy.

Peter adds a final line that is a repetition of Joel's first line. This not only highlights '*the act of prophesying*' as the focal point of the Spirit's outpouring, it provides literary bookends that frame this section. In other words, it creates an *inclusio*—which, in turn, implies that the '*visions*' and '*dreams*' mentioned between the bookends should be regarded as subdivisions of prophesying. This is not surprising since dreams and visions were often given to Old Testament prophets, not merely to understand God's character and will, but for the purpose making known this revelation to people.[11] Nevertheless, it is the infrequent mention of these phenomena in Acts that is revealing. '*Visions*' in Acts are rare (9:10-11; 10:3, 17; 16:9-10; 18:9). '*Dreams*' are never mentioned. And, in fact, only a few individuals are designated '*prophets*' in the traditionally understood sense (11:27-28; 13:1; 15:32; 21:9-10). Therefore, the question that begs to be asked is: *To what, then, does this* '*prophesying*' *refer*—here promised as the universal experience of all people who are indwelt with the Spirit of God?

The answer becomes obvious when careful consideration is given to: 1) the principal theme of Acts—the missionary agenda that Jesus has assigned to His followers; 2) Jesus' instruction

---

11. Visions (*e.g.,* Num. 24:4; Isa. 1:1; Ezek. 1:1). Dreams (*e.g.,* Gen. 37:5; 1 Sam. 28:15; Dan. 1:17).

that the inauguration of this agenda is dependent upon the reception of the Holy Spirit; and, 3) the consequential display of the Spirit's reception—unbelievers hear 'the wonders of God' declared in their own languages. All of this combines to necessitate a broadened understanding of *'prophecy'* in this text—what Stott refers to as 'an umbrella-use of the verb to "prophesy".'[12] In distinction from the Old Testament epoch in which the Spirit was given to a select few for the purpose of making known God's word, Pentecost means that all of God's people are now enabled to declare the fulfillment of God's salvation plan in Jesus Christ. Just as Christians have been made kings and priests, so, too, the Spirit-indwelt followers of Jesus are now prophets. This is the realized meaning in Jesus' words: 'I tell you, among those born of women there is no one greater than John; yet the one who is least in the kingdom of God is greater than he' (Luke 7:28). Turner is insistent:

> ... from the perspective of these key Lukan sections the promise of the Spirit to the disciples is especially focused as prophetic empowerment for witness. This alone makes sense of the explicit statements concerning the heavenly 'power' they will receive in Lk. 24:49 and Acts 1:8, of the undoubted reference in 'the promise of my/ the Father' to Joel's promise of the 'Spirit of prophecy', and of the *mission* given to the church to fulfill the role of the prophetic 'servant' of Isa. 49:6 ... The disciples have already implicitly experienced 'forgiveness of sins', they have fully enjoyed the benefits of 'the kingdom of God' (in so far as that was present in Jesus' ministry) and of 'salvation', and they have attained the fullness of Christian faith in the crucified and risen Lord. What is left to them now is to receive the Spirit as a prophetic empowering to extend this message and its benefits to Israel and beyond.[13]

This is the fulfillment of Joel's ancient prophecy, and that to which Peter here refers: every Christian has been granted

---

12. Stott, *The Message*, p. 74.

13. Turner, *Power from on High*, p. 343.

the indwelling Holy Spirit as the unique empowerment for witness during this time between '*the last days*' and '*the day of the Lord.*' It serves to underscore the church's vocation by implying that the present time for God's people is not a season for waiting, but one set apart for mission. The eschatological clock is ticking.[14]

> I will show wonders in the heavens above and signs on the earth below, blood and fire and billows of smoke. The sun will be turned to darkness and the moon to blood before the coming of the great and glorious day of the Lord. (vv. 19-20)

It is not uncommon for people to read passages like this through a predisposed lens; in particular, the lens provided by Hollywood's ever-increasing reservoir of post-apocalyptic movies (*e.g.*, *The Day After, The Book of Eli, The Hunger Games*). On a more respectable level, there are fine scholars who do approach such passages with a strict literalism—and, as in this case, seek to provide a direct historical correspondence for each these cosmic expressions.[15] While some of their conclusions appear plausible (*e.g.*, the darkening of the sun is a reference to the crucifixion, Luke 23:45), others are strained beyond certainty. A few are reserved entirely for the period just preceding the final day. Yet all of these are drawn from a common quarry of traditional apocalyptic images; indeed, they are 'stock metaphors for God's action in judging and saving.'[16] They serve to personify creation, picturing it in turmoil and upheaval, breaking apart and imploding in a kind of de-creation that results from the act of God's fierce judgment. Use of such cosmic disturbances is not exclusive to the final judgment, however; throughout the history of Israel they are associated with other days of judgment as well (*e.g.*,

---

14. Bock, *Acts*, p. 117.

15. See Eckhard J. Schnabel, *Acts*, ECNT (Grand Rapids: Zondervan Publishing House, 2012), pp. 138-139.

16. Ryken, *et al*, 'Day of the Lord,' *Biblical Imagery*, p. 197.

Isa. 13:9-22; Ezek. 32:1-10; Amos 8:9-14; Joel 2:10-12). In each case, they induce an intensified terror among the potential recipients by amplifying their awareness of the severity of coming judgment; perhaps, as a means of arousing repentance among them.

Peter's point is that the pouring out of the Spirit of prophecy on God's people has signaled the entrance into 'the last days'—the eschatological period that is also distinguished by these cosmic, pre-judgment judgments. It is not just a season of unprecedented blessing, but of heightened distress; in particular, because the launch sequence to final judgment has begun. 'The last days' anticipate the last day, the event Peter refers to as: 'the great and glorious day of the Lord.' It is 'great'[17] because of its significance: the new age will be consummated. It is 'glorious'[18] because of its conspicuousness: the final judgment will be an unmatched revelation of God's glory. But this does compel a corollary question of practical significance: Should the imminent revelation of God's glory in judgment be anticipated fearfully? Joel adds:

> And everyone who calls on the name of the Lord will
> be saved. (v. 21)

Robert Wall has stated: 'Typically, the most important phrase of a quoted text is the last one read, which lingers in the auditor's ear.'[19] If this is true, the most important phrase Peter cites from Joel's prophecy is aimed at relieving distress in his hearers. It is to assure them that the event of final judgment need not be a cause of fear; rather, that a gracious opportunity has been allocated for those living in 'the last days.'

What is the essence of this opportunity? It is the future experience of being 'saved.' The Greek term could just as easily

---

17. The word megas can pertain to being 'superior in importance.' Bauer, Greek-English Lexicon, p. 624.

18. Louw and Nida suggest the following meaning of epiphanes in Acts 2:20: 'Pertaining to being glorious or wonderful, in view of being conspicuous and self-evident.' Greek-English Lexicon, vol. 1, p. 696.

19. Wall, Acts, p. 65.

be translated 'rescued,' or 'delivered.' Whichever English term is used, each presupposes a condition necessitating intervention. In this case, people are *'saved'* from the eternal condemnation meted out upon God's enemies on the *'the great and glorious day of the Lord.'* Salvation is the epicenter of God's message in the Bible, a repeated theme in Luke's writings (*e.g.,* Luke 1:69; 2:11; 7:50; 19:9-10; Acts 2:40; 4:12; 15:11; 28:28). Accordingly, it is this experience that lies at the heart of the mission Jesus has assigned to His people.

Who may avail themselves of this opportunity? Peter (citing Joel, who is quoting Yahweh) extends this to *'everyone.'* In the present context this includes: 'Fellow Jews and all of you who live in Jerusalem,' (v. 14), 'Fellow Israelites,' (vv. 22, 29), 'all Israel,' (v. 36), 'every one of you,' (v. 38), 'you and your children and ... all who are far off' (v. 39). Elsewhere in the New Testament, this portion of Joel's text will be extended ever further (*e.g.,* Rom. 10:13; 1 Cor. 1:2).

How may people benefit from this opportunity? The passive voice of the verb–*'will be saved'*–indicates that salvation on the day of final judgment is an experience that can only be granted, not self-achieved. As such, it must not be assumed. While *accessible* to everyone, it is only *accessed in actuality* by everyone *'who calls on the name of the Lord.'* What does this mean? The word that is here rendered–*'calls'*–typically implies: 'an appeal for aid ... to ask for help.'[20] But is this all that Peter means? At the conclusion of his sermon–in response to the earnest inquiry of his hearers ('... what shall we do?' v. 37)—Peter provides a reply that serves as an exposition of his meaning here: 'Repent and be baptized ... in the name of Jesus Christ' (2:38). In other words, to call on the Lord's name is synonymous with submitting oneself in repentance and faith to baptism in the name of Jesus. This raises a significant issue. In Joel's original prophecy, the Lord who executes final judgment and grants salvation is Yahweh. Is this who Peter has in mind in these last days?

---

20. Louw and Nida, *Greek-English Lexicon,* vol. 1, p. 408.

The King Has Been Enthroned

> 'Fellow Israelites, listen to this: Jesus of Nazareth was
> a man accredited by God to you by miracles, wonders
> and signs, which God did among you through him,
> as you yourselves know. This man was handed over to
> you by God's deliberate plan and foreknowledge; and
> you, with the help of wicked men, put him to death by
> nailing him to the cross.' (vv. 22-23)

Peter's sermon now progresses into its next stage. His agenda
is still intact: to provide an explanation for the Pentecostal
event. But doing so requires him to advance from its *prophetic
basis* in ancient Scripture to the *redemptive cause* of its present
fulfillment. Consequently, his attention moves from the Holy
Spirit (who is not mentioned again until v. 33, and once
more in v. 38) to Jesus of Nazareth. This not only serves to
realize the Spirit's anticipated ministry (John 15:26; 16:14),
it provides a model of apostolic witness. Since this is not a
comprehensive transcript of Peter's sermon, it is prudent to
assume that the content provided is not arbitrary but serves
an exemplary purpose.[21]

This not a testimony that recounts a dramatic *first person*
conversion experience. It is an address that unambiguously
calls attention to a *third person*; more specifically, to key
historical events in His unique life and ministry that are
corroborated by firsthand eyewitnesses. Ajith Fernando
provides an appropriate reminder: 'Christianity is Christ.'[22]
Accordingly, Peter begins by asserting that Jesus was an
authentic person–'*a man*'–identified by His Galilean roots–
'*from Nazareth*' (a fact that, by itself, may have discredited Him
as the Messiah, *cf.* John 1:46; 7:52). Moving forward, Peter

---

21. 'Luke has provided us with carefully selected representative speeches–the point
of which appears to be to provide us with models/patterns/examples for how the
gospel was proclaimed and defended among various audiences that Christians met
as the gospel spread.' Thompson, *Acts of the Risen Lord*, p. 89.

22. Fernando, *Acts*, p. 107.

declares that God exhibited[23] the kind of man Jesus was by the displays He empowered through Him: *'miracles'* (mighty works that evidence a supernatural potency and kingly power—'If I drive out demons by the finger of God, then the kingdom of God has come upon you,' Luke 11:20), *'wonders'* (so designated because of the astonishment they effect—'I will show wonders in the heavens above,' Acts 2:19), both of which may be regarded as *'signs'* (pointing beyond themselves to the significance of the one performing them—'Rabbi, we know that you are a teacher who has come from God. For no one could perform the signs you are doing if God were not with him,' John 3:2).[24] Additionally, these displays are a matter of public record, Peter implies. He reminds his hearers that God's exhibition of Jesus occurred *'... among you ... as you yourselves know'*—even more pointedly, that God's display has been directed *'to you'*—that is, for their benefit.

Peter then proceeds to establish the death of this man, Jesus. He does so by explicitly identifying each of the responsible parties. *First,* he ascribes full blame to the people of Israel: *'and you ... put him to death.'* Certainly many among his listeners would know this to be an appropriate accusation, given the various expressions of Jewish wrongdoing: the seething jealousy of the religious leaders, the long-standing greediness of Judas, the trumped-up charges submitted by false witnesses, the kangaroo court comprised of hypocritical priests, the vicious mockery of the temple guard, the bloodthirsty fickleness of the mob, and the insidious manipulation of Pontius Pilate. But Jesus was not executed by the sole actions of Israel. *Second,* Peter indicates that their agenda was attained *'... with the help of*

---

23. The verb *apodeiknymi* means: 'To show forth the quality of an entity ... to display.' Bauer, *A Greek-English Lexicon*, p. 108.

24. 'Signs and wonders' is a repeated expression in the Old Testament, used almost exclusively with regard to the Exodus event (e.g., Exod. 7:3; Deut. 4:34; Ps. 135:9). Appropriated here with relationship to Jesus, it anticipates a redemptive act of similar significance; perhaps, a typological fulfillment.

wicked men ...' (literally, 'lawless men')[25]—a fact made evident in the Gospel accounts. Roman centurions torture and scourge Jesus. The Roman governor, despite protestations from his wife, sentences Jesus to death by a means of execution that is distinctly non-Jewish—*'nailing him to the cross'*—during which time the attending Roman executioners expose their indifference in a narcissistic display: they cast lots to determine the beneficiary of Jesus' tunic.

Peter's indictment for the murder of Jesus is unmistakably clear: it is the achievement of a coordinated evil on the part of Jews and Gentiles.[26] N. T. Wright succinctly captures the significance of this:

> The anointed king would come to the place where evil was reaching its height, where the greatest human systems would reveal their greatest corruption (Rome, with its much vaunted system of justice, revealing itself rotten at the core; Israel, with its celebrated Temple and hierarchy, revealing itself hollow at its heart), and where this accumulated evil would blow itself out in one great act of unwarranted violence against the person who, of all, had done nothing to deserve it.[27]

Nevertheless, without diminishing any onus of responsibility (and, perhaps, anticipating the possibility of forgiveness for it), Peter elevates the meaning of this death by indicating that such was possible only because Jesus *'was handed over to you by God's deliberate plan and foreknowledge.'* In the Greek text, this statement actually precedes Peter's accusations of the Jews and Gentiles. His point is to make clear that standing behind the crucifixion of Jesus is the eternal purpose of God Himself:

---

25. This is not a reference to those without any moral code, but to those outside the Mosaic tradition.

26. One could argue that this comprises the entire human race distinguished and divided representatively by their covenantal association with Yahweh.

27. N. T. Wright, *Acts for Everyone* (Louisville: Westminster John Knox Press, 2008), vol. 1, pp. 38-39.

'God foreknew it, decided it, and planned it.'[28] Yet, even at this point, it must be understood that God's predetermined plan in the death of Jesus was not dependent on His foreknowledge of what human beings would do. Rather, what human beings did was based on God's foreknowledge and predetermination[29] as expressed throughout the prophetic writings. This is a fact to which Jesus and the apostles repeatedly appeal:

> Jesus took the Twelve aside and told them, 'We are going up to Jerusalem, and everything that is written by the prophets about the Son of Man will be fulfilled. He will be handed over to the Gentiles. They will mock him, insult him and spit on him; they will flog him and kill him.' (Luke 18:31-33)

> He said to them, 'How foolish you are, and how slow to believe all that the prophets have spoken! Did not the Messiah have to suffer these things and then enter his glory?' And beginning with Moses and all the Prophets, he explained to them what was said in all the Scriptures concerning himself ... Then he opened their minds so they could understand the Scriptures. He told them, 'This is what is written: the Messiah will suffer ...' (Luke 24:25-27, 45-46)

> Now fellow Israelites, I know that you acted in ignorance, as did your leaders. But this is how God fulfilled what he had foretold through all the prophets, saying that his Messiah would suffer. (Acts 3:17-18)

> You spoke by the Holy Spirit through the mouth of your servant, our father David: 'Why do the nations rage and the peoples plot in vain? The kings of the earth rise up and the rulers band together against the Lord and against his holy one.' Indeed Herod and Pontius Pilate met together with the Gentiles and the people of Israel in this city to conspire against your

---

28. C. K. Barrett, *A Critical and Exegetical Commentary on the Acts of the Apostles*, ICC (Edinburgh: T & T Clark, 1994), vol. 1, p. 142.

29. God's foreknowledge is grounded in His predetermined plan. For a helpful explanation of the relationship between *horismene boule* and *prognosei*, see Wallace, *Greek Grammar*, p. 288.

> holy servant Jesus, whom you anointed. They did what
> your power and will had decided beforehand would
> happen. (Acts 4:25-28)

> This is the passage of Scripture the eunuch was reading:
> 'He was led like a sheep to the slaughter,
>   and as a lamb before its shearer is silent,
>   so he did not open his mouth.
> In his humiliation he was deprived of justice.
>   Who can speak of his descendants?
>   For his life was taken from the earth.'
> The eunuch asked Philip, 'Tell me, please, who is the
> prophet talking about, himself or someone else?' Then
> Philip began with that very passage of Scripture and
> told him the good news about Jesus. (Acts 8:32-35)

> The people of Jerusalem and their rulers did not
> recognize Jesus, yet in condemning him they fulfilled
> the words of the prophets that are read every Sabbath.
> Though they found no proper ground for a death
> sentence, they asked Pilate to have him executed.
> When they had carried out all that was written about
> him, they took him down from the cross and laid him
> in a tomb. (Acts 13:27-29)

The death of Jesus, perpetrated by Jews and Gentiles,
was an act of incalculable wickedness for which they were
entirely accountable. Simultaneously, asserts Peter, it was the
fulfillment of God's eternal plan. What is the warrant for
such an outrageous claim? Not only the prophetic testimony
of Scripture, but the indisputable fact that this predetermined
death has been answered by a foreordained display of
resurrection. Death will not have the final word in the case of
Jesus of Nazareth. Peter declares that God will not allow it by
virtue of who Jesus is.

> But God raised him from the dead, freeing him from
> the agony of death, because it was impossible for death
> to keep its hold on him. (v. 24)

Death is 'agony' because it holds its victims in captivity from
which there is no escape. The Psalmist cries: 'The cords of

death entangled me; the torrents of destruction overwhelmed me. The cords of the grave coiled around me; the snares of death confronted me' (Ps. 18:4-5; cf. 116:3). Peter's point is that God intervenes to free Jesus from death's bondage. Yet his language expresses a metaphor that is mixed. The word translated *'agony'* normally applies to the intense sufferings of childbirth.[30] Used here, it conveys the notion that death's agony actually becomes its birth pangs. That just as a child must come forth, having been confined to its mother's womb for nine months, so, too–*'because it was impossible for death to keep its hold on him'*–must Jesus come forth from the womb of the earth. It is as if death was in labor and unable to hold back the 'delivery' of Jesus.[31] But why is this the case? Because God's predetermined plan for Jesus must be fulfilled, a point Peter now makes by citing a Davidic psalm that he introduces as follows: *'For David says'* (ESV).[32]

As mentioned earlier, the apostles have come to interpret Old Testament references to David and his royal seed as finding their ultimate fulfillment in Jesus. This may occur through typological means (something occurs in David's life that serves to anticipate a fuller experience in the life of Jesus),[33] or through the means of verbal prediction (an explicit statement is made that finds its consummate fulfillment in Jesus). Both of these are displayed in the Psalms. In particular, Psalm 16 is a declaration of David's trust in Yahweh in which he confesses his loyalty to Yahweh (16:1-4) and his assurance of Yahweh's provision (16:5-11). Peter's use of it focuses

---

30. Louw and Nida, *Greek-English Lexicon*, vol. 1, p. 287. ESV: 'loosening the pangs of death.'

31. 'The abyss can no more hold the Redeemer than a pregnant woman can hold the child in her body.' Georg Bertram, 'ωδιν,' *TDNT*, vol. IX, p. 673.

32. The explanatory force of this is obscured by the NIV which, unfortunately, omits the explanatory conjunction *'for'* at the outset of v. 25.

33. See 'Pt. 6: How Did the New Testament Authors Use Typology?' in G. K Beale, ed., *The Right Doctrine from the Wrong Text: Essays on the Use of the Old Testament in the New* (Grand Rapids: Baker Book House, 1994).

attention on 16:8-11 which serves to substantiate his assertion
that death could not contain Jesus:

> I saw the Lord always before me.
> Because he is at my right hand,
> I will not be shaken. (v. 25)

David's trust is grounded in the God of the covenant, the God
who is ever present at his *'right hand'* (the place of support) and
whose care is certain. Consequently, he has nothing to fear.
What is the tangible result of this security?

> Therefore my heart is glad and my tongue rejoices;
> my body also will rest in hope, because you will not
> abandon me to the realm of the dead, you will not let
> your holy one see decay. (vv. 26-27)

This is a confidence that has joyful bearing on his entire being:
his heart, his tongue—even, says David, his body. Yet, it is at
this point that David begins to speak of something *beyond* the
boundaries of his own horizon, an event that will transcend
his own experience.[34] It will be the resurrection of *'the holy
one' par excellence*—the Messiah—a God-wrought resurrection
that will be immediate since Messiah's death will not be
sufficiently prolonged to allow the process of decomposition
to occur. David summarizes:

> You have made known to me the paths of life; you will
> fill me with joy in your presence. (v. 28)

While David is speaking of himself qualitatively (that he
possesses an abundant life in fellowship with Yahweh), this

---

34. 'The resolution of the tension between the historical horizon where Psalm 16
refers to David and the apostles' horizon where it refers to Christ is best solved by
interpreting Psalm 16 as a typico-prophetic psalm. As heir of the David covenant
David is a type of the quintessential Fulfillment of that covenant. But beyond
that typology David, while possibly using hyperbole with reference to himself,
prophesies that the body presumably of his final Heir—God's fully devoted one,
though experiencing death, will not experience decay ... this means deliverance
from the grave, not deliverance from a premature death.' Bruce K. Waltke and
James M. Houston, *The Psalms as Christian Worship: A Historical Commentary* (Grand
Rapids: William B. Eerdmans Publishing Company, 2010), p. 339.

has ultimate reference to a quantitative abundant life (*i.e.,* eternal life). Peter's application of it refers to the consequence of resurrection: God revealing the way of life, rather than allowing the Messiah to endure abandonment in the realm of the dead and the inevitable dissolution of the flesh. This leads to one glorious end: everlasting joy in the immediate company of the divine. This is not to infer that Psalm 16 has no literal application to David, but that as 'the recipient and conveyor of God's ancient but ever-renewable promise'[35] it extends beyond David to the one David's life and ministry anticipates, as Peter now explains:

> Fellow Israelites, I can tell you confidently that the patriarch David died and was buried, and his tomb is here to this day. (v. 29)

Peter's comments bespeak an immovable assurance grounded in indisputable evidence: the tomb in which David was buried, subsequent to his death, is still in plain view for any Jew to see.[36] Moreover, an examination of it would reveal that its inhabitant has not been removed and, that the decomposition process has had its full effect. Peter's point, then, becomes unmistakably obvious: someone other than David must qualify as the ultimate subject of Psalm 16. It is a prophetic declaration of the future experience of David's royal son, the Messiah. Accordingly, Peter further explains of David:

> But he was a prophet and knew that God had promised him on oath that he would place one of his descendants on his throne. (v. 30)

Not only did David possess prophetic powers (*cf.* 1:16), he was the recipient of God's covenantal promise. One of his sons would reign on his throne forever:

---

35. W. C. Kaiser, Jr., *The Uses of the Old Testament in the New* (Chicago: Moody Press, 1985), p. 34.

36. This tomb was located on the slope of Ophel near the pool of Siloam (*cf.* 1 Kings 2:10; Neh. 3:15-16).

> The LORD swore an oath to David, a sure oath he will
> not revoke: 'One of your own descendants I will place
> on your throne.' (Ps. 132:11)

This hearkens back to the historical account of God's original
pledge to David:

> The LORD declares to you that the LORD himself will
> establish a house for you: when your days are over
> and you rest with your ancestors, I will raise up your
> offspring to succeed you, your own flesh and blood,
> and I will establish his kingdom. He is the one who
> will build a house for my Name, and I will establish
> the throne of his kingdom forever. (2 Sam. 7:11b-13)

Three hundred years later Isaiah the prophet reiterates and
advances this promise:

> For to us a child is born,
>   to us a son is given,
>   and the government will be on his shoulders.
> And he will be called
>   Wonderful Counselor, Mighty God,
>   Everlasting Father, Prince of Peace.
> Of the greatness of his government and peace
>   there will be no end.
> He will reign on David's throne
>   and over his kingdom,
> establishing and upholding it
>   with justice and righteousness
>   from that time on and forever.
> The zeal of the LORD Almighty
>   will accomplish this. (Isa. 9:6-7)

It is the angel, Gabriel, who brings this prophecy to the brink
of realization in the Annunciation:

> You will conceive and give birth to a son, and you are
> to call him Jesus. He will be great and will be called
> the Son of the Most High. The Lord God will give him
> the throne of his father David, and he will reign over
> Jacob's descendants forever; his kingdom will never
> end. (Luke 1:31-33)

Throughout the history of redemption this great promise was repeated on many occasions and in various ways. One could argue that its fulfillment would be realized in an ongoing succession of kings from David's line that would follow him to the throne. However, following the Babylonian exile, there were no more Davidic kings. Thus, the haunting question that had to be faced: Has God's covenant with David been invalidated? It is here on the day of Pentecost—in response to David's prophecy—that Peter is now granted the unique privilege of heralding its ultimate fulfillment, tying together the promise of the Messiah and bodily resurrection in the person of Jesus of Nazareth:

> Seeing what was to come, he spoke of the resurrection of the Messiah, that he was not abandoned to the realm of the dead, nor did his body see decay. God has raised this Jesus to life, and we are all witnesses of it. (vv. 31-32)

Peter's listeners must have heard the staggering shift in his language. Rather than repeat David's future tense verbs as originally cited—'*you will not abandon me to the realm of the dead, you will not allow your holy one to see decay*' (v. 27)—Peter now adjusts these same verbs to the aorist tense—'*he was not abandoned to the realm of the dead, nor did his body see decay.*' The adjustment serves to underscore the fulfillment of David's prophecy—that what was promised has now taken place. Moreover, it explains the reason it was impossible for death to restrain Jesus (v. 24): He is the descendant of David who will reign forever in keeping with God's messianic promises contained in the record of prophetic Scripture. Thus, He *had* to be raised from the dead. Not only is this God's validation of Jesus as the Messiah, it is the only way a descendent of David could rule forever over God's people.[37] It is for this reason that 'witness' now becomes a predominant emphasis in the ministry of the apostles (1:22; 2:32; 3:15; 4:33; 5:30-32;

---

37. Peterson, *The Acts*, p. 149.

10:39-41; 13:29-31; 22:14-15; 26:15-16). To sharpen the focus, Peter's declaration–'*we are all witnesses of it*'–reveals that the apostolic Christians occupy the role of witness in a double sense: they have not only *seen* the bodily-resurrected Jesus, they *testify to* the bodily-resurrected Jesus.[38] This is a witness that will not allow resurrection to be regarded as a metaphor, a literary description of a disembodied spirit ascending into heaven while leaving a physical counterpart behind in a tomb. This witness to the resurrection of Jesus is the proclamation of a concrete historical reality. It is the announcement that the physical body put to death is the physical body raised to life.

This is what defines the essence of authentic Christian witness: the declaration of the life, death, and resurrection of Jesus Christ. Contemporary 'gospel' conversations with unbelievers, however, often assume a form that has little resemblance to the apostolic pattern. They are substantively vague and, thus, bereft of redemptive value. The following, for example, is not atypical:

> 'Have you ever considered becoming a Christian? It's a real thing, you know. It will help you navigate life's challenges. And then, when you come to the end of your life, you can be certain that all will turn out well. Just believe in Jesus.'

It cannot be surprising when such expressions of 'witnessing' are met with responses that correspond in kind:

> 'Does this mean I have to stop sleeping with my boyfriend?'

> 'Does this mean I can no longer practise a gay lifestyle?'

Such responses are telling, but not of the one *responding to the witness*. They are telling of the inadequate substance *contained in the witness*—of how little unbelievers have been asked to embrace; a witness that, for all intents and purposes, has conveyed nothing that is distinctly Christian. To the contrary, when un-

---

38. Witherington, *The Acts*, p. 147.

believers are brought to understand the atoning death of Jesus Christ, and God's validation of His death on the third day by means of bodily resurrection, they are faced with a reality of infinitely greater significance than an experience of premarital sex or of a homosexual lifestyle. They are confronted with one who bears the rightful claim as the living Lord—which, if believed, will serve to place all other perceived priorities in their proper perspective. This is not to dismiss the necessary call to repentance. Rather, this is to place repentance in a greater gospel context—one in which it can be regarded as an appropriate response to the resurrected King, rather than a resented afterthought as a result of a bait-and-switch presentation of Christianity.

Peter's witness to Jesus has included His God-authenticated life and ministry, His violent death divinely purposed and preordained, and His bodily resurrection effected by God that now serves to confirm Him as the promised Messiah. But none of this signals Peter's point of conclusion. He must provide an explanation for the events witnessed by these celebrants of Pentecost; specifically, hearing the wonders of God declared in their native languages as a result of the advent of the Spirit. *What does this mean?*

> Exalted to the right hand of God, he has received from the Father the promised Holy Spirit and has poured out what you now see and hear. (v. 33)

The bestowal of the Spirit is a bestowal by Jesus. But the granting of this gift does not occur during His earthly ministry. It is the consequence of His resurrection, a point blunted by the NIV in its omission of the Greek inferential conjunction 'therefore' near the beginning of this sentence ('Therefore having been exalted to the right hand of God ...' NASB). Neither does the pouring out of the Spirit occur at some period between Jesus' resurrection and ascension. Rather, it is the exaltation of Jesus that triggers the reception of '*the promised Holy Spirit*' for the purpose of pouring Him out.[39] These two events coincide, while the second serves as the consequence of the first.

To any person in the ancient world, the right hand of a monarch was regarded as a position[40] of supreme authority and sovereignty. For a person acquainted with the Old Testament, 'the right hand of God' was regarded as the source from which divine power and salvation are displayed (e.g., Exod. 15:6; Ps. 60:5; 98:1). Use of such a phrase with regard to Jesus would naturally arouse implications associated with deity. But Peter's sermon moves beyond mere implication. In his original citation of Joel, he accurately names 'God' as the one who will pour out the Spirit on all people. Now, he assigns this divine act to the resurrected and exalted Jesus; that the accompanying audiovisual displays–'what you now see and hear'–are the manifestations of the glory and power and deity that are uniquely His as the exalted Lord.

To reinforce this, Peter once again appeals to David:

> For David did not ascend to heaven, and yet he said, 'The Lord said to my Lord: "Sit at my right hand until I make your enemies a footstool for your feet."' (vv. 34-35)

This quotation is taken from the opening of Psalm 110. Peter draws upon it here for two reasons. First, it shares a link with the earlier reference from Psalm 16 (v. 25)–'at my right hand'–thus inferring common subject matter.[41] Second, this shared phrase

---

39. The aorist participle–'exalted'–is temporal and, thus, calls attention to the time when the risen Jesus received the Holy Spirit from God for the purpose of pouring Him out on 'all people' (v. 17).

40. While some commentators (e.g. F. F. Bruce, Acts, p. 66) translate this as an instrumental dative–'exalted by God's right hand'–Peter supports his argument by appealing to Ps. 110:1, which clearly identifies a location signifying status. Thus, this is better understood as locative dative. See also Acts 5:31.

41. This is an example of an exegetical principle referred to as gezerah shawah (i.e., equal ordinance), in which one text is 'interpreted in the light of another text to which it is related by a shared word or phrase.' David Instone Brewer, Techniques and Assumptions in Jewish Exegesis Before 70 CE (Tubingen: Mohr Siebeck Publishing Company, 1992), p. 18.

seeks to establish a prophetic basis for Peter's prior claim that Jesus has been exalted to the right hand of God. It does so by stimulating in the hearer an unspoken question: Since David did not ascend into heaven, to whom is Yahweh speaking when He urges this person to sit at His right hand until His enemies are entirely subjugated?[42] To discover the identity of this individual, it is essential to discriminate between the two uses of 'Lord' in this verse, neither of which can refer to David since he is named as the narrator. In the first instance, David makes reference to a Lord who speaks: 'the Lord.' In the second instance, David identifies a Lord who is addressed: 'my Lord.' Clearly, reference is being made to two distinct persons. Furthermore, as the drama unfolds 'the Lord' installs 'my Lord' into the throne at His right hand—both of whom, once again, are clearly superior to David since he refers to each of them as 'Lord.' So who is 'the Lord'? God Himself. He is actually referred to as Yahweh in Psalm 110:1. Who, then, is 'my Lord'? Only someone greater than David; yet, according to v. 30, He is a descendant of David who would one day be placed on David's throne by God Himself. It is an unambiguous reference to the Messiah, the one previously mentioned as resurrected from the dead and identified as 'this Jesus' (v. 31-32).

He is the enthroned one: a fact stated explicitly in v. 33a—'exalted to the right hand of God'—and again in v. 34b when God asks Him to 'sit at my right hand.'[43] Beyond this, and framed in between these statements of Jesus' exaltation, is Peter's explanation for the events of Pentecost: 'he has received from the Father the promised Holy Spirit and has poured put what you now see and hear' (v. 33b). His point is inescapable: the outpouring of the Holy Spirit is the irrepressible consequence of the enthronement of Jesus the Messiah.

---

42. The word *hypopodion* means 'to be under the complete control of someone.' Louw and Nida, *Greek-English Lexicon*, vol. 1, p. 473. It is metaphorical for the subjugation of enemies (cf. Josh. 10:24; 1 Kings 5:3; Isa. 51:23).

43. Jesus' presence at the right hand of God finds frequent mention in the New Testament (Luke 20:42-44; 22:69; Acts 7:55-56; Rom. 8:34; Eph. 1:20; Col. 3:1; Heb. 1:3, 13; 8:1; 10:12-13; 12:2; 1 Peter 3:22).

The Deliverer Has Been Identified

The advent of the Holy Spirit, with the subsequent heralding of God's wonders in languages not learned by the speakers, has raised the pressing question of Pentecost: *'What does this mean?'* (v. 12). What does this mean, *indeed?* Peter's sermon has set out to provide an answer. And it does so successfully by displaying these events as fulfillments of biblical prophecy that have been woven into the script of God's salvation plan. Specifically, the events of Pentecost mean that *'the last days'* of salvation's history have now been inaugurated in anticipation of its climax—*'the great and glorious day of the Lord.'* Moreover, they signify that the long-awaited Messiah, raised from the dead, has now been exalted to God's right hand in fulfillment of God's promise to David. Finally, they indicate that He has demonstrated His royal status in the divine act of deluging all of God's people with the Holy Spirit, just as these God-fearing worshippers have observed. Yet, Peter is not preaching solely for the purpose of furnishing his inquirers with a more thoroughly developed biblical theology. He is preaching for a verdict, driving them to the response that should be generated by a true understanding of Jesus, especially in the wake of their prior rejection of Him:

> Therefore let all Israel be assured of this: God has made this Jesus, whom you crucified, both Lord and Messiah. (v. 36)

Throughout his entire sermon, Peter has subtly revealed God to be the supporting figure in the life of Jesus, a reality that has manifested itself in the following ways:

His supernatural displays of power—

> ... a man accredited by God to you by miracles, wonders and signs which God did among you through him. (v. 22)

His crucifixion—

> This man was handed over to you by God's deliberate plan and foreknowledge. (v. 23)

His resurrection—

> ... God raised him from the dead ... God raised this Jesus to life. (vv. 24, 32)

His exaltation and outpouring of the Spirit—

> Exalted[44] (by God) to the right hand of God, he has received from the Father the promised Holy Spirit (v. 33, parenthesis mine).

and His enthronement—

> ... 'The Lord said to my Lord: 'Sit at my right hand until I make your enemies a footstool for your feet'' ... God has made this Jesus ... both Lord and Messiah. (vv. 34-36)

God's immediate participation in the ministry of Jesus, culminating in His enthronement, has progressively revealed who Jesus is: 'Lord and Messiah.' This is no adoptionist Christology (the notion that God 'adopted' Jesus and made Him Lord and Messiah sometime after His death; or, perhaps, on the basis of it). Contrarily, on many occasions prior to His resurrection Jesus was referred to as 'Lord' and 'Messiah' (Luke 1:43; 2:11, 26; 4:41; 9:20; 10:1; 11:39; 12:42; 20:41-44; 22:61). Hence, Luke's Christology here is not ontological, but functional. Jesus has not become Lord, but is revealed to be Lord by His resurrection and exaltation. As Schnabel has said: '... the Messiah-designate has now become the Messiah-enthroned.'[45] Nevertheless, upon claiming to be the 'Messiah,' Jesus was rejected and immediately condemned to death by Israel's judges (Mark 14:61-64). Peter's point here is that the ultimate judge has unequivocally overturned their ruling by raising Jesus from the dead and installing Him into David's throne, thereby vindicating Jesus' claim. Furthermore, God has revealed Him to be the bearer of the name that is above every other name—the ineffable name of the God of Israel: 'Lord.'

---

44. This participle is a divine passive (i.e., this exaltation is performed by God).

45. Schnabel, Acts, p. 151.

Given the testimony of Scripture upon which this entire sermon has been established, Peter insists to his listeners that God's declaration of Jesus must now be embraced without reservation; that, in fact, 'All Israel' must 'be assured'[46] of it. In fact, the language Peter employs–(literally, 'all the house of Israel,' ESV)–is highly evocative, once again raising reminiscences of Ezekiel 36-37. There the prophet references the return of the exiles (36:24; 37:21), the resurrection of the nation by the impartation of the Spirit (37:9-14), the reunification of the northern and southern kingdoms (37:15-22), the reign of the Davidic king (37:24-25), and reestablishment of the Temple in their midst (37:26-27). All of it speaks clearly of the restoration of Israel. Consequently, when Peter's call to 'All Israel' is combined with the distinct events of Pentecost, a clarion signal is being sounded: Israel's prophesied restoration has begun (and, by implication, her mission). All of it turns on the enthronement of Jesus as Lord and Messiah.

Yet it is precisely at this point that the haunting echo of culpability reverberates in Peter's recapitulation of their guilt regarding Jesus–'whom you crucified.' Now, with a reality and intensity never before experienced, the graphic images suddenly explode upon the consciousness of those hearing Peter's sermon: the blood and fire and billows of smoke– the sun turned to darkness and the moon turned to blood. Could there be anything more unnerving to God-fearing practitioners of Judaism than to learn that they have killed their own Messiah? Could anything else arouse such a feeling of dread than to become aware that they have effected the crucifixion of this one who now shares the throne of God– Israel's true King and, thus, the world's true Lord? How devastating a confrontation this must be, especially in the context of being told that they have just been ushered into the final days of salvation's history–the days that anticipate the

---

46. 'pertaining to being certain ... to known beyond a doubt.' Bauer, A Greek-English Lexicon, p. 147.

last day when the eternal judgment of every human being will be determined by 'the Lord'? (v. 20).

Do you recall the ending of Joel's prophecy? Peter's citation reveals that it does not conclude with a terrifying fear of future condemnation, but with a gracious expression of saving invitation: 'And everyone who calls on the name of the Lord will be saved' (v. 21). Do you hear the universality in this promise? 'Everyone'—even Messiah-killers. Do you hear the redemption in this promise? '... will be saved.' The assurance is definite. Do you hear the simplicity in this promise? Everyone who 'calls on the name of the Lord.' This is eminently good news for people who know they are guilty. But who is this 'Lord' that will return in judgment on the great and glorious last day (v. 20)? Who is this 'Lord' that will effect the salvation of all guilty people who call upon Him (v. 21)? Peter has identified Him. Better yet, God has identified Him. The 'Lord' is none other than the resurrected and enthroned Jesus (v. 36). He is the deliverer of all who call upon Him.

What does Pentecost mean? It means that the promise of the Father has fulfilled. It means that the Holy Spirit has been poured out. It means that the last days have begun. It means that the last day is coming. It means that the Lord has been revealed. It means that the Messiah has been enthroned. It means that Israel is being restored. It means that her mission has commenced. It means that salvation is now to be extended to the ends of the earth.

This is what Pentecost means: Salvation from final judgment is found in King Jesus who is the Lord.

This is the message that defines our mission.

6

WHAT RESPONSE DOES PENTECOST DEMAND?

The sin of people today put Jesus to death
just as surely as the sinful hatred of first-century people.
With Peter's first audience,
we must return to the scene of the crime, the cross.
We must face up to our guilt before almighty God, the Judge.
We must throw ourselves on his mercy, asking,
What shall we do?
WILLIAM J. LARKIN, JR.

~~~~~~~~~~~~~~~

The question is not, shall I repent?
For that is beyond a doubt.
But the question is,
shall I repent now, when it may save me;
or shall I put it off to the eternal world
when my repentance will be my punishment?
SAMUEL DAVIES

~~~~~~~~~~~~~~~

Peter is asked by his audience to relate
the practical relevance of the gospel proclamation just given.
He offers no helpful hints on living a more fulfilling life,
no useful projects to work on, no feel-good platitudes;
rather, he calls people to conversion.
ROBERT W. WALL

~~~~~~~~~~~~~~~

[37]When the people heard this, they were cut to the heart and said to Peter and the other apostles, 'Brothers, what shall we do?'
[38]Peter replied, 'Repent and be baptized, every one of you, in the name of Jesus Christ for the forgiveness of your sins. And you will receive the gift of the Holy Spirit. [39]The promise is for you and your

children and for all who are far off—for all whom the Lord our God will call.'

⁴⁰With many other words he warned them; and he pleaded with them, 'Save yourselves from this corrupt generation.' ⁴¹Those who accepted his message were baptized, and about three thousand were added to their number that day.

(Acts 2:37-41)

The Missionary Spirit

It has been one of my favorite texts for a very long time. It contains a promise that has often replenished me with fresh feelings of expectancy when I have found myself discouraged in ministry:

> Very truly I tell you, whoever believes in me will do the works that I have been doing, and they will do even greater things than these, because I am going to the Father. (John 14:12)

You may recognize these as the words of Jesus, spoken to His original followers just hours before His arrest in the Garden of Gethsemane. It is not the first occasion Jesus addressed the subject of His impending departure with them. Yet, on this evening in the Upper Room, the implications of His leaving are pressed into their consciousness more deeply than ever before. It was a night they would never forget, marked by an upheaval of emotions: thoroughgoing confusion, heartbreaking grief, immobilizing apprehension. In turn, Jesus compassionately applies the balm of comfort to their open wounds. He provides the disciples with instruction that is among the most intimate and significant of His entire ministry. Beyond this, He seamlessly weaves reinforcing promises into His teaching that will prove to be sustaining as they face the prospect of advancing His ministry apart from His physical presence.

John 14:12 is one of these promises—a promise that is nothing short of staggering. Appreciating it fully, however, necessitates an answer to a question: To what is Jesus referring when He speaks of the *'greater things'* to be done by those who believe in Him? Many are quick to propose the notion that this must be a reference to miracles (*e.g.*, healings, exorcisms, supernatural displays of power). This sounds plausible, until one remembers that Jesus employs an adjective of comparison–*'greater'*–indicating that believers will not merely do *what* He has done, but that they will do *greater* than He has done. Accordingly, it must be asked: Have Christians performed *'greater'* miracles than those displayed by Jesus during His earthly ministry? The negative conclusion leads many of the initial proponents of this view to rescind their earlier proposal.

What, then, is the essence of this promise? A step closer to the answer is taken when attention is given to the subordinate clause that expresses the cause of the related verbal action: 'they will do even greater things than these, *because I am going to the Father'*–a phrase that is shorthand for Jesus' death, resurrection, ascension, and exaltation. What is the point of connection between these two? Asked differently, why is the former–*'greater things'*–the consequence of the latter–*'because I am going to the Father'*? This becomes plain when Jesus expands His comments further in the conversation:

> But very truly I tell you, it is for your good that I am going away. Unless I go away, the Advocate will not come to you; but if I go, I will send him to you. When he comes, he will prove the world to be in the wrong about sin and righteousness and judgment. (John 16:7-8)

This is an indisputable reference to the advent of the Holy Spirit, a subject of Old Testament prophecy brought to fruition by Jesus' redemptive accomplishments that climax in His enthronement as Lord and Messiah. This marks a shift in salvation-historical categories, a movement into an age of increased clarity and power. Thus, the Spirit will indwell Jesus' followers for the purpose of attending their witness with His convicting effects that will arouse the guilty to seek refuge in Jesus. But this interpretation, too, must bear the scrutiny of the obvious question: Are these effects of the Spirit's coming comparatively *'greater'* than those experienced during the ministry of Jesus? The testimony of Scripture provides the answer. Prior to Pentecost, one hundred and twenty followers are gathered in His name. Subsequent to the outpouring of the Holy Spirit, the number immediately multiplies twenty-six times. The conclusion appears to be unassailable. The conversions of people are the *'greater things'* that have been promised by Jesus to those who believe in Him. The consequences of His *'going to the Father'* are missionary consequences associated with the inauguration of the new age.[1]

Not surprisingly, then, nearly early every mention of the Holy Spirit in Acts bears a connection to the missionary witness of the church. This, of course, begins with the programmatic declaration of Jesus:

> But you will receive power when the Holy Spirit comes on you; and you will be my witnesses in Jerusalem, and in all Judea and Samaria, and to the ends of the earth. (1:8)

This missionary witness is then launched in the initial Pentecostal display:

> All of them were filled with the Holy Spirit and began to speak in other tongues as the Spirit enabled them. (2:4)

Moreover, it is this Spirit of prophecy who is given to those who respond in repentance and faith to the apostolic testimony:

---

1. Carson adds: 'The contrast itself (*i.e.*, the greater things performed by the followers of Jesus over against those accomplished by Jesus) ... turns not on raw numbers but on the power and clarity that mushroom after the eschatological hinge has swung and the new day has dawned.' D. A. Carson, *The Gospel According to John*, PNTC (Grand Rapids: William B. Eerdmans Publishing Company, 1991), p. 496 (parenthesis mine).

> Repent and be baptized, every one of you, in the name
> of Jesus Christ for the forgiveness of your sins. And
> you will receive the gift of the Holy Spirit. (2:38)

When two apostles are brought before the Sanhedrin to explain the source of healing a disabled man, Peter supplies a striking witness to Jesus as the result of being—

> ... filled with the Holy Spirit. (4:8)

Upon being released by the authorities, Peter and John return to the company of Christians for prayer, after which—

> ... they were all filled with the Holy Spirit and spoke
> the word of God boldly. (4:31)

Later, when facing intensified persecution from the Sanhedrin, the apostles acknowledge the Spirit's work in tandem with their own missionary ministry:

> We are witnesses of these things, and so is the Holy
> Spirit, whom God has given to those who obey him.
> (5:32)

Preaching before hostile opponents, Stephen roots their rejection of Jesus in an expression of defiance:

> ... you always resist the Holy Spirit! (7:51)

When the people of Samaria embrace the good news of the kingdom of God as a result of the missionary preaching of Philip, they also—

> ... received the Holy Spirit. (8:17)

Upon the completion of his ministry in Samaria, Philip is dispatched to the road leading from Jerusalem to Gaza. While on his way, in anticipation of his witness to an Ethiopian eunuch:

> The Spirit told Philip, 'Go to that chariot and stay
> near it.' (8:29)

Philip preaches the gospel to the eunuch who, in turn, responds with a request for baptism. After this—

> ... the Spirit of the Lord suddenly took Philip away
> (8:39)

—after which he preached the gospel in the towns between
Azotus and Caesarea.

Following a period of persecution, the church in Judea, Galilee
and Samaria enjoyed a time of peace and refreshment—

> Living in the fear of the Lord and encouraged by the
> Holy Spirit, it increased in numbers. (9:31).

Upon Ananias' explanation to Saul that he was to be—

> ... filled with the Holy Spirit (9:17)

—Saul immediately

> began to preach in the synagogues that Jesus is the Son
> of God. (9:20)

The Holy Spirit prompts Peter's first missionary witness to the
Gentiles:

> ... the Spirit said to him, 'Simon, three men are looking
> for you. So get up and go downstairs. Do not hesitate
> to go with them, for I have sent them.' (10:19-20)

Barnabas and Saul are sent on their first missionary journey,
but not until—

> the Holy Spirit said, 'Set apart for me Saul and
> Barnabas for the work to which I have called them
> ...' The two of them, sent on their way by the Holy
> Spirit, went down to Seleucia and sailed from there to
> Cyprus. (13:2, 4)

At the Jerusalem Council, Peter's contribution to legitimize
the conversion of Gentiles apart from the Mosaic Law turns
on the Gentile reception of the Spirit:

> God, who knows the heart, showed that he accepted
> them by giving the Holy Spirit to them, just as he did
> to us. (15:8)

On two occasions during their missionary endeavors, Paul and Silas are restrained from missionary witness before being redeployed to Macedonia:

> ... having been kept by the Holy Spirit from preaching the word in the province of Asia ... they tried to enter Bithynia, but the Spirit of Jesus would not allow them to. (16:6-7)

The historical record established by Acts reveals that the advent of the Holy Spirit is inextricably tied to the massive missionary movement that steadily progresses throughout its narrative. Luke reveals the Holy Spirit to be a radically missionary Spirit. Moreover, this is in keeping with his contribution to the Bible's larger storyline. As indicated previously, Pentecost reveals that the restoration of Israel is being inaugurated. But this restoration, it should be remembered, is only penultimate—rather, that at the heart of it is 'the renewal of the vocation of Israel to be a light to the nations to the end of the earth ...'[2] Consequently, Jesus' promise of the *greater things* associated with the Spirit's outpouring serves as assurance that the vocation assigned to revived Israel will prove successful. A strategic display of this is now seen in Acts 2:37-41, which answers a remaining question: *What response does Pentecost demand?*

Is it a question you have considered? Pentecost is not merely a moment in ancient history to be pondered with sentimental affection. Nor is it a phenomenon to be scrutinized carefully by New Testament scholars whose sole concern is to explain the mysterious nature of its various manifestations. Pentecost is an event that demands a response that carries with it an eternal consequence. What response does Pentecost demand from you?

---

2. D. L. Tiede, 'The Exaltation of Jesus and the Restoration of Israel in Acts 1,' *Harvard Theological Review* 79, (1986), p. 286.

The Desperate Plea

> When the people heard this, they were cut to the heart
> and said to Peter and the other apostles, 'Brothers,
> what shall we do?' (v. 37)

Many years ago, following a Sunday evening service during
which I had preached the gospel, an older gentleman sought me
out and said in genuine disappointment: 'Had you concluded
your sermon with an invitation, brother, I am certain that
people would have been saved tonight. Now, unfortunately, it's
little more than a lost opportunity.' I had no reason to doubt
that he meant well. In fact, I was certain of it. The heartbreak
in his voice and deep grief in his eyes were unmistakable. Like
many well-meaning evangelicals, he had been schooled in an
approach to evangelism (whether by precept or pattern) that
unknowingly substituted religious technique for the power of
God. In the brief conversation that followed, he articulated
his firm conviction: the likelihood of success in conversion
turns, almost exclusively, on the preacher's direct appeal;
more specifically, on his skillful 'invitation' to the unbelievers
being addressed. The more he spoke, however, it became
increasingly evident that he was defining the gospel by the
invitation—that the invitation was the gospel—and, therefore,
I would continue to be unfaithful to the gospel until I said to
the unbelievers within the congregation: 'Would you like to
receive Jesus Christ as your Savior? You may do so right now.
Step into the aisle and come forward to the altar. I'll pray a
prayer of salvation that you may repeat after me.'

While someone might argue the point—that Peter's sermon
does include a public 'invitation'—a closer examination reveals
it to be an appeal not initiated by the preacher, but one
demanded by the congregation: 'Brothers, what shall we do?'[3]

---

3. 'It is unclear whether Peter's listeners interrupt his speech, as many assume, or
whether Peter had concluded his speech with the explanation of the miraculous
manifestations among the followers of Jesus. Since he had demonstrated that Joel's
promise of the coming of the Holy Spirit and David's promise of the coming of the

It is a rational response to the content preached: ...' Willimon insightfully explains:

> The *kerygma* has the power to evoke that which it celebrates ... this is not Peter's homiletical ability to work the crowd up into an emotional frenzy or in the crowd's sincere inner determination to get themselves right with God ... True, the crowd responds, asking what they should do now. But their action is response, not initiative ... Here is salvation, not as earnest human striving but salvation beyond such striving, salvation which only comes as the call and work of the Spirit which both testifies to and enacts salvation among the crowd. The Spirit that inspired prophets like Joel now inspires Peter to tell what has happened for Israel. God's restoration of a prophetic people has begun.[4]

What is the content of this effectual *kerygma?* It is little more than the clear and cogent articulation of historical events: the life, death, resurrection, and exaltation of the Lord Jesus—realities, Peter displays, that are deeply embedded in the fertile soil of Old Testament revelation. Furthermore, he includes an exposition of the meaning of these events: 1) the last days have commenced (ultimately concluding in final judgment); 2) Jesus is the Davidic Messiah enthroned at God's right hand (evidenced by His resurrection from the dead and the subsequent outpouring of the Holy Spirit); and, 3) He is the Lord to whom everyone may call for salvation from judgment. But a sermon filled with strong gospel content is not a cerebral *cul de sac.* Its intent is to evoke something more—*a response*—as it does here. Peter's listeners are *'cut to the heart.'* It is not a literal description, of course. The *'heart'* is a metaphorical designation that refers to a person's internal control center, the source of thoughts, feelings, motivations, and actions (*e.g.,* Luke 6:45; 16:15; Acts 5:3; 7:39).

Messiah had both been fulfilled in the life, resurrection, and exaltation of Jesus of Nazareth, Peter might have wanted to end his speech at this point, waiting to see what would happen.' Schnabel, *Acts,* p. 161.

4. Willimon, *Acts,* pp. 36-37.

This is not unlike a recognition scene (anagnorisis) in a Greek tragedy, the moment of critical discovery when a character finally recognizes the truth—and along with it, in many cases, the realization that he has previously acted against his own best interests (e.g., when Oedipus discovers that he has unknowingly killed his father and married his mother). Here, at Pentecost, these people now recognize that their prior actions against Jesus have placed them in an impossible situation: they crucified the one who is now revealed to be the ascended Lord and enthroned Messiah. As a result, they experience something akin to a sharp pain or a deep stab. Though this verb translated—'they were cut'—is only used here in the New Testament, its use in the Septuagint to translate several different Hebrew terms reveals the strong emotions contained within its semantic range: 'remorseful' (Gen. 27:38), 'indignant' (Gen. 34:7), 'struck silent' (Lev. 10:3), 'brokenhearted' (Ps. 109:16). In the present context it means: 'to experience acute emotional distress.'[5] And here, it is this very experience of conviction that, in turn, begets their plea of desperation: 'Brothers, what shall we do?'

This is a phenomenon that seems strangely absent from a great deal of present-day evangelism. It is not uncommon, in fact, for current evangelistic methodologies to be designed with the intention of ensuring that feelings of conviction are not experienced. This may be, in part, a reaction to approaches of the past that erred in the opposite direction: the fidelity of a gospel presentation measured by the extent of the remorse generated by it. This, too, deserves thoughtful critique, though this is rarely of significant relevance to contemporary practices of evangelism in Western contexts. The evangelistic deficiency far more pertinent to a context saturated in postmodern inclusivity is the conspicuous vacuum of conviction. Given the present text, then, it would be irresponsible not to ask: Is it possible for a person to be

---

5. Louw and Nida, *Greek-English Lexicon*, vol. 1, p. 319.

authentically converted without feeling the sting of being 'cut to the heart'? Can anyone be saved who has not, in desperation, asked: 'What must I do? Am I doomed to experience God's condemnation? How do I alleviate myself of this guilt and the judgment it demands?'

Have you ever been so conscience-stricken? Have *you* experienced the phenomenon of being 'cut to the heart'? Pursuit of a Savior will seem superfluous apart from an awakened awareness of guilt. Of course, your immediate reply to this may be: 'But *I* am not responsible for the crucifixion of Jesus. That is the unique wickedness of the people to whom Peter is preaching.' True, you are not guilty of actually applying the scourge to Jesus' back. Nor are you guilty of hammering the nails through His hands. You were not present with the frenzied mob screaming, 'Crucify him.' But physical absence from Golgotha is not synonymous with moral innocence. It was your sin (and mine) that made Jesus' death necessary—not only your specific sins, but the ultimate sin that is shared by every human being: the refusal to acknowledge Jesus as God's Messiah and Lord. This is what you share with the guilty people listening to Peter's sermon on Pentecost.

'Brothers,[6] what shall we do?' This plea of desperation on the part of these people is not the outcome of Peter's adroit manipulations as a preacher. It is their own awareness of a deserved condemnation, a product of the promise made by Jesus with reference to the Holy Spirit:

> When he comes, he will prove the world to be in the wrong about sin and righteousness and judgment: about sin, because people do not believe in me ... (John 16:8-9)

---

6. The crowd's plea is not just directed to Peter, but to the other apostles as well (*cf.* 2:14; Luke 22:30). This may be Luke's indication that 'already the Twelve were fulfilling their role in relationship to their fellow Jews that they were intended to play.' Witherington, *The Acts*, p. 153.

Pentecost provides an efficacious demonstration of this divinely effected conviction. But its purpose, most assuredly, is not to taunt and torment—

> 'Twas grace that taught my heart to fear,
> and grace my fears relieved.

Is there a slender hint of hope to be discerned in their cry– 'Brothers, what must we do?' They have heard Peter herald the promise from Joel: 'And everyone who calls on the name of the Lord will be saved' (v. 21). And also, without undermining responsibility or diminishing blame, Peter has explained that Jesus' death was a manifestation of 'God's deliberate plan and foreknowledge' (v. 23). Might there be a possibility of deliverance from the judgment appropriate to such a heinous crime?

The Explicit Reply

> Peter replied, 'Repent and be baptized, every one of you, in the name of Jesus Christ for the forgiveness of your sins. And you will receive the gift of the Holy Spirit. The promise is for you and your children and for all who are far off—for all whom the Lord our God will call.' (vv. 38-39)

'The gospel is not something simply to be discussed. It is a message that demands a personal response ...'[7] Yes, but for those who have become truly cognizant of their profound neediness, it is a response exercised with eagerness. Peter's explicit reply is a balm of healing for the raw wounds that have been opened by the Spirit's convicting work. It will be helpful to consider four aspects of this reply under the following headings: 1) the gospel stipulation; 2) the gospel result; 3) the gospel scope; and, 4) the gospel sign.

The gospel stipulation: 'Repent.' A person acquainted with the Synoptic Gospels will not find this stipulation unusual.

---

7. Fernando, Acts, 118.

Luke describes the ministry of John the Baptist as follows: 'He went into all the country around the Jordan, preaching a baptism of *repentance* for the forgiveness of sins' (Luke 3:3). Luke later includes a specific excerpt from John's preaching: 'Produce fruit in keeping with *repentance*' (Luke 3:8). Matthew's summary of John's ministry is even more pointed: '*Repent*, for the kingdom of heaven has come near' (Matt. 3:2). Echoing the Baptist, Jesus Himself proclaimed this same stipulation: '*Repent*, for the kingdom of heaven has come near' (Matt. 4:17). To the Pharisees and teachers of the Law who criticized Him for eating with 'sinners,' Jesus defined His ministry as follows: 'I have not come to call the righteous, but sinners to *repentance*' (Luke 5:32). To clarify that no one will escape divine judgment, Jesus said on one occasion: '... unless you *repent*, you too will perish' (Luke 13:3).[8] Here, Peter's call to '*repent*' is a fulfillment of Jesus' prophecy made subsequent to His resurrection: '... the Messiah will suffer and rise from the dead on the third day, and *repentance* for the forgiveness of sins will be preached in his name to all nations, beginning at Jerusalem' (Luke 24:46-47). Consequently, Luke's narrative in Acts steadily displays '*repentance*' as a key component in apostolic preaching:

> *Repent*, then, and turn to God ... (3:19)

> God exalted him to his own right hand as Prince and Savior that he might bring Israel to *repentance* ... (5:31)

> *Repent* of this wickedness ... (8:22)

> So then, even to Gentiles God has granted *repentance* that leads to life. (11:18)

> In the past God overlooked such ignorance, but now he commands all people everywhere to *repent*. (17:30)
> I have declared to both Jews and Greeks that they must turn to God in *repentance* ... (20:21)

> ... I preached that they should *repent* and turn to God and demonstrate their repentance by their deeds. (26:20)

---

8. See also Luke 10:13; 11:32; 15:7, 10; 16:30; 17:3-4.

'I've always regarded "*belief*" to be the gospel stipulation,' someone might reply at this point. 'Aren't we supposed to urge people to "*believe*" in the Lord Jesus Christ? Which is it: repentance or belief?' Given that these terms are mutually interpreting—'two sides of the same coin'[9]— no exclusive choice should be made. The concept contained within each term is inclusive of the other (*cf.* 3:19)—a fact that becomes evident later when those who have repented are referred to as 'believers' (v. 44), even though there is no direct indication Peter specifically articulated belief as a stipulation. Is it possible that the confusion at this point stems from a reductionistic understanding of repentance; the idea that it is little more than 'feeling badly about sin'? Certainly, the people in this crowd are in a state of anguish over their guilt. They have, after all, been '*cut to the heart.*' But the grief they feel cannot be synonymous with repentance, otherwise there would be no need for Peter to call them to something more. Their desperate plea—'*Brothers, what must we do?*'—would be answered with the simple assurance: 'But you've already done it: you feel guilty.' Repentance, however, is not a religious equivalent for remorse. It is an about-face in one's thinking that produces an about-face in one's living—a radical reorientation that is nothing short of conversion.[10] Thus, Peter is not only exhorting these Jews to forsake their former thoughts and attitudes about Jesus that resulted in their rejection and crucifixion of Him, but to now fully embrace Jesus in recognition of who He is: Lord (upon whom they must call for salvation) and Messiah (God's enthroned king). But how is this possible? Do these people possess the *capacity* to exercise such an extreme change? It is beyond question that this is a responsibility required of them (and all people!). But responsibility is not interchangeable with

---

9. Marshall, *The Acts*, p. 81.

10. 'Investigation of the history of the term up to NT days has shown ... and exposition of the theological usage of the NT will pursue this to its destination, namely, that μετανοεω and μετανοια are the forms in which the NT gives new expression to the ancient concept of religious and moral conversion.' J. Behm, 'μετανοεω,' *TDNT*, vol. IV, p. 1000.

capability. The actual exercise of repentance, Luke elsewhere explains, necessitates a divine enablement. For example, of Jesus he writes: 'God exalted him at his right hand as Leader and Savior, to *give repentance* to Israel and forgiveness of sins' (5:31, ESV; *cf*. 3:26; 11:18; 2 Tim. 2:25). Repentance is the gospel stipulation, but Jesus bestows it on His enemies in celebration of His enthronement.[11]

The gospel result: *'... for the forgiveness of your sins. And you will receive the gift of the Holy Spirit.'* Peter announces two results for those who meet the prerequisite of repentance: the forgiveness of sins and the reception of the Spirit. What is this *'forgiveness'*? The word itself means: 'to release from legal or moral obligation or consequence, cancel, remit, pardon,'[12] with specific attention focused upon the guilt of the wrongdoer. 'The event of wrongdoing is not undone, but the guilt resulting from such an event is pardoned. To forgive, therefore, means essentially to remove the guilt resulting from wrongdoing.'[13] Accordingly, as is the case in v. 38, the apostles' preaching is not only distinguished by their call to repentance, but by their repeated proclamation of *'forgiveness'* as the accompanying consequence of repentance. For example:

> *Repent*, then, and turn to God, so that your *sins may be wiped out*, that times of refreshing may come from the Lord. (3:19)

Repentance and forgiveness are clearly tied together, the latter being God's promised response to the former. Further apostolic testimony may be considered:

> God exalted him to his own right hand as Prince and Savior that he might bring Israel to *repentance* and *forgive* their sins. (5:31)

---

11. Johnson, *The Message*, p. 25.

12. Bauer, *A Greek-English Lexicon*, p. 156.

13. Louw and Nida, *Greek-English Lexicon*, vol. 1, p. 503.

Repentance and forgiveness are again mentioned in tandem, both as gifts of the exalted Christ, with repentance being the implied precursor to forgiveness. On yet another occasion, Peter conveys a similar message in a confrontation with a practitioner of the occult:

> *Repent* of this wickedness and pray to the Lord in the hope that he may *forgive* you for having such a thought in your heart. (8:22)

Here the hope of forgiveness is explicitly contingent upon Simon's immediate repentance and prayer.

In each of these cases, the experience of the forgiveness of sins is inextricably connected to repentance as the exclusive prerequisite. This is not an apostolic innovation, but a faithful display of their allegiance to Jesus' design for mission: '... *repentance for the forgiveness of sins* will be preached in his name to all nations ...' (Luke 24:47). Precept and pattern are unmistakable: God's removal of the guilt accrued by sin is His gracious answer to repentance, a wiping away of the basis for condemnation, a full pardon for law breaking.

The gospel result includes more than the purging away of sin and guilt from the past, however. It includes a transformation that begins in the present by releasing its recipients into the freedom of being all that God has intended. It includes the creation of a new heart, a new appetite, a new orientation (*e.g.*, Jer. 31:31-34; Ezek. 11:19-20; 36:26-27)—all as the result of receiving '*the gift of the Holy Spirit*'—or, more precisely, '*the gift*' which consists of '*the Holy Spirit.*'[14] *Even more to the point— and in keeping with what Peter has already affirmed regarding the outpouring of the Spirit of prophecy in the last days—this is the gift that will enable the fulfillment of the mission that has been assigned to the renewed people of God and reiterated by Jesus: '... you will receive power when the Holy Spirit comes on you; and you will be my witnesses ...' (1:8).*

---

14. The genitive is epexegetical, which distinguishes this from the gifts that the Spirit imparts (*cf.* 1 Cor. 12:7-11).

For Peter's listeners who were—'cut to the heart'—these were the most glorious and hope-filled words they had ever heard, far beyond anything they deserved or for which they could even wish. David Gooding writes:

> They had murdered God's Son; he was offering them his Spirit. They had crucified the Second Person of the Trinity; he was offering to them the Third. They had thrown God's Son out of the vineyard in the hope of inheriting the vineyard themselves; now he was inviting them to receive God's Spirit not just into their vineyard but into their very hearts, to be their undying life, to be the earnest and guarantee of an infinite and imperishable inheritance.[15]

This is the gospel result for those who meet the gospel's stipulation: the forgiveness of all guilt, and the gift of the transformational presence of the Holy Spirit.

The gospel scope: *'The promise is for you and your children and for all who are far off—for all whom the Lord our God will call.'* It is this claim that exhibits the vast intention of God's saving purpose, and that exposes the breadth of the missionary vocation that is now assigned to His people. All boundaries that might have restricted the offer of *'the promise'*—the pardon of guilt and the gift of the Spirit—have been removed. Most amazingly, Peter indicates that this promise is firstly—*'for you'*—the very people antecedently identified in his sermon as those who *'crucified'* Jesus (v. 36) and *'put him to death'* (v. 23). Is this possible? To suggest they are unworthy of this promise would be an exercise in gross understatement. They are people culpable for an offense that will be forever distinguished by its inestimable wickedness. To declare that this promise is for them is to stretch the notion of divine grace to a point that dwarfs even the most generous of human conceptions.

Furthermore, Peter expands the scope of this to include all of their succeeding generations—*'and your children.'* It is the

---

15. Gooding, *True to the Faith*, p. 67.

converse to the covenant threat formula: 'I, the LORD your God, am a jealous God, punishing the children for the sin of the parents to the third and fourth generation of those who hate me' (Exod. 20:5; *cf.* 34:7). When seen in this light, it becomes clear that Peter's reference in this promise is not 'little children' or 'infants,' but any person viewed in relationship to parents; more specifically, 'descendants from a common ancestor.'[16] The broader context affirms this (v. 17 speaks of children old enough to prophesy; v. 38 addresses those who receive forgiveness and the gift of the Spirit, neither of which seem to be inclusive of infants). Peter, then, is referring to 'not to one's immediate descendants or offspring (that is to say, to one's sons or daughters) but to a successive series of such persons, one's descendants.'[17] Consequently, this serves as the echo of God's covenantal promises to *Noah*–

> I now establish my covenant with you and with your descendants after you ... (Gen. 9:9)

Abraham–

> 'All the land that you see I will give to you and your offspring forever ... I will establish my covenant as an everlasting covenant between me and you and your descendants after you for the generations to come, to be your God and the God of your descendants after you. The whole land of Canaan, where you now reside as a foreigner, I will give as an everlasting possession to you and your descendants after you; and I will be their God.' Then God said to Abraham, 'As for you, you must keep my covenant, you and your descendants after you for the generations to come. This is my covenant with you and your descendants after you, the covenant you are to keep: every male among you shall be circumcised.' (Gen. 13:15; 17:7-10)

and *David*–

---

16. Bauer, *A Greek-English Lexicon*, p. 994.

17. Louw and Nida, *Greek-English Lexicon*, pp. 115-116.

He gives his king great victories;
  he shows unfailing love to his anointed,
  to David and to his descendants forever.

The LORD swore an oath to David,
  a sure oath he will not revoke:
'One of your own descendants
  I will place on your throne.
If your sons keep my covenant
  and the statutes I teach them,
then their sons shall sit
  on your throne for ever and ever.'
(Ps. 18:50; 132:11-12).

Peter's delineation of the gospel's scope reveals that God has not forgotten or forsaken Israel. Rather, He is restoring her in keeping with His ancient promises. This, too, is redolent of an extraordinary grace, especially when the former cry of the Jewish mob is replayed—their self-condemning retort to Pilate's profession of innocence in relationship to the execution of Jesus: 'His blood is on us and on our children!' (Matt. 27:25). It is an irony of grace that those so willing to impute the death of Jesus to themselves and their posterity should experience the redeeming benefits that result from it—benefits, says Peter, that are now extended to *you and your children.*

Yet even this is not the full extent of the gospel's scope. This is a promise—*for all who are far off—for all whom the Lord our God will call.* Commentators are universally agreed that the phrase—*'far off'*—is an allusion to Isaiah 57:19, where the prophet writes: '"Peace, peace, to those far and near," says the LORD. "And I will heal them."' Given the spatial implications of this adverb, along with Peter's obvious reticence toward movement in a Gentile direction until his vision in Acts 10, some have concluded that Peter's reference to those who are—*'far off'*—is an effort to encompass Jews living in distant lands.[18] However, both the immediate and distant contexts argue

---

18. Wall, '*The Acts,*' p. 68; Witherington, *The Acts,* pp. 155-156.

more effectively for a meaning that is universal, one extending to Gentiles.

To begin with, the setting of Acts 2 should be kept in mind. Luke has already indicated that Peter's Pentecostal audience is comprised of Jews *'from every nation under heaven'* (v. 5). As such, these 'Diaspora Jews' are the very group Peter is addressing in the first two parts of this three-part sentence: *'The promise is for you and your children.'* The third part of this sentence– *'and for all who are far away'*–is not a reference, then, to Jews scattered around the world (who have already been included in the scope of this promise), but a group distinct from them; i.e., Gentiles.[19] This interpretation is further strengthened in Acts when Luke later uses the same term to narrate Paul's commission to ministry by the Lord: 'Go; I will send you *far away to the Gentiles'* (22:21). In a more distant context, Paul also employs this language with reference to God's missionary agenda for the Gentiles: 'But now in Christ Jesus *you who were once far away* have been brought near by the blood of Christ ... He came and preached peace to *you who were far away* and peace to those who were near' (Eph. 2:13, 17).[20] Finally, while it is certainly true that Peter required significant persuasion before he could enter the house of a Gentile (Acts 10), it is also true that he acknowledges God's purpose to send the resurrected Jesus to Israel *'first'* (3:26), thus implying an awareness of a subsequent Gentile benefit associated with the salvation that commences with the restoration of Israel.

The scope of this promise, therefore, is universal–a fact amplified by Peter in his summarizing clause: *'for all whom the Lord our God may call.'* It is here that Peter returns to the text in Joel 2 for a final appeal. To appreciate the significance of

---

19. Pao, *Acts*, pp. 230-232.

20. 'Gentiles were "far away," not in terms of geographical distance, but in terms of exclusion from God's covenant with Israel (Eph. 2:12). In Christ, the barrier that kept Gentiles at a distance, barred from God's sanctuary, was dismantled. Aliens now have access to God's holy place "through the blood of Christ" (Eph. 2:13).' Johnson, *The Message*, p. 121.

this requires a brief reminder of the ending of Joel's original text:

> And everyone who calls on the name of the Lord will be saved; for on Mount Zion and in Jerusalem there will be deliverance, as the LORD has said, even among the survivors whom the LORD calls. (Joel 2:32)

Peter's earlier citation of Joel (vv. 17-21) concluded with the phrase: *'And everyone who calls upon the name of the Lord will be saved.'* Now, in his resumption of it, he bypasses an intervening line and skips ahead to the final clause: *'for all whom the Lord our God may call.'* The point is that Peter has obviously omitted the concerns related to Mount Zion and Jerusalem and has, instead, inserted the phrase–*'all who are far off.'* It highlights an application of this promise that is universal in scope and, thus, indicative of a mission that will intentionally seek the conversion of Gentiles.[21] It provides the theological basis, for example, upon which Paul can declare boldly to the philosophers of Athens: '... now he [God] commands *all people everywhere* to repent' (17:30).

Some pushback, however, should be expected at this point: 'This actually appears to set limits on those who receive God's promise ... that the forgiveness of sins and the gift of the Spirit are only for those whom *"the Lord our God calls."* Is God really the one who summons people to salvation?' Earlier in this sermon, as Peter comes to a temporary stopping point in his citation of Joel, he clearly sets forth the promise (with its implicit invitation): *'everyone who calls upon the name of the Lord will be saved'* (v. 21)—more specifically (in the subsequent light of Peter's preaching, vv. 22-38), any who exercise repentance in relationship to Jesus. Here, in v. 39 (as he resumes quoting the words of Joel), Peter provides the complementary perspective: *'for all whom the Lord our God will call.'* These are not competing

---

21. Luke's adjustment of Joel's plain relative clause (*hous kyrios proskekletai*) to an indefinite relative clause (*hosous an* further implies an extent without limits and, thus, reinforces an expansion inclusive of Gentiles.

realities. They are completing realities, the latter underscoring that the initiative in salvation belongs to God. It is His call to sinners that enables their calling upon Him—a fact implied elsewhere in Acts when Luke indicates that even repentance and faith are God's gifts (3:16, 26; 5:31; 11:18). Far from imposing any insecurity, this would be a cause of great assurance for Peter's listeners. Were they to cast themselves upon Jesus in a plea for salvation, there would be no cause to doubt His saving response. Why? Their call is a responsive act. His call will have initiated theirs. Says Barrett: '… there is no possibility that men will save themselves except in the sense that they call upon him who has already called them.'[22] *Nevertheless, a word of caution is necessary.* To use this text for the aim of establishing a strict exclusivism runs the risk of missing Peter's point. It is not his intent to provide a dogmatic *apologia* for limitations within God's saving sovereignty, but to spotlight God's gracious initiative in the outworking of a promise that is universal in scope.

The gospel sign: '… *be baptized, every one of you, in the name of Jesus Christ* …' How does '*baptism*' intersect with the reception of this promise? It is now pertinent to recall the 'aside' made previously when consideration was given to the other Acts passages that address the experience of forgiveness, along with the commission provided by Jesus Himself in Luke 24:45-47. Mention of baptism is wholly absent from these texts. Why, then, does Peter include it here in v. 38? That there exists a tight connection between the internal reality (the reception of the promise) and the external sign (baptism) is undeniable, as will soon be explained. Yet the former is not *dependent* upon the latter. This becomes evident in a brief consideration of the shift that Luke/Peter makes in the use of the verbs in v. 38:

---

22. Barrett, *Acts*, vol. 1, p. 156.

'Repent ...'
(The plural form of the verb is used. Peter is addressing the entire crowd.)

'be baptized, *every one of you, in the name of Jesus Christ ...*'
(A shift is made to the singular form of the verb. Peter adjusts to address each individual.)

'*for the forgiveness of your sins. And you will receive the gift of the Holy Spirit ...*'
(He shifts back to the plural form of the verb. Peter is once again addressing the entire crowd. Moreover, he uses the plural pronoun in association with forgiveness—'your sins'.)

When this shift is given appropriate consideration, the phrase—'*for the forgiveness of your sins*'—is seen to be subordinate only to the verb—'*repent*'—and not to the verb—'*be baptized.*' To reflect this emphasis, the sentence may be structured as follows: 'Repent for the forgiveness of your sins, and you will receive the gift of the Holy Spirit—and be baptized, every one of you, in the name of Jesus Christ.' Admittedly, this distinction is subtle. To not make it, however, leaves two significant obstacles to overcome: 1) baptism appears to be a prerequisite for the forgiveness of sins and the reception of the Spirit (at odds with New Testament theology); and, 2) it creates an irreconcilable barrier between this and the other passages in Luke/Acts that tie the experience of forgiveness to the act of repentance solely.[23]

Baptism is not a criterion that must be met before a person can receive the gospel promise. But neither, for this

---

23. Schnabel has attempted to reconcile this difficulty by appealing to a causal use of the preposition *eis*. Thus, the translation would be as follows: 'Repent and be baptized, every one of you, in the name of Jesus Christ *because of* the forgiveness of your sins.' In other words, forgiveness of sins is the cause of baptism. *Acts*, pp. 154-155. See also Nigel Turner, 'Syntax,' *A Grammar of New Testament Greek*, ed. James Hope Moulton (Edinburgh: T & T Clark, 1963), vol. 3, p. 266. Wallace, while affirming the theological instincts that compel such a consideration (*i.e.*, that baptism is not the cause of salvation), strongly argues against it on the basis of weak linguistic support. *Greek Grammar*, pp. 369-371.

reason, is it an optional act, related to a status of comparative insignificance. In anticipation of the new age, John the Baptist announced: 'I baptize you with water. But one more powerful than I will come, the straps of whose sandals I am not worthy to untie. He will baptize you with the Holy Spirit and fire' (Luke 3:16). It would not have been illogical to assume that immersion in water would cease to be practised once the outpouring of the Spirit occurs. Yet this does not become the case. Jesus makes water baptism an essential expression of the Great Commission (Matt. 28:19), and the apostles practise it so consistently that no intentional exceptions or delays are explicitly recorded.[24] The New Testament never entertains the notion of a follower of Jesus who remains unbaptized. It is the reason for the particular emphasis Peter stresses as he urges baptism '*in the name of Jesus Christ.*' This is not a denial of the Trinitarian formula prescribed by Jesus (Matt. 28:19). The preposition used here–'*in*'–means 'on the basis of.' It may, in fact, suggest that the person being baptized actually confessed the name of Jesus publicly, affirming Him as the basis or ground upon which submission to baptism was occurring– 'acknowledging his claims, subscribing to his doctrine, engaging in his service and relying on his merits.'[25] While it is theologically orthodox to assert that baptism is not an indispensible prerequisite for salvation, it is equally orthodox to acknowledge that a decision to remain unbaptized is akin to the choice not to be a Christian. It is to refuse the sign of allegiance to Jesus.

What is the gospel stipulation? It is repentance. Have *you* 'repented'? Have *you* experienced the internal, intellectual act

---

24. This is not to suggest that baptism is always mentioned in every reference to Christian conversion (*e.g.*, 5:14; 6:7). To refrain from mentioning it, however, is not synonymous with the conclusion that baptism was not required, postponed for a later occasion, or refused by a professing follower of Jesus. It is rarely, if ever, Luke's agenda to provide a comprehensive portrait of the actual experience of salvation.

25. J. A. Alexander, *A Commentary on the Acts of the Apostles* (Carlisle: The Banner of Truth Trust, 1963), vol. 1, p. 85.

of exchanging old beliefs for new beliefs regarding Jesus Christ that, in turn, has resulted in a reorientation of your life?

What is the gospel result? It is the forgiveness of sins and the indwelling of the Holy Spirit. Have these unique and gracious gifts of the new covenant been granted to *you*? Have they made *you* into a different kind of person?

What is the gospel scope? It is the universal extension of the promise, a sovereign call initiated by the Lord God Himself. Have *you* been called by the Lord Jesus? Have *you*, in response to His initiation, called upon Him to save you?

What is the gospel sign? It is baptism in water, the definitive public affirmation that expresses an internal reality that has already occurred. Have *you* been baptized as a self-evident expression of your experience of salvation, aligning yourself with Jesus Christ and His work as the basis for your baptism?

These four—repentance, forgiveness/gift of Spirit, baptism, calling[26]—comprise Peter's explicit reply to the desperate plea of this crowd that has been '*cut to the heart*' by an awareness of their guilt.

The Concluding Summary

> With many other words he warned them; and he pleaded with them, 'Save yourselves from this corrupt generation.' Those who accepted his message were baptized, and about three thousand were added to their number that day. (vv. 40-41)

Several years ago, following a lecture I had given on preaching, a student asked me: 'How do you generate passion when you preach?' At the time, admittedly, I was completely caught off guard by this question, in that I had never given any self-conscious thought to it. Immediately, questions of my own raced through my mind: 'Is this student asking me for something formulaic; a methodology, perhaps, that would

---

26. These are listed in the sequence in which they have been explained above. This is not an attempt to establish an *ordo salutis*.

create urgency during the sermon's most strategic moments?
Does he suspect that earnestness can be manufactured by
including, at the appropriate points, notes of direction in the
margin of a preaching manuscript: "Raise voice here; pause
strategically now; close eyes and appear pensive; gesticulate
wildly with arms"?' Thankfully, all of these thoughts remained
unspoken as I attempted to provide this student with a cogent
answer. Later in the day, however, I did wonder to myself: 'Why
is so much contemporary preaching devoid of urgency? Why
is it that preaching today, by and large, is insipid and tepid?'
Preaching, after all, addresses human beings made in the image
of God. Moreover, in relationship to such people, it is taken
up with the issues of eternal vindication and judgment. A lack
of urgency on the part of the preacher exposes an inadequate
estimation of the significance of the event and conveys a
disqualifying indifference that betrays both the subject and
objects of the preaching. It is the Puritan Richard Baxter who
still, most succinctly, reflects the essence of this:

> I preached, as never sure to preach again,
> and as a dying man to dying men![27]

Peter's ministry to his audience on the day of Pentecost has
included much more content than is included in Luke's
narrative record. This has already been acknowledged. Luke's
selection of material for inclusion (and omission) has been
chosen in keeping with his purpose for writing. At this
point, then, the particulars related to the ongoing events of
Pentecost are now summarized and concluded, including
Peter's preaching. Nevertheless, Luke's summary does contain
two verbs that characterize the demeanor of Peter's–'*many
other words*'–both of which convey a sense of urgency.[28] In the

---

27. Richard Baxter, *Poetical Fragments* (Ann Arbor: University of Michigan Library DLPS, 1689), p. 40.

28. 'The earnestness of Peter's words is connoted by the prepositions in the verbs *diamartyromai* ("warned") and *parakaleo* ("pleaded"), which tends to strengthen the usual verbs for "witness" (*martyreo*) and "call" (*kaleo*)." Longenecker, '*Acts*,' p. 286.

first instance, Luke writes that Peter—'*warned them.*' Though
the ESV has softened this significantly—'*he bore witness*'—the
word used here means: 'to exhort with authority in matters of
extraordinary importance ... frequently with reference to higher
powers and/or suggestion of peril, solemnly urge, exhort,
warn.'[29] Paired with this, Luke indicates that Peter—'*pleaded
with them.*' It is a verb that not only communicates intensity;
more to the point, it speaks of Peter making an earnest request
of his listeners, of pleading with them and appealing to them
to respond appropriately.[30] Furthermore, Luke's use of this
verb in the imperfect tense signifies that Peter's appeals were
repeated again and again. Longenecker writes: 'What we have
here is the vision of an evangelist—a vision that is all too often
lost as the gospel is acclimated to the world ...'[31]

What is the general thrust of these appeals? '*Save yourselves
from this corrupt generation.*' This is the rehearsal of an Old
Testament phrase that would immediately strike a resonant
chord in the hearts of those to whom Peter is speaking. It
was a description of their ancestors, the people of Israel, who
rebelled against God in the wilderness were and subsequently
barred from the Promised Land (Deut. 32:5; Ps. 78:8). In the
New Testament, it is used by Jesus to refer to those who refused
to believe in Him (Luke 9:41; 11:29-32). Peter now applies this
language to His audience, urging them to be delivered from
their rejection of 'God's second great act of liberation,'[32] the
new exodus. This is a deliverance that involves rescue from a
'*generation.*' It refers not to a period of time, but to a people
who exhibit common characteristics[33]—a culture. Peter's
accusation—'*Save yourselves from this corrupt generation*'—is not just

---

29. Bauer, *A Greek-English Lexicon*, p. 233.

30. 'To ask for something earnestly ... to request, to plead for, to appeal to.' Louw
and Nida, *Greek-English Lexicon*, vol. 1, p. 408.

31. Longenecker, 'Acts,' p. 286.

32. Schnabel, *Acts*, p. 167.

33. Bauer, *A Greek-English Lexicon*, pp. 191-192.

directed at a heinous act (in this case, the rejection of Jesus)—
rather, that this heinous act was a telltale sign of an entire way
of life: *'corrupt'*–crooked, perverse, and unscrupulous.[34] It is
from this *'corrupt generation'* that Peter urges these people–*'save
yourselves'*–or, perhaps, better–'allow yourselves to be saved,'
with the permissive passive calling attention to the Lord who
must effect this salvation.

Why is this the substance of Peter's importunity? This culture
and the people shaped by it have an appointment with destiny:
they will face judgment on the great and glorious day of the
Lord. This hearkens back to the quotation of Joel—which also,
accordingly, provided a gracious assurance for those seeking
deliverance: *'And everyone who calls on the name of the Lord will
be saved'* (v. 21). It is to be remembered that the salvation
God promised through Joel, though made to all Israel, was
only enjoyed by a remnant of the whole people. Presently, as
Peter appeals to these Jewish worshippers on Pentecost, he is
urging them to make certain *they* belong to the remnant being
delivered from their fallen culture, and this notwithstanding
their Hebrew ancestry. The twofold implications of this are
profound: 1) insiders (Jews) are as much in need of salvation
as outsiders (Gentiles); and, 2) a new community is being
established, the nucleus of which is the believing remnant of
old Israel—which is, simultaneously, the nucleus of a restored
Israel. Stott captures the implications:

> Peter was not asking for private and individual conver-
> sions only, but for a public identification with other
> believers. Commitment to the Messiah implied com-
> mitment to the Messianic community, that is, the
> church. Indeed, they would have to change communi-
> ties, transferring their membership from one that was
> old and corrupt to one that was new and being saved.[35]

---

34. This term expresses 'the nature of the man who does not walk in the straight-
ness and uprightness which God has ordained for him but who in a way which is
guilty and worthy of punishment is crooked, cramped, distorted and hence corrupt.' Georg Bertram, 'σκολιος,' *TDNT*, vol. VII, p. 406.

35. Stott, *The Message*, pp. 78-79.

Until the day of Pentecost, this was a nucleus of one hundred and twenty people. Yet Jesus had been explicit with disciples: *'because I am going to the Father'*–believers would do even *'greater things'* than He had done. Of course, there would be many other events on many other days that would serve as fulfillments of Jesus' eschatological promise. But none would ever be as foundational as the events of the first day when, as a result of Peter's ministry: *'... and about three thousand were added to their number that day.'*

Conspicuously, in this immediate expansion from 120 to 3,120, there is no mention of a sound like the blowing of a violent wind, no mention of anything like tongues of fire resting upon each convert, no mention of speaking in unlearned languages. These, apparently, were among the phenomenal features unique to the initial stage of Pentecost. The phenomena that *are* seen and heard are those features that prove perpetual throughout the entirety of the last days: *'Those who accepted his message were baptized.'* It was the immediate expression of accepting the apostolic message, not the later ratification of a decision made on an earlier occasion.

This is what happened on the day of Pentecost. The Spirit of God came down. The gospel was proclaimed. The mission of the church began. To what end? Pentecost demanded a response from its first listeners. It is the same response that Pentecost continues to demand from us:

Repent
—and be baptized, every one of you, in the name of
Jesus Christ—
for the forgiveness of your sins.
And you will receive
the gift of the Holy Spirit.

7

SPIRIT-REVIVED COMMUNITY
(Part 1)

This summary of the activity of the church
focuses our attention away from preoccupation with individual actors
toward the true concern of the story—
the community.
WILLIAM E. WILLIMON

The higher we value our personal privacy
and freedom from commitments,
the shallower our grasp of fellowship will be—
reduced to moments of idle chitchat over steaming coffee
before or after a worship service.
DENNIS E. JOHNSON

Have you received this apostolic doctrine? I can test you simply.
If you have believed this and received it,
you have new, spiritual life,
and that will show itself in this way:
You will be hungering and thirsting for more.
It will become the greatest interest of your life.
D. MARTYN LLOYD-JONES

*42They devoted themselves to the apostles' teaching and to fellowship,
to the breaking of bread and to prayer. 43Everyone was filled with
awe at the many wonders and signs performed by the apostles. 44All
the believers were together and had everything in common. 45They
sold property and possessions to give to anyone who had need. 46Every
day they continued to meet together in the temple courts. They
broke bread in their homes and ate together with glad and sincere
hearts, 47praising God and enjoying the favor of all the people. And*

the Lord added to their number daily those who were being saved.
(Acts 2:42-47)

The Displays of Life

> If there is one thing the history of evolution has taught
> us, it's that life will not be contained. Life breaks
> free. It expands to new territories. It crashes through
> barriers. Painfully ... maybe even dangerously. But ...
> well, there it is. Life finds a way.[1]

These are the words of Dr. Ian Malcolm, the eccentric chaos
theoretician from the original blockbuster film *Jurassic Park*.
The movie is fiction (sourced in Michael Crichton's novel of
the same name), creatively constructed upon a foundation
of evolutionary presuppositions. Nonetheless, an aspect of
truth *is* encompassed in Dr. Malcolm's apprehension that
actually antedates the innovation of natural selection. It is
a phenomenon evidenced on the pages of Scripture itself:
The life God gives, conveyed through the gospel of Jesus Christ, will
not be contained. Sourced in God's own life, the eternal life
that is given to the followers of Jesus possesses a vitality and
exuberance that defies any attempt to contain it. In various
ways and through various means it expands to new territories,
crashes through longstanding barriers ... sometimes painfully,
sometimes even dangerously. But this life does find a way.

Pentecost has proved it—this unique fulfillment of God's
great last days' promise: the establishment of a new age and
a new kingdom that would commence in and among Israel,
spreading from Israel and by Israel, to encompass the entire
world. Firmly rooted in Old Testament revelation, Peter's
sermon is his effort to persuade the Pentecost celebrants
that the events they have just witnessed—the wonders of God
declared in their own languages—signal the inauguration of
this eschatological epoch. How has this come to pass? Jesus,

---

1. *Jurassic Park,* directed by Steven Spielberg (1993; Los Angeles: Universal Studios
Home Entertainment, 2003), DVD.

whom they crucified, has been subsequently raised from the dead, installed into David's throne, and acknowledged by God as Lord and Messiah. Seated at God's right hand, He has now dispensed the Holy Spirit upon all of His followers—which, in turn, has served to herald the beginning of the Messianic age. Horrified by the stark realization of their culpability for His execution, Peter's listeners express their desperation accordingly: 'What shall we do?' Heeding Peter's unambiguous and ever-relevant response, three thousand people accept his message and are baptized, as the remnant of Israel multiplies twenty-six times and becomes the Spirit-filled body of Jesus Christ.

A former epoch has ended and a new epoch has been inaugurated. A barrier has been crashed, and it will only be the first of many. Consequently, from this point on, the movement in Acts is fast paced and steadily progressing, with the gospel relentlessly advancing like an unstoppable locomotive hurtling forward on its tracks: *Jerusalem ... Judea ... Samaria ... the ends of the earth.* Intermittently, however, Luke reduces the speed of the movement—briefly pausing in the storyline of the church's *exterior mission*—for the purpose of providing a cameo, a tantalizing summary passage[2] of the church's *interior life*. Acts 2:42-47 is Luke's initial cameo. Like those that follow (*cf.* 4:32-37; 5:12-16), it reveals that Spirit-produced life is uncontainable. Coming on the heels of 2:1-41, this vignette implies that the display of community among these believers is the result of the transforming power of the Spirit; indeed, it is the beginning of the renewed society that was not only anticipated in Mosaic legislation (*e.g.*, Deut. 24:17-22), but envisioned by Old Testament prophets in their repeated pleas that urged the covenant people to repent of their failure to care for the needy among them (*e.g.*, Isa. 1:17; Jer. 5:26-29;

---

2. Witherington helpfully distinguishes between 'summary passages' and 'summary statements,' the latter of which are included to chronicle the growth and spread of the Christian community (6:7; 9:31; 12:24; 16:5; 19:20). *Acts*, pp. 157-160.

7:5-7; Micah 6:7-8; Zech. 7:9-10; Mal. 3:5). This is a portrait of Israel restored. Conspicuously, the summary cameo in 4:32-37 also follows an explicit reference to the Spirit's activity among believers in 4:31. Is this repetition *coincidental?* More than likely, it is *paradigmatic;* that, in each case, Luke spotlights these powerful displays of the renewed people of God in community *as the consequence of the unique presence and influence of the Holy Spirit.*

> Acts 2:42-47 follows so immediately (with 2:41) upon Peter's promise, that the reader naturally assumes the state of affairs described there as a measure of the impact of the promised Spirit on the community. The lack of any specific comment about the Spirit in 2:42-47, to earth the tense expectation built up from 2:1-11 through to 2:38-39, serves only to strengthen the reader's assumption. If one does not presume that the Spirit underlies the overall picture of the community here (and/or individual elements of it), then the silence on the Spirit in 2:42-47 becomes astonishingly incongruous, a sharp dissonance in the narrative and thematic development. The second summary (4:32-37) follows almost equally hard on the account of the 'Little Pentecost' in 4:31, though here there is at least a change of subject between 4:31 and 4:32. Once again there is literally 'not a syllable' to indicate that the Spirit is behind the life of the community depicted there, though in this case the Spirit would evidently be presumed to be the source of the 'great power' with which the apostles gave their testimony (4:33; cf. Luke 24:49; Acts 1:8), and so might equally plausibly be supposed, while unmentioned, behind other aspects of the community life, especially its communal generosity.[3]

Spiritual life has found a way. Eschatological Christianity, introduced by the power of the Spirit, has set itself on display in these portraits of community. Not an idealized life together, which is reserved only for the consummated new creation, but a community life that *is* indicative of an existence set in the

---

3. Turner, *Power*, p. 414.

overlap between the 'already' and the 'not yet.' Therefore, specific to Acts 2:42-47, it must now be asked: *What are the distinguishing activities of a Spirit-revived community? What are the telltale signs of a corporate life that has been brought into existence by Jesus' gift of the Holy Spirit?* Luke reveals four features, the first two of which will be examined in the remainder of this chapter, followed by the final two that will be considered in the last chapter.[4]

Distinguishing Activity #1: The Community Persistently Learns

> They devoted themselves to the apostles' teaching and to fellowship, to the breaking of bread and to prayer. (v. 42)

How many times have I read this terse, compact sentence? Hundreds of times? Without ever making an attempt to memorize it, I know it by heart. The same may well be true of you. Yet each time I read it, despite its familiarity, it startles me into a heightened alertness—like a pebble striking the windshield of my car—reorienting me back to the simplicity, the utter lack of complexity and sophistication, that marks this Spirit-revived community. This is not an expression of an early Christian liturgy, determining the four activities to be adhered to in every gathering. This is a summary expression: v. 42 listing four elements, with vv. 43-47 serving as an elaboration. As the remainder of the paragraph demonstrates, some of these activities occur at different times and in different places. Two facts, nonetheless, are to observed: 1) each of these activities are preceded by the definite article— '*the* apostles' teaching,' '*the* fellowship,' '*the* breaking of bread,' '*the* prayers'—highlighting the fact that when Acts was written, each of these had become well-known and distinctive features

---

4. These four activities seem to be listed in two pairs defined by their connecting conjunctions: 'to the apostles' teaching *and* to fellowship, to the breaking of bread *and* to the prayers.'

of Christian gatherings;[5] and, 2) one verb governs each of these four activities–'they *devoted themselves*'–which speaks of doing something with intense effort,[6] suggesting a steadfast fidelity. Moreover, the verb appears in a form that indicates a dedication that is constant and unrelenting,[7] as if what is in view is a holy stubbornness on the part of these Christians in their attention to these activities. Listed first is their devotion to–'*the apostles' teaching.*'

This is one of the decisive manifestations of people who have been authentically born again: the possession of a genuine hunger for the truth, an ongoing demand for the nourishment derived from divine revelation, in the same way that a decreased appetite for the truth is a sure indication of spiritual declension. For this reason, Peter elsewhere urges Christians: 'Like newborn babies, crave pure spiritual milk, so that by it you may grow up in your salvation, now that you have tasted that the Lord is good' (1 Peter 2:2-3). Perceiving themselves to be mature, Christians must not quickly dismiss Peter's exhortation as irrelevant on the ground that they have developed beyond the stage of spiritual infancy. A careful examination of Peter's words will reveal that the nub of his analogy does not turn on the *simplicity of substance* digestible by an infant (*i.e.*, mere milk over against meat; *cf.* 1 Cor. 3:2), but on the healthy infant's *insatiable demand* to digest pure milk. So, too, will this be the case for healthy Christians at *every* stage of maturity: they will deeply desire the unadulterated word.

Throughout the years, it has not been unusual to hear a Christian wistfully express to me a familiar concern: 'I'm not sure what we should do. Though my family and I are active members in our local church, we find ourselves starved for

---

5. Wallace, *Greek Grammar*, p. 225.

6. Louw and Nida, *Greek-English Lexicon*, vol. 1, p, 663. The same verb is used in 1:14; 2:46; 6:4; 8:13; 10:7.

7. This is a periphrastic construction–(the imperfect verb *esan* and the present participle *proskartereo*)–which stresses the ongoing nature of this activity.

the word of God.' In one sense, ironically, it is an encouraging concern, in that their professed hunger for nourishment is a conspicuous sign of their possession of genuine life. In a larger sense, however, it is heartrending—though consistently attending services each week that ostensibly schedule 'preaching,' the followers of Jesus find themselves at various stages of undernourishment. What is the frequent problem in these churches? Not the absence of an ordained person who is recognized as 'the preacher.' The problem is that not all that passes itself off as preaching *is* preaching. Here, in Acts 2:42, these revived people are undeniably engaged in learning. But a more focused observation necessitates a more pointed question: To which *curriculum* are they persistently devoted? Luke identifies it as—'*the apostles' teaching.*' The Holy Spirit, as it were, opens a school on the day of Pentecost,[8] with its faculty comprised of the Twelve[9]—their credentials having been established by Jesus' direct appointment and instruction. Three thousand new students matriculate into the kindergarten on the very first day which, frighteningly, represents a student-to-teacher ratio of 250:1.

Little imagination is required to ponder the demand associated with this work: the preaching, teaching, counseling—the barrage of seemingly endless questions from these Christians, eager to learn. No doubt, each evening the apostles would collapse exhaustedly into their beds, only to recognize that the next day would require more (and even greater) displays of the same. Their students were not unduly sluggish learners, possessing no familiarity with the Scriptures. They were Hebrews, after all, members of the old covenant community. Nevertheless, in the light of the coming of Jesus Christ, their orientation toward the Scriptures required no insignificant adjustment. They needed to be furnished with

---

8. This is an image proposed by Stott, *The Message*, p. 82.

9. The phrase—'*the apostles' teaching*'—is a subjective genitive; *i.e.*, the apostles were the ones performing the teaching.

the capacities necessary to hear and read the Old Testament in a manner consistent with the knowledge of the Savior who has now come. The apostles were well aware of this, having been the beneficiaries of this illumination themselves. Furthermore, they understood the significance of this moment in redemptive history: their calling, in part, was to *reform* Israel—or, to say it differently, to *form* the Christian community. The point, albeit implicit, should not be missed: not only had the new followers of Jesus—'*devoted themselves to the apostles' teaching*'—the apostles themselves were persistently devoted to teaching them. It is a theme Luke mentions repeatedly in the next few chapters:

> They were greatly disturbed because the apostles were *teaching* the people, *proclaiming* in Jesus the resurrection of the dead. (4:2)

> Then they called them in again and commanded them not to *speak* or *teach* at all in the name of Jesus. (4:18)

> At daybreak they entered the temple courts, as they had been told, and began to *teach* the people. (5:21)

> Then someone came and said, 'Look! The men you put in jail are standing in the temple courts *teaching* the people.' (5:25)

> 'We gave you strict orders not to *teach* in this name,' he said. 'Yet you have filled Jerusalem with your *teaching* ...' (5:28)

> Day after day, in the temple courts and from house to house, they never stopped *teaching* and *proclaiming* the good news that Jesus is the Messiah. (5:42)

As the church in Jerusalem progressively increases, so, too, do the responsibilities and conflicts that accompany such expansion. Consequently, the Twelve delegate the care and management of these responsibilities to another group of spiritually qualified people. What is their rationale for doing so? The conviction that they must be persistent in their devotion to preaching and teaching:

> It would not be right for us to neglect the *ministry of the word of God* in order to wait on tables ... We will turn this responsibility over to them and will give our attention to prayer and the *ministry of the word* (6:2-4).[10]

Of course, it must not be forgotten that Luke's cameo in Acts 2 is one of a community uniquely revived by a fresh outpouring of the Holy Spirit. By comparison, not many seasons of ministry are distinguished by such a visitation, a fact made plain by any honest reading of the remainder of the New Testament, let alone the record of church history and the actual experience of most Christians. It is to be expected, then, that the respective appetites for truth on the part of congregations and preachers may vary. For example, it has not been unusual for congregations that crave the truth to find themselves associated with preachers who fail to supply a sustaining diet. Nor is it a rare exception that preachers who exhaust themselves in the weekly provision of a biblical feast find themselves standing before congregations without a corresponding palate. A faithful preacher will, nevertheless, persist in this task despite the fluctuation in a congregation's desire, knowing that the ministry of the word is not only the means of satisfying a healthy spiritual appetite, but that it can serve as the Spirit-appointed means of stimulating one. As such, Paul urges Timothy to this relentless task:

> In the presence of God and of Christ Jesus, who will judge the living and the dead, and in view of his appearing and his kingdom, I give you this charge: preach the word; be prepared in season and out of season; correct, rebuke and encourage – with great patience and careful instruction. For the time will come when people will not put up with sound doctrine. Instead, to suit their own desires, they will gather round them a great number of teachers to say

---

10. This apostolic ministry of teaching is not confined to Jewish contexts solely, but expresses itself in Gentile settings as well (*e.g.*, 11:25-26; 18:11; 19:9-10; 20:7-12, 20-21, 28-32; 28:30-31). Clearly, the primitive Christian community regards teaching as an expression of ministry that is transcultural.

what their itching ears want to hear. They will turn
their ears away from the truth and turn aside to myths.
But you, keep your head in all situations, endure
hardship, do the work of an evangelist, discharge all
the duties of your ministry. (2 Tim. 4:1-5)

During extraordinary seasons of awakening, as in Acts 2, a *reciprocal persistence* can occur—a convergence of preachers and
people with respect to their attitudes toward, and appetites for,
the truth. But what, more specifically, is—'*the apostles' teaching*'?
It is *nothing less* than the deposit of truth that is now contained
in the New Testament, with Jesus Christ as its principal subject. It is a record of His incarnation, ministry, and teaching—
with particular attention given to His crucifixion, resurrection,
ascension, exaltation, and return. It includes the implications
of these events for the eternal salvation of human beings, along
with a body of practical ethics that correspond to and are motivated by His redemptive accomplishments (*e.g.*, ethics related
to marriage, money, work, sexuality). Is it then to be inferred
from this that Christians are now free to disengage from *Old
Testament* Scripture? While—'*the apostles' teaching*'—is *nothing less*
than New Testament revelation, the actual ministries of the
apostles display it to be *something more*. Nearly everything they
preach, teach, and write is an allusion to or exposition of a
portion of the Hebrew Scriptures—a fact that should no longer
prove surprising, given that Jesus displayed Himself to be their
ultimate focal point (*cf.* Luke 24:27, 45-47). For this reason,
nearly every paragraph in the New Testament inevitably redirects a Bible student to the Old Testament—if, for no other
reason, than the former apart from the latter constitutes a fulfillment without a promise; as it were, the provision of answers
to a test without an awareness of the questions asked. The apostolic sermons in Acts establish this pattern emphatically.[11]

---

11. An intentional study of the extended sermons recorded in Acts will prove
invaluable for a serious preacher, especially a careful consideration of the apostles'
use of the Old Testament.

So what does this mean for contemporary congregations and their preachers? Their collective and constant attention to–'*the apostles' teaching*'–will mean a display of persistent submission to the authority of the Christ-centered Scriptures. For the preacher, in particular, this means that his chief priority each week must be the work of prayerfully preparing a gospel meal for the nourishment of the congregational family–that the deep-seated joy unique to his calling is unattained until he has exhausted himself in the painstaking task of sermon preparation for the Lord's Day. For the congregation, this means that they must fervently intercede for the preacher and themselves in anticipation of the banquet, that they ready themselves to eat heartily by avoiding malnourishing foods that can compromise their digestive abilities, and that when the meal is finally set before them they dine with pleasure in the awareness of the sustaining benefits they will derive from the meal prepared for them. When this reciprocal persistence to–'*the apostles' teaching*'–is a distinguishing feature of a congregation's life together, it is a clear indication of a Spirit-revived community. *The Spirit reigns where the word of Jesus Christ reigns.*

Unfortunately, a glaring disjunction frequently reveals itself at this very point, expressing itself in something akin to the following: 'I'm not really into the serious study of the Bible. I don't mind dipping in, occasionally, to find a good thought for the day. But to figure out what words mean and how they relate to each other? And then, to ponder their connection to other ideas in Scripture so that I might better appreciate the Bible's main storyline–God's salvation of the human race through His son, Jesus–it's not for me. My preference is to be led by the Spirit.' But to such perspectives, a question must be posed: Does this assumed alternative (which appears to be more of an antithesis) bear any semblance to the Spirit-birthed Christianity that expresses itself in Acts 2:42? It could be argued that if ever such a dichotomy were to be seen, one would expect an expression of it here on the heels of the greatest outpouring of the Holy Spirit in history. Yet there is not the slightest hint of favoring mystical experiences, even in the name of the Spirit, over against the apostles' ministry of teaching. It could be asked at this point: How many of these three thousand converts speak in tongues? Even if some did, apparently Luke did not regard it as significant enough to note. And how many of these three thousand perform miracles? While Luke does indicate that–'*Everyone was filled with awe at the many wonders and signs performed*' (v. 43)–he is equally explicit as to their source–'*by the apostles.*' These were the means, in part, of identifying the apostles as heirs of Jesus' authority, whose own life and ministry God validated by–'*miracles, wonders and signs*' (v. 22). It is not fortuitous, then, that these two references to the apostles–their teaching (v. 42) and their miracles (v. 43)– appear in such close proximity, in that the latter were designed to confirm the former (*cf.* Rom. 15:19; 2 Cor. 12:12; Heb. 2:1-4).[12] The preoccupation of these Spirit-revived Christians is clearly focused on–'*the apostles' teaching.*' It is for this purpose they gathered publicly–'*Every day they continued to meet together in the temple courts*' (v. 46; 3:11-26; 5:21). Moreover, this implies that the reception of the Holy Spirit did not convince these Christians to summarily eliminate all human teachers as unnecessary.

---

12. This was essential, given their unique role as 'the medium and guarantors of the teaching–presumably focused on fresh interpretation of the Scriptures (as in 2:14-36) and beginning to order the memories of Jesus' teaching and ministry into forms suitable for instruction, worship, and proclamation.' Dunn, *The Acts*, p. 35. All of this is not to suggest that only the apostles perform miracles, though only two people are said to perform miracles in Acts outside of those identified as apostles: Stephen (6:8) and Philip (8:13). Nor is this to imply that miracles do not occur presently. However, a quick scan will reveal that miracles are not distributed evenly throughout the Bible, but occur in concentrated pockets and are connected to individuals granted a unique authority as God's spokesmen (Moses, Elijah, Jesus, the apostles). To expect the same density of miracles today is probably unwise in the light of these observations.

None of this is to suggest that all followers of Jesus should attend Bible college or seminary, or that all serious-minded Christians should learn to read Greek and Hebrew. It is to say that the anti-intellectualism that characterizes so much of evangelical spirituality is at cross-purposes with the fullness of the Spirit. It is to assert that real life cannot be contained; in this case, particularly, that people brought to life by the Spirit crave the truth. In fact, when professing Christians prove to be devoid of this appetite, when there is no internal compulsion toward a deeper appreciation of the Bible and how it points to the glorious Savior who has not spared Himself to save them, it is impossible *(and irresponsible)* to assure such people that they are authentically born again of the Spirit.

Undergirding all of this is the ministry and mandate of Jesus Himself, for whom teaching was a defining activity (Luke 4:15, 31-32; 5:3, 17; 6:6; 13:10, 22; 19:47; 20:1, 21; 21:37; Acts 1:1). He actually claimed, on one occasion, that the purpose of His coming was to teach and preach (Mark 1:38), and that it was for this very reason He was anointed with the Spirit (Luke 4:18-19). Not surprisingly, then, His orders for the apostles subsequent to His resurrection encompassed this same emphasis:

> All authority in heaven and on earth has been given to me. Therefore go and make disciples of all nations, baptizing them in the name of the Father and of the Son and of the Holy Spirit, and teaching them to obey everything I have commanded you. (Matt. 28:18-20)

To be sure, the result of this 'going' and declaring the Lordship of Jesus would result in responses of faith that would be appropriately displayed in baptism. Does this signal the completion of the apostles' mission? Yes ... if the aim of their efforts is *decision-making* over against *disciple-making*. But baptism is not where Christian discipleship concludes, only where it commences. It progresses forward by the following means: 'teaching them to obey everything I have commanded you' (Matt. 28:20)–a lifelong process, given that the goal is not merely that Christians master the gospel, but that they are mastered by the gospel with all of its theological, ethical, and social implications. Stated differently, discipleship's end is that the followers of Jesus 'obey everything' He has commanded.

Persistent devotion to–'*the apostles' teaching*'–is not only a telltale sign of a corporate life that has been birthed by the Holy Spirit. It is a display of fidelity to the word of the universal Lord. These are not to be regarded as alternative options between which Christians may choose. As indicated in Acts 2, the thrust of the Spirit will always advance the people of Jesus into a greater devotion to the revealed word. This is a distinguishing activity of a Spirit-revived community.

Distinguishing Activity #2: The Community Selflessly Shares

> They devoted themselves to the apostles' teaching and
> to fellowship ... (v. 42)

While there are those who mistakenly seek the subjective mysticisms of the Spirit as a preferred alternative to diligent Bible study, equally errant are those who tend to equate the Spirit's reviving work with phenomena that are exclusively cerebral: the reading of the right books, written by the approved theologians, who espouse an acceptable confession of historic Christian orthodoxy ... along with the almost inescapable cultivation of a fastidiousness over doctrinal minutiae that expresses itself in an eagerness to be pugnacious and separatist. But being *quarrelsome* is not the relational manifestation of a Spirit-revived community. '*Fellowship*' is a virile and robust New Testament concept that has been undermined by applications of it that are banal and insignificant. For example, imagine two, nearly identical scenarios. Scenario #1: A Christian and a non-Christian meet at a local coffee shop for enthusiastic conversation about a recent football game, while each enjoying a pumpkin-spiced latte. Scenario #2: The non-Christian is substituted for a Christian, while all the other details remain unchanged—the location, the coffee, the substance of the conversation. Why is the former encounter most typically labeled 'friendship,' while the latter is defined as 'fellowship'? Is there a difference between 'friendship' and 'fellowship'? And, if so, does the difference consist solely in *the spiritual status* of the conversation partners? What is Luke highlighting in Acts 2:42 when he indicates that these Christians were giving their constant attention to—'fellowship'?

The word translated—'fellowship'—was originally employed in commercial contexts, often in specific reference to those who were partners in business (*cf.* Luke 5:10)—a 'close association involving mutual interests and sharing ...'[13] In secular Greek, it was commonly drawn upon to describe the kind of mutuality that occurs in marriage. So, too, its New Testament usage comprehends qualities more specific and substantive than mere acquaintance or friendship. It means 'to share with someone in something ... to give someone a share in something'[14]—that is, above and beyond the relationship itself. Certainly 'fellowship' is nothing less than friendship, but it is also something much more. To summarize the New Testament notion succinctly: 'fellowship' means a *sharing in* and a *sharing out*.

When a person becomes a Christian, an eternal partnership with the Triune God is established that transcends the mere declaration of a right status. The New Testament writers indicate that Christians *share in*—'fellowship ... with the Father and with his Son, Jesus Christ' (1 John 1:3; *cf.* 1 Cor. 1:9), and that they also *share in*—'fellowship of the Holy Spirit' (2 Cor. 13:14; *cf.* Phil. 2:1). But this eternal boon of *sharing in* the life of God and His blessings is not a terminus. It effects a *sharing out* with those in fellowship with God through the gospel.[15] It is this

---

13. Bauer, *A Greek-English Lexicon*, p. 552.

14. Friedrich Hauck, 'κοινωνια,' *TDNT*, vol. III, pp. 798-809.

15. 'We should be cautious about using different occurrences of any word in the Bible to arrive at a general meaning of it, as words take different meanings accord-

194 SPIRIT EMPOWERED MISSION

Luke calls to attention when he notes that these Spirit-revived people were persistently devoted to–'*the fellowship*' (the definite article in the Greek text indicates a reference to something specific). What does Luke have in mind?

Consider how this term–'*fellowship*'–is frequently employed elsewhere in the New Testament:

> For Macedonia and Achaia were pleased to make a *contribution* for the poor among the Lord's people in Jerusalem. (Rom. 15:26)

> ('*Contribution*' is a translation of the same Greek word used for '*fellowship*' in Acts 2:42.)

> And now, brothers and sisters, we want you to know about the grace that God has given the Macedonian churches. In the midst of a very severe trial, their overflowing joy and their extreme poverty welled up in rich generosity. For I testify that they gave as much as they were able, and even beyond their ability. Entirely on their own, they urgently pleaded with us for the privilege of *sharing in* this service to the Lord's people. (2 Cor. 8:1-4)

> ('*Sharing in*' is a translation of the same Greek word used for '*fellowship*' in Acts 2:42.)

> This service that you perform is not only supplying the needs of the Lord's people but is also overflowing in many expressions of thanks to God. Because of the service by which you have proved yourselves, others will praise God for the obedience that accompanies your confession of the gospel of Christ, and for your generosity in *sharing* with them and with everyone else. (2 Cor. 9:12-13)

> ('*Sharing*' is a translation of the same Greek word used for '*fellowship*' in Acts 2:42.)

> Moreover, as you Philippians know, in the early days of your acquaintance with the gospel, when I set out

---

ing to the context on which they appear. But the nineteen occurrences of *koinonia* in the New Testament suggest that the church used this word for the unique sharing that Christians have with God and with other Christians.' Fernando, *Acts*, p. 120.

> from Macedonia, not one church *shared* with me in
> the matter of giving and receiving, except you only;
> for even when I was in Thessalonica, you sent me aid
> more than once when I was in need. (Phil. 4:15-16)

> ('*Shared*' is the verbal form of the same Greek word
> used for '*fellowship*' in Acts 2:42.)

Even a minimal exposure to these texts leads to the realization
that a counterfeit meaning of '*fellowship*' has infused itself
into the minds of many evangelicals, ultimately undermining
their experience of its sanctifying benefits. A corrective from
the New Testament reveals this *sharing in* to be something
costlier than idle conversation that occurs among Christians
over espresso and scones in the church's *Fellowship Hall*. It is
a partnership in the sharing of economic resources. Speaking
most practically, it implies that the wallets and purses belonging
to these Christians are open.

This is Luke's emphasis in v. 42, made evident by his
expanded description of '*fellowship*' in the verses that follow:
'*All the believers were together ... Every day they continued to meet
together ...*' (v. 44a, 46a). *All* of them? *Every* day? Even the most
spiritually-minded Christians would regard this as excessive.
Why do this? Some might suggest that this must have been
the standing order of the apostles—that full participation was
required at daily meetings. If this is so, however, Luke never
mentions it. Others might explain this as a display of the
old adage: 'Birds of a feather flock together'—that people of
similar tastes congregate in groups. But given the significant
diversity expressed earlier (vv. 9-11), the obvious question
would quickly follow: What similarities *could* these people
share? Do they all belong to the same socio-economic class?
Do they all embrace the same cultural values (the Jerusalem
Jews and the Diaspora Jews)? Do they all share the same
skin pigmentation? Do they all speak the same dialect?
What *are* the bases upon which their radical togetherness is
established?

Though many have acknowledged (without much regret) that the church growth movement has passed its prime, one of its principal concepts remains indelibly fixed in the minds many evangelicals: indispensable to numerical growth is a commitment to congregational homogeneity. Though this may take the form of an ethnic uniformity, the concept is not confined to such limitations. Congregations may unite and expand on the basis of a common dislike of a political agenda, or a shared conviction that parents should school their children at home. Their concord may be grounded in a mutual appetite for reading Reformation theologians, or a reciprocal enthusiasm for hip-hop music, tattoos, and body piercings. Christian fellowship, however, is not an exercise in cloning. Moreover, when such as these are bases of unity, even among an assembly of Christians, it is certain that the community has been sown with the seeds of its own demise—that little time will pass before indications of inbreeding begin to display themselves and the congregation implodes.

At the risk of oversimplification, two clues embedded in the text serve to explain the level of frequency and participation that distinguished these meetings. First, Luke refers to these Spirit-revived people as—'believers' (v. 44).[16] In other words, the basis of their conspicuous unity is that they share a common faith—a surprising means of identification given that 'belief' is not explicitly set forth in this account as a qualification for membership in this community. But in whom, specifically, has their faith been placed? This calls attention to a second clue: the use of the conjunction—'And'—near the beginning of v. 42. Left untranslated in the NIV, it implies that the expression of community in vv. 42-47 is not a disassociated phenomenon, but in continuity with the events that have preceded it. God has raised Jesus from the dead, exalted Him to heaven, and enthroned Him as Lord and Messiah in fulfillment of Old

---

16. This becomes a common means of identification employed by Luke (e.g., 4:32; 5:14; 15:1-5; 19:18; 21:20, 25; 22:19).

Testament revelation. The recognition of this moves Peter's hearers to repentance that, in turn, results in the experience of forgiveness, a public identification with Jesus Christ in baptism (the external demonstration of faith), and the reception of the new covenant gift of the Holy Spirit. The faith they have come to share as 'believers' rests on Jesus, the enthroned Messiah who has poured out the Holy Spirit. All of this, then, accounts for the zeal displayed in their common commitment to assemble together daily.

Admittedly, this *is* a season of revival—'the inaugural revival of the New Testament epoch'[17]—an unusual occasion in which everything is exponentially heightened for a period of time (when wise and experienced pastors, without quenching the Spirit's awakening work, will need to help people avoid reckless and detrimental excesses).[18] Yet, it must be asked: Is there not a real sense in which this is the distinctive disposition of *all* genuine Christians? Is this *your* disposition? Have you changed *your* mind about Jesus Christ? Have you recognized His saving majesty and Lordship? Have you gone public with your allegiance to Him, calling upon His name in baptism? Have you experienced the unique freedom of a full forgiveness and been given the gift of the indwelling Spirit? If these are your claims, then there ought to be seismic tremor in your conscience if you possess no internal urge to meet with people

---

17. Sinclair B. Ferguson, *The Holy Spirit* (Downers Grove: InterVarsity Press, 1996), p. 90.

18. The New Testament never mandates that Christians should meet together daily as they did immediately following Pentecost. Considering the responsibilities to witness, family, and vocation, it is not advisable for churches to schedule required events with a frequency that undermines other activities that are essential expressions of authentic Christianity. The events surrounding Pentecost mark a *season* of revival, not the ongoing expectation of all Christians throughout the entirety of church history. Moreover, the uniqueness of this time in salvation history should be remembered: a transition of epochs has occurred which involves the restoration and reformation of the entire covenant community. Given this necessary qualification, Christians should nevertheless aspire to gather together consistently and frequently.

who have known the same gospel benefits. 'Although I am a Christian, I am strictly the non-churchgoing type.' This was the testimony of a man, recorded in a London newspaper, to which Dr. Martyn-Lloyd Jones responded: 'According to the book of Acts ... such a man is not a Christian.'[19]

Where the gospel is genuinely embraced, the gospel dynamically controls. And when the gospel controls, it unites the one controlled by it to everyone else for whom it is the controlling influence. One hundred pianos all tuned to the same tuning fork will automatically prove to be tuned to one another. They are pitched in unity, not because they have been tuned to each other, but because they have been tuned to another standard to which each one must individually submit. Likewise, when members of the Christian community steadily look to Jesus Christ they experience a greater intimacy with one another than if they suddenly become 'unity conscious' and avert their preoccupation from Jesus to themselves for the sake of 'creating' a greater unity of fellowship. It is their deeply shared allegiance to Jesus as Messiah and Lord that constitutes the basis and motivation of '*all the believers*' to be together '*every day.*' But what is Luke's purpose for highlighting this? He does so because the frequent meeting together of Christians is an essential platform for something beyond itself: '*All the believers were together and had everything in common*' (v. 44). What does Luke mean by this? He provides an explanation in the following verse: '*They sold property and possessions to give to anyone who had need*' (v. 45). The point is as obvious as it is simple: efficacy of fellowship is dependent upon proximity to the fellowship. Intentional and consistent engagement with the community of faith is a chief prerequisite for meaningfully addressing the needs of those within the community.

It is precisely at this point that authentic fellowship remains a mystery to so many. Their participation in the

---

19. D. Martyn Lloyd-Jones, *Authentic Christianity* (Wheaton: Crossway Books, 2000), p. 92.

church is erratic at best; ironically, in many cases, because their notions of fellowship are interpreted through the grid of self-centeredness. Such folk may sporadically visit on a Sunday morning, but given their insatiable and omnivorous appetite for self-gratification (who could ever meet their desires?), they typically leave the congregation with biting criticism on their lips: 'There's no real fellowship at that church.' To experience Christian fellowship requires community members who are enthusiastic givers, not ravenous consumers. Four points of clarification, however, are necessary.

First, Luke's account is not the provision of welfare relief for the poor and needy unbelievers in the broader Jerusalem community. He is describing–'*fellowship*'–a term used exclusively for the sharing Christians experience with God and each other. It is a covenantal phenomenon (1 John 3:17; *cf.* James 2:14-16). *Second*, this is not charity for Christians who refuse to work, even if their refusal is couched in ostensible expressions of piety. According to Paul, such an idea is reprehensible and decidedly contrary to Christian teaching (2 Thess. 3:6-13). *Third*, this is not a once-for-all disposal of private property, with the proceeds placed into a common fund and dispensed appropriately among all believers. It is not enforced sharing, a primitive expression of an economic communism. The clear implication of v. 46 is that Christians maintained their homes. Later in his narrative, Luke introduces Mary, the mother of John Mark, whose large home is used for ministry (12:12). Other portions of the New Testament reveal Christians like Gaius (Rom. 16:23), Aquila and Priscilla (1 Cor. 16:19), Nympha (Col. 4:15), and Philemon (Philem. 1-2), all of whom exercised effective ministry by the means of their affluence. Acts does not evidence a renunciation of private property. It displays a renunciation of personal possessiveness. *Fourth*, this is not an alternative manifestation of the Christian mission, the exchange of social benevolence for the preaching of the gospel. These Christians are persistently devoted to—'*the apostles' teaching*'—that is, the proclamation of the love of God in the gospel of Jesus Christ that results in practical demonstrations of this love within the context of the gospel community. In fact, in a later cameo provided by Luke (4:32-37), squeezed between two strong statements regarding the church's generosity (v. 32 and vv. 34-37), Luke writes: 'With great power the apostles continued to testify to the resurrection of the Lord Jesus' (4:33).

How, then, is this—'*fellowship?*'—to be understood? A close examination of the verbs—'*sold*' and '*give*'—reveal them to be iterative imperfects, indicating repeated actions that are occasional in their display.[20] This can be illustrated by the image of a horizontal line on a plane. Rather than the image of an unbroken line that begins at a point in the past and runs along a surface uninterruptedly (a customary or habitual imperfect), the iterative imperfect envisions a line that begins at some past moment and then pauses. It then resumes at a later point and then pauses again, only to begin once more and then pause. The point made by the force of these verbs indicates, therefore, that this selling and distributing were repeated, but intermittent actions. What occasioned their necessary display? They were activated in response—'*to anyone who had need.*' Rather than claiming exclusive rights to their assets, these Christians parted with a portion of their '*property*' or their '*possessions*'[21]—thus diminishing the strength of their own economic security—for the sake of addressing the needs of their fellow believers. It was an eloquent generosity, a decided bias toward sharing in both the burden of poverty and the blessing of wealth. These were voluntary expressions of sacrificial generosity in response to specific needs. The early

---

20. Wallace, *Greek Grammar*, pp. 546-547.

21. 'The word κτημα (*ktema*) literally means a possession of any kind, but it came to be restricted to "landed property," "a field," or "a piece of ground." Its synonym υπαρξις (*hyparxis*) when used in tandem with *ktema* likely signifies more what we would call personal possessions apart from real estate.' Longenecker, 'Acts,' p. 292.

church father, Tertullian c. (A.D. 155-240), wrote about this in his day:

> Though we have our treasure-chest, it is not made up of purchase-money, as of a religion that has its price. On the monthly day, if he likes, each puts in a small donation; but only if it be his pleasure, and only if he be able: for there is no compulsion; all is voluntary. These gifts are, as it were, piety's deposit fund. For they are not taken thence and spent on feasts, and drinking-bouts, and eating-houses, but to support and bury poor people, to supply the wants of boys and girls destitute of means and parents, and of old persons confined now to the house; such, too, as have suffered shipwreck; and if there happen to be any in the mines, or banished to the islands, or shut up in the prisons, for nothing but their fidelity to the cause of God's Church, they become the nurslings of their confession. But it is mainly the deeds of a love so noble that lead many to put a brand upon us. See, they say, how they love one another ... [22]

It is akin to the instinct unique to a family comprised of members who readily make great sacrifices for other family members. It is no coincidence that in Acts, while Luke refers to the followers of Jesus as 'the saints' (four times), 'the believers' (five times), 'the church' (twenty-two times), 'the disciples' (twenty-three times), it is his reference to Christians as 'brothers and sisters' he employs most frequently (twenty-five times). 'By the grace of God,' concludes Dennis Johnson, 'they had been born into a family that could call God "Father" (Luke 11:2). How could they not, then, treat each other as brothers and sisters (whatever their previous lineage)?'[23] It is this expression of family generosity that is repeated in various forms throughout Luke's narrative:

> All the believers were one in heart and mind. No one claimed that any of their possessions was their own,

---

22. Tertullian, *Apologeticus*, 39. See *The Apology of Tertullian for the Christians*, T. H. Bindley, ed. (Oxford: Parker and Company, 1890), pp. 64-54.

23. Johnson, *The Message of Acts*, pp. 74-75.

but they shared everything they had. With great power the apostles continued to testify to the resurrection of the Lord Jesus. And God's grace was so powerfully at work in them all that there were no needy persons among them. For from time to time those who owned land or houses sold them, brought the money from the sales and put it at the apostles' feet, and it was distributed to anyone who had need. Joseph, a Levite from Cyprus, whom the apostles called Barnabas (which means 'son of encouragement'), sold a field he owned and brought the money and put it at the apostles' feet. (4:32-37)

In those days when the number of disciples was increasing, the Hellenistic Jews among them complained against the Hebraic Jews because their widows were being overlooked in the daily distribution of food. So the Twelve gathered all the disciples together and said ... 'Brothers and sisters, choose seven men from among you who are known to be full of the Spirit and wisdom. We will turn this responsibility over to them ...' (6:1-4)

During this time some prophets came down from Jerusalem to Antioch. One of them, named Agabus, stood up and through the Spirit predicted that a severe famine would spread over the entire Roman world. (This happened during the reign of Claudius.) The disciples, as each one was able, decided to provide help for the brothers and sisters living in Judea. This they did, sending their gift to the elders by Barnabas and Saul. (11:27-30)

You yourselves know that these hands of mine have supplied my own needs and the needs of my companions. In everything I did, I showed you that by this kind of hard work we must help the weak, remembering the words the Lord Jesus himself said: 'It is more blessed to give than to receive.' (20:34-35)

After an absence of several years, I came to Jerusalem to bring my people gifts for the poor ... (24:17)

Are *you* engaging in authentic, Christian–'*fellowship*'? Is your *congregation* exercising similar kinds of expressions of partnership and sharing to those described in Acts? Some, musing in response, might actually dare to suggest the following: 'Well, maybe it *would* be better to turn this into an enforced mandate; that all the members of our congregation liquidate everything they own and accumulate their resources together in a common church fund that is dispensed accordingly. At least, then, we wouldn't have to worry about our responsibilities for each other' (which, translated, may actually mean: 'At least we wouldn't have to feel guilty about ignoring our responsibilities for each other'). In one sense, provision in this manner could be made for brothers and sisters without requiring careful thinking, compassionate feeling, and openhearted praying— never having to wrestle with issues of conscience when faced with questions like: 'How much sharing *is* enough? Do I give to the point of jeopardizing my own security? How does all of this intersect with the needs of my family? Do I really need the new car? Should I buy a new Lexus or will a used Hyundai suffice? And what about the Hawaiian vacation we've been planning? The remodeling of our kitchen? The pair of designer jeans priced at $150?' The Scriptures do not provide universal and unambiguous answers to these kinds of questions—that is, right or wrong responses that are always appropriate for every Christian in each of these situations. This is, in large part, because the Lord of the church does not want His people to disengage from the burden of making their monetary decisions in the light of the neediness of brothers and sisters to whom they belong in covenant community.

> This is how we know what love is: Jesus Christ laid down his life for us. And we ought to lay down our lives for our brothers and sisters. If anyone has material possessions and sees a brother or sister in need but has no pity on them, how can the love of God be in that person? (1 John 3:16-17)

'What we do or do not do with our material possessions is an indicator of the Spirit's presence or absence.'[24] It was stated earlier: the Spirit reigns where the word reigns. The following must also be added: *the Spirit reigns where selflessness reigns*—which makes logical sense, given that the greatest display of selflessness was manifest in the saving life and death of the ultimate Spirit-filled man, Jesus Christ. Real life cannot be contained. Real life finds a way.

What are the distinguishing activities of a Spirit-revived community? Acts 2:42 has revealed that such a community persistently learns and selflessly shares. To say it a bit differently, a Spirit-revived community displays theological fidelity and relational beauty—a pairing of activities that is particularly relevant, given that very few postmodern people will believe a congregation's theological fidelity until they observe a congregation's relational beauty. While it may be granted that their conclusions are skewed and self-serving, they are nevertheless more right than some care to admit. It should be remembered that Jesus Himself threatens to extinguish the lampstand that signifies the church in Ephesus. For all of their commendable vigilance to guard orthodoxy, they have simultaneously failed in their vigilance to love. Apart from repentance, Jesus warns, He will remove their capacity to bear witness. Why? Their testimony to the gospel is a distortion of the gospel. The witness they bear is a false witness. There is no lasting theological fidelity apart from relational beauty.

The Spirit reigns where selflessness reigns. It was (and continues to be) true of Jesus Christ. It was (and continues to be) true of His Spirit-revived followers as well.

Real life cannot be contained. Real life finds a way.

---

24. Gerhard Krodel, *Acts* (Minneapolis: Augsburg Publishing House, 1986), p. 95.

8

SPIRIT-REVIVED COMMUNITY
(Part 2)

The physical presence of other Christians
is a source of incomparable joy and strength to the believer ...
The believer feels no shame,
as though he were still living too much in the flesh,
when he yearns for the physical presence of other Christians.
DIETRICH BONHOEFFER

Those first Jerusalem Christians were not so preoccupied
with learning, sharing, and worshipping,
that they forgot about witnessing.
For the Holy Spirit is a missionary Spirit
who created a missionary church.
JOHN R. W. STOTT

Ultimately, God is the evangelist.
AJITH FERNANDO

*42They devoted themselves to the apostles' teaching and to fellowship,
to the breaking of bread and to prayer. 43Everyone was filled with
awe at the many wonders and signs performed by the apostles. 44All
the believers were together and had everything in common. 45They
sold property and possessions to give to anyone who had need. 46Every
day they continued to meet together in the temple courts. They
broke bread in their homes and ate together with glad and sincere
hearts, 47praising God and enjoying the favor of all the people. And
the Lord added to their number daily those who were being saved.
(Acts 2:42-47)*

Replacing a Wish Dream

Innumerable times a whole Christian community has broken down because it had sprung from a wish dream. The serious Christian, set down for the first time in a Christian community, is likely to bring with him a very definite idea of what Christian life together should be and try to realize it. But God's grace speedily shatters such dreams. Just as surely as God desires to lead us to a knowledge of genuine Christian fellowship, so surely must we be overwhelmed by a great disillusionment with others, with Christians in general, and, if we are fortunate, with ourselves.

By sheer grace, God will not permit us to live even for a brief period in a dream world. He does not abandon us to those rapturous experiences and lofty moods that come over us like a dream ... Only that fellowship which faces such disillusionment, with all its unhappy and ugly aspects, begins to be what it should be in God's sight, begins to grasp in faith the promise that is given to it. The sooner this shock of disillusionment comes to an individual and to a community the better for both. A community which cannot bear and cannot survive such a crisis, which insists upon keeping its illusion when it should be shattered, permanently loses in that moment the promise of Christian community. Sooner or later it will collapse. Every human wish dream that is injected into the Christian community is a hindrance to genuine community and must be banished if genuine community is to survive. He who loves his dream of a community more than the Christian community itself becomes a destroyer of the latter, even though his personal intentions may be ever so honest and earnest and sacrificial.

This applies in a special way to the complaints often heard from pastors and zealous members about their congregations. A pastor should not complain about his congregation, certainly never to other people, but also not to God. A congregation has not been entrusted to him in order that he should become its accuser before God and men. When a person becomes alienated

> from a Christian community in which he has been
> placed and begins to raise complaints about it, he had
> better examine himself first to see whether the trouble
> is not due to his wish dream that should be shattered
> by God ... [1]

These poignant and pungent words, borrowed from the pen
of Dietrich Bonhoeffer, were among the gracious instruments
used by God to rescue me from a very dark season during my
early days as a pastor. I was not altogether unlike other men
new to pastoral ministry, both those prior and subsequent to
me: exceedingly aware of the glaring flaws and inconsistencies
that characterized every Christian congregation with which I
had been acquainted—and keenly aware of the manifold ways
they each fell miserably short of the idyllic community set
forth in the book of Acts. 'How can they not see it?' I often
wondered. 'Their imperfections are so obvious.' Of course,
the unspoken implication embodied in my expressions
of contempt was hardly inconspicuous: I was convinced I
could do better. But after two difficult years of pastoring a
congregation I had planted, it was painfully evident I had not
recreated the garden of Eden. I was deeply discouraged, and
more painfully aware of my own inadequacies than I had ever
been of anyone else's.

My suffering, in no small part, was the consequence of
cherishing a 'wish dream'—in my own case, a devastating
mixture of good intentions (genuinely), youthful arrogance
(unknowingly), and a distorted perception (egregiously).
Though the first two of these, generally speaking, have been
shared by most (thus requiring no explanation), what *was* this
'distorted perception' that plagued me? It was the mistaken
notion that the primitive Christian community in Acts was
pristine, free from the failings that distinguished every other
expression of community life I had ever known. I realize now,

---

1. Dietrich Bonhoeffer, *Life Together* (New York: Harper & Brothers Publishers,
1954), pp. 26-27, 29-30.

retrospectively, that I was suffering from an inebriated idealism (an over-realized eschatology)—that I had inadvertently distorted reality by means of a fantasy. Though I was a confessing Augustinian, I was operating as a functional Pelagian. I had lost sight of the fact (practically speaking, not theologically) that Christian theology is explicit about the influence of residual depravity in the followers of Jesus; moreover, that the clear and inescapable data contained within the narrative of Acts itself scarcely allow for the distortion I had developed. In Acts 5, the Christian community is forced to confront lying and greed within its membership, resulting in a severe demonstration of church discipline. In Acts 6, the apostles are met with massive congregational grumbling that is associated with the ethnic differences resident within the body of believers. Serious theological controversy erupts in Acts 15, threatening to decimate the church in irreparable division. Though truth prevails within the fellowship and unity is preserved, the conclusion of the same chapter is marked by such strong and polarizing opinions that a rift ensues between the two leaders who had previously experienced effective ministry together during the church's first missionary journey. All of this has yet to recollect the remaining New Testament record regarding the congregational life of the early Christians: divisions (e.g., 1 Cor. 1:10-17), immoralities (e.g., 1 Cor. 5:1-5), lawsuits (e.g., 1 Cor. 6:1-8), heresies (e.g., 2 Tim. 2:16-18), materialism (e.g., Rev. 3:17), syncretism (e.g., Rev. 2:14-15), favoritism (e.g., James 2:1-7), mysticism (e.g., Col. 2:18-19), nominalism (e.g., Rev. 3:2-3), legalism (e.g., Gal. 3:1-6), antinomianism (e.g., Jude 8), slothfulness (e.g., 2 Thess. 3:6-13), drunkenness (e.g., 1 Cor. 11:20-21), abusive leadership (e.g., 3 John 9-10), and one-upmanship (1 Cor. 12:21-26).

How is that for pristine?

Have you, as I had, expected something other than these kinds of failings in the local church of which you are a member? Have you been infected with the virus of idealism, the belief that you and the other members of your congregation are beyond vulnerability to such compromises? Is it your expectation that good theology and strong gospel preaching will eventually ensure a congregational experience that can nearly approximate life in the new creation? Identify your aspiration for what it is: a 'wish dream' that will eventually destroy you with disappointment unless God graciously destroys it for you.

'But what you are suggesting ... it's so *deflating*.'

This may appear to be the case right up to the moment God mercifully reveals that your dream has never been anything more than a mirage. At that point, the real-life account of Acts 2:42-47 becomes exhilarating, precisely because it is *not* Shangri La. These primitive followers of Jesus are not sanctified just shy of the full experience of glorification. They are a community of Christians akin to us—born again, to be sure—yet still bearing the effects of their remaining sin and, therefore, always inconsistent and flawed; at times, even ugly.

'This is exhilarating?'

Most certainly—in the sense that this display of Spirit-revived community is not beyond the possibility of our experience. Certainly Pentecost will not be repeated (for the reasons established earlier), but neither has it been rescinded. 'The inaugural outpouring of the Spirit creates ripples throughout the world as the Spirit continues to come in power. Pentecost is the epicenter; but the earthquake gives forth further after-shocks.'[2] The congregational life in Acts 2, then, is not to be regarded as *exclusive*, but *authentic*—and, thus, the prayerful aspiration of every Christian congregation. This is *not* a wish dream. It is a display of the Spirit-filled, yet imperfect followers of Jesus Christ in life together. As such, it hearkens back to the question posed in the prior chapter: *What are the distinguishing activities of a Spirit-revived community?* We have already considered the initial pair of these—'They

---

2. Ferguson, *Holy Spirit*, p. 91.

devoted themselves to the apostles' teaching and to fellowship'–and summarized them accordingly: 1) a Spirit-revived community persistently learns; and, 2) a Spirit-revived community selflessly shares. Attention will now be given to the remaining pair of activities, along with the elaboration that accompanies them in the subsequent verses.

Distinguishing Activity #3: The Community Joyfully Eats

> They devoted themselves to the apostles' teaching and
> to fellowship, to the breaking of bread ... (v. 42)

Fine students of the Bible regard–'*the breaking of bread*'–as a technical reference to the Lord's Supper, the covenantal meal Jesus gave to His followers by which they remember His sacrifice and proclaim His return. It is unlikely, however, that this ongoing rite of the church is the subject Luke is spotlighting here in v. 42.

At the outset, this expression–'*the breaking of bread*'–was commonly employed in Jewish households to describe the initiation of every meal. Thanks to God would be expressed, the loaf would be broken by hand, and the meal would commence with the distribution of the bread.[3] Luke's usage of this term corroborates this meaning. For example, when Jesus prepares to feed the five thousand, He takes the five loaves and–'looking up to heaven, he gave thanks and *broke them*. Then he gave them to the disciples to distribute to the people' (Luke 9:16). Following an encounter with two disciples on the road to Emmaus, the resurrected Lord Jesus shares a meal with them. Luke adds: 'When he was at the table with them, he took bread, gave thanks, *broke it* and began to give it to them' (Luke 24:30). While sailing across the Adriatic Sea en route to Rome, Paul's vessel encounters a fierce storm that threatens the lives of those on board. Confident of God's

---

3. Murray J. Harris, 'Baptism and the Lord's Supper,' *In God's Community: Essays on the Church and Its Ministry*, ed. David J. Ellis and W. Ward Gasque (Wheaton: Harold Shaw Publishers, 1978), p. 21.

providence and protection, Paul urges the hungry crew and passengers to take necessary nourishment, after which—'... he took some bread and gave thanks to God in front of them all. Then he *broke it* and began to eat' (Acts 27:35). Each of these is a reference to an ordinary meal. Of course, Luke does indicate that Jesus, at what subsequently came to be regarded as the Lord's Supper—'took bread, gave thanks, and *broke it,* and gave it to them, saying ...' (Luke 22:19). But—*'the breaking of bread'*— is not the distinguishing feature of the Lord's Supper. It was the manner in which *every* Jewish meal was initiated.[4] It is not until the second century (after the New Testament had been written) that the phrase—*'the breaking of bread'*—is adopted as a formal title for the Lord's Supper.[5] Here, in Acts 2:42, it means simply: 'to eat together.'[6]

Luke's elaboration in v. 46 contributes to this understanding: *'Every day they continued to meet together in the temple courts. They broke bread in their homes and ate together with glad and sincere hearts.'* A more literal translation will identify the primary

---

4. 'It might be argued that the reference to the meeting of the Christians in Troas "on the first day of the week" in order to break bread (*klasai arton*) is a pointer to a formal Sunday gathering for the purposes of the Lord's Supper (20:7). Paul's discussion with them, however, occupied their attention until after midnight and again after the meal, suggesting that it was a very unstructured and informal meeting. When Luke mentions that that Paul finally broke bread (perhaps on behalf of everyone present) he adds "and when he had eaten, he engaged in much further conversation until dawn" (v. 11, lit.). It is really quite artificial to suggest the meal by which Paul satisfied himself after such a long time was somehow distinct from "the breaking of bread". Since Christian meetings were largely held in the context of private homes, it is natural that they expressed their fellowship in terms of eating together.' David Peterson, *Engaging with God: A Biblical Theology of Worship* (Downers Grove: InterVarsity Press, 1992), p. 156.

5. Cf. *Didache* 14:1. See Cyril C. Richardson, ed. *Early Christian Fathers* (New York: Macmillan Publishing Company, n.d.), p. 178. Ignatius, *Ephesians* 20:2. See J. B. Lightfoot, *Apostolic Fathers: Clement, Ignatius, and Polycarp,* 5 vols. (Grand Rapids: Baker Book House Press, 1981), vol. 2, p. 550.

6. 'The breaking of bread is simply a customary and necessary part of the preparation for eating together. It initiates the sharing of the main course in every meal ... Acts 2:42, 46 refers to the daily fellowship of the first Christians in Jerusalem and has nothing to do with the liturgical celebration of the Lord's Supper ...' J. Behm, 'κλαω,' *TDNT,* vol. III, pp. 727-730.

clause by the main verb: '(they) ate together with glad and sincere hearts.' This is preceded by two participial clauses: 'they continued to meet together in the temple courts'—and—'they broke bread in their homes.'[7] Together this can be rendered: '... while they were meeting in the temple courts and while they were breaking bread, they always took their meals with glad and sincere hearts.' This clarifies the principal emphasis of the verse: these Christians were regularly eating their meals together, whether in the temple complex or in private homes. There is nothing here that indicates a liturgical celebration. If vv. 43-47 are an elaboration of v. 42, it would seem highly unnatural to interpret the prior mention of—'the breaking of bread' (v. 42)—as a reference to the Lord's Supper. Eating communally, then, was a tangible manifestation of the reviving work of the Spirit, a clear sign of the spiritual and social solidarity enjoyed by the early Christians, despite their external differences. Without doubt, it was the phenomenon the apostles themselves experienced as a result of Jesus' frequent meals with them (e.g., Luke 24:35, 41-43; Acts 1:4).[8]

Admittedly, it was not until the relatively recent past when I first began to understand the significance of this communal eating. For several months prior to the formal establishment of Trinity Church in Portland (where I pastor), a group of us met on Wednesday evenings for prayer, singing, and Bible study related the New Testament's instruction for local churches. Earlier in the afternoons, a smaller nucleus of folk would meet for purpose of rehearsing the music we would sing later in the evening with the entire church planting team. To ease

7. Both participles (proskarterountes, klontes) are circumstantial and possess a temporal force. Moreover, their use in the present tense suggests action that is contemporaneous to that of the main verb (metelambanon). Wallace, Greek Grammar, pp. 622-626.

8. Luke's citations of Jesus' 'table fellowship' are often scenes of controversy (e.g., Luke 7:36-50; 11:37-54; 14:1-24). Nevertheless, the apostles repeatedly witness Jesus' expressions of acceptance and friendship to individuals who are regarded by the religious establishment as unacceptable. Hence, the subsequent questions and accusations: 'Why do you eat with tax collectors and sinners?' (Luke 5:30). 'This man welcomes sinners and eats with them' (Luke 15:2).

the demand of the extended afternoon and evening, we soon began to provide meals for the musicians and singers before the others arrived. It was during this time that something palpable began to happen; so much so that after only a few of these meals I found myself filled with anticipation for the following Wednesday evening. I found this interesting at the time, since none of the people involved were new to me. I had actually known each one in various, prior contexts. However, during these months of eating a weekly meal together, my affections for each one began to increase. I found myself caring for them in newer and deeper ways. Sharing dinner together seemed to refresh and enhance our intimacy as a gestating community. Looking back, the fingerprint of Trinity Church was being formed during these meals.

Why did this happen? Why *does* this happen? Is it, in part, because people are more relaxed when eating together? Is it because there is a mutual vulnerability demanded in this kind of sharing—a collective disarming in the presence of food and drink? At times, the experience of table fellowship can possess a quality that is nearly sacramental—something that has very little to do with the proper arrangement of the place settings, or the quality of the meal, or the décor of the dining room. Frankly, I have never found table fellowship compromised because of a home's unattractive color scheme, or because the roast beef had been overcooked. Quite to the contrary, at the conclusion of many such evenings I have been left with an overwhelming sense of refreshment and exhilaration. I may have gone home tired, and weary at the thought of an alarm waking me early the next morning. But the *community* we shared—the togetherness, the storytelling, the talk of the Lord and the wonders of the gospel—was so profoundly satisfying, so joy-infusing, that I knowingly remained longer than I should have because the benefits accrued were worth more to me than the sleep I would lose. My Christianity was strengthened. It was a means of grace.

Has it crossed your mind that one of the reasons God has provided you with a home or an apartment (which, in most cases, takes the largest portion of your income) is to furnish you with an effective platform for ministry? Some may be quick to reply at this point: 'I could never invite anyone to our home. It's so small and cluttered. I have no eye for decorating. The sofa is old and the carpet is stained. What's more, I've never had a knack for putting together elegant meals—not like some of the people in our congregation.' But these excuses are both lame and irrelevant. When Christians use such reasons to refrain from using their homes for table fellowship, they not only expose their pride; they prove that they have *missed the point entirely*. The Christians who are most effective in using their homes for ministry are not those who have mastered the art of entertaining. However humble or extravagant their homes may be, their effectiveness is rooted in the humility and selflessness (*i.e.*, Christlikeness!) they display in the act of serving people—their expressions of care and compassion. Christians must remember that hospitality is not a suggestion for those in the congregation with domestically oriented gifts. It is a responsibility commanded of all congregational members (*e.g.*, Rom. 12:13; 1 Peter 4:9).[9]

A pertinent and related observation is that these gatherings of Spirit-revived Christians reflect a healthy balance of large meetings (more corporate in their orientation) and small meetings (more intimate in their emphasis). Luke writes: '*Every day they continued to meet together in the temple courts*' (v. 46a). These were public and corporate meetings convened for prayer and praise and preaching, frequently at a location referred to as 'Solomon's Colonnade' (*cf.* 3:1, 11-26; 5:12, 21; Luke 24:53)—a long, marble-columned porch, running the eastern side of the outer court of the Temple, that possessed

---

9. See Alexander Strauch, *The Hospitality Commands: Building Loving Christian Community, Building Bridges to Friends and Neighbors* (Littleton: Lewis & Roth Publishers, 1993).

the capacity of accommodating large gatherings of people. Luke also mentions smaller, more private meetings: 'They broke bread in their homes ...' (46b). It stands to reason that the form and demeanor of these meetings most likely reflected the uniqueness of their respective locations, some being more formal and structured, others taking on more informal and spontaneous qualities. Their gatherings in homes, for example, were undoubtedly much more relaxed—as we might say today, 'Take off your sandals and feel free to lay your coat on the bed. Pick up a plate and help yourself to some food. We'll start singing when everyone's finished eating.' The effectiveness of a home setting is enhanced by its informality. On the other hand, the sheer numbers at their large meetings would necessitate greater formality, without which effectiveness in such settings is undermined.

Sadly, it has become an all-too-common phenomenon in recent days for Christians to advocate vigorously for their preferences at this very point: 'I favor the informal context of a small group.' Another asserts: 'I think that the formal gathering of the entire congregation is better.' Both perspectives are naïve. To polarize one from the other for the purpose of exclusively choosing either is to sacrifice the benefits of the context that is disregarded. It is highly improbable that a Christian will develop meaningful and intimate relationships with three thousand people gathered in a corporate setting. It is equally dubious that a Christian will be transfixed by Spirit empowered preaching while lounging in a recliner in a dimly lit family room. These early followers of Jesus continually participated in this combination of meetings (large and small) and experienced the benefits of both, each of which was distinguished by the sharing of their meals. Theirs was a common and intimate life together that proved spiritually refreshing, a fact made even more conspicuous by the invigorating qualities that accompanied their eating together. They—'ate together with glad and sincere hearts ...' (v. 46c).

Their being–'*glad*'–is a description of something more
than mere appreciation for the provision of their daily needs.
It speaks of 'a state of intensive joy ... extreme gladness'[10]–
an overwhelming quality that is nearly transcendent. These
are people who have recognized that they are living in the
inaugurated fulfillment of the eschatological age[11] and that,
as a result, they are enjoying the benefits of the promised
Messianic salvation: the forgiveness of sins, the indwelling
presence of the Holy Spirit, and the privilege of being the
nucleus of a revived Israel that is now demonstrating itself in
a community life distinguished by generosity and liberality. It
is understandable, then, that Luke would describe their meals
as being eaten with–'*sincere hearts.*' This is a Greek noun that is
used only here in the New Testament. However, it is apparently
related to another commonly used noun that conveys sincerity
and generosity. It suggests that this sharing together was not
associated with any sense of double-mindedness or grudging
envy.[12] Rather, they were pure expressions of self-giving
liberality–the expected redemptive responses from people
who are cognizant of the undeserved blessings that have been
lavished upon them. It is not surprising, then, that there is
this uncontainable gladness and sincere generosity.

Are these qualities in keeping with your understanding
of Christian piety? Needless to say, there are more than a
few followers of Jesus who deliberately seek to display their
Christianity by a somberness that is defiant of any expression
of delight or pleasure. But this is a spurious piety in most cases–
if, for no other reason, than it is too self-conscious. Moreover,
it is important to be reminded of Jesus Himself who, because

---

10. Louw and Nida, *Greek-English Lexicon*, vol. 1, p. 303.

11. 'The term "gladness" (*agalliases*) is one that suggests eschatological joy in the
presence of the Lord (see Luke 1:14, 44, 47; 10:21, and compare LXX Pss. 9:2; 12:5;
20:1; 30:7; 39:16; 44:7; 80:1; 83:1; 99:2; 117:15).' Luke Timothy Johnson, *The Acts
of the Apostles* (Collegeville: The Liturgical Press), p. 59.

12. 'The term *aphelotes* ... appears related to *haplotes* (see Luke 11:34; Rom. 12:8;
2 Cor. 8:2; 9:11, 13; Eph. 6:5; Col. 3:22; James 1:5).' *Ibid.*, p. 59.

He conspicuously enjoyed meals with people, was accused of being a glutton and a drunkard (Luke 7:34). He was neither. But that He was accused of such things indicates that Jesus openly enjoyed good friends, good food, and good drink. This is not to disregard him as 'a man of sorrows' (Isa. 53:3, ESV), but it is to acknowledge that experiences of joy and gladness were essential to His completeness as a human being.

Few would dispute the claim that we belong to a society that is rabidly hedonistic. We find ourselves surrounded by people pursuing pleasure at all costs, even via means that violate their essential humanity—sinful means that will, ultimately, prove to be self-destroying. But the Christian answer is never asceticism. It is not the repudiation of extreme gladness and joy by refusing the pleasures God has created. A full-orbed Christianity acknowledges that God is the creator of our capacity for joy. It recognizes that even though we have sinned against Him, He offers us an immediate and comprehensive forgiveness in the gospel of Jesus Christ, the true experience of which results in freedom—a freedom that is intended to display itself in the refreshing benefits of joyful and openhearted table fellowship with others who have experienced the same forgiveness.

Frequently overlooked, this is a most beautiful display of Spirit-revived Christianity: *the community joyfully eats.* It is an activity that not only unites us to salvation's history (*e.g.,* the Old Testament feasts mandated in Israel, the ministry of table fellowship exercised by Jesus), but it also foreshadows the ultimate Messianic banquet when, in keeping with Jesus' promises, His followers will—'eat and drink at my table in the kingdom' (Luke 22:30; *cf.* Rev. 19:9). Eating together now as the followers of Jesus is a present enjoyment that anticipates the consummation.

What are the distinguishing activities of a Spirit-revived community? It persistently learns. It selflessly shares. It joyfully eats. Finally—

Distinguishing Activity #4: The Community Intentionally Prays

> They devoted themselves to the apostles' teaching and
> to fellowship, to the breaking of bread and to prayer
> (v. 42)

Is it possible to conceive of a spiritually awakened congregation that does not give its constant attention to prayer? Not if the Pentecostal community of Christians provides the definitive paradigm. Prayer displays itself immediately as an activity to which these Christians are persistently devoted. Yet an important nuance needs to be observed. This does not, first and foremost, call attention to the spontaneous praying of individual Christians (*e.g.*, Phil. 1:3; James 5:13)–which, to be sure, is the great privilege of a person who has become a child of God. The context indicates this to be a *community* at prayer. No doubt *one* expression of this took place in homes, given that their eating together included–'*praising God.*' It is not illogical to infer that this would have also included praying together, seeking God's provision for their needs and those of other Christians. The emphasis of the Greek text, however, appears to be pointing to something more specific: 'They devoted themselves to ... *the prayers.*' The plural form with the definite article implies particular–'*prayers*'–rather than a more extemporaneous kind of praying. The context suggests planned occasions, at predetermined venues, for particular purposes–all of which implies a strong intentionality. To what is this referring?

This early community of Christians, it should be remembered, is comprised of exclusively Jewish people who are living in Jerusalem. They have not ceased to be Jewish, and neither has Luke indicated their desire to make a radical break from Judaism. In fact, Peter's Pentecostal sermon and, by extension, the apostles' ongoing teaching, has revealed Christianity to be the consummation of Judaism. It is highly probable, then, that these Jewish followers of Jesus regard themselves as the remnant of a restored Israel. Accordingly, they have not ceased attending the Temple for the traditionally scheduled meetings of prayer (9:00am, 12:00pm, 3:00pm; *cf.* 3:1)—meetings in which established prayers were employed that, for Christians, were now being filled with newfound meaning. Furthermore, the ongoing narrative of Acts displays the Christian community assembling for its *own* occasions of intercession, in which the set prayers from Judaism were not used.[13]

This persistent devotion to prayer in various congregational settings is a telling feature of the early Christian community. It reveals that Jesus' followers did not regard the gift of the Spirit and His power as the basis upon which dependent prayer may now be dismissed as irrelevant, particularly with relationship to the accomplishment of the mission Jesus has assigned them. Unfortunately, the opposite has frequently been the case in contemporary evangelistic and church planting endeavors. Though never stated explicitly, the neglect of an emphasis on intentional and concerted prayer implicitly reveals the source of missionary confidence: the establishment of strategic plans utilizing the latest technological apparatus, expertise at contextualization to ensure that the gospel is marketed appropriately to its target audience. This is not to suggest that a constant dedication to prayer diminishes the need for wise planning, careful research, and sensitivity to cultural uniqueness. It is to recognize the church as a missionary body seeking to convert human beings—an impossibility apart from God's exclusive and effectual initiation. Therefore, the constant dependence of the church must conscientiously rest on His sovereign good pleasure and omnipotence, not on the vast potentialities of human prowess.

---

13. 'The earliest believers not only viewed the old forms as filled with new content, but also in their enthusiasm they fashioned new vehicles for their praise. In addition, it is not difficult to envision the earliest believers using extemporaneous prayers built on past models—such as Mary's *Magnificat* (Luke 1:46-55), Zechariah's Song of Praise (Luke 1:67-79), or Simeon's *Nunc Dimittis* (Luke 2:28-32).' Longenecker, 'Acts,' p. 290.

Jesus Himself, the ultimate Spirit-filled man, provides the definitive model of a persistent devotion to prayer:

> Very early in the morning, while it was still dark, Jesus got up, left the house and went off to a solitary place, where he prayed. (Mark 1:35)

> But Jesus often withdrew to lonely places and prayed. (Luke 5:16)

> ... Jesus went out to a mountainside to pray, and spent the night praying to God. (Luke 6:12)

> Once when Jesus was praying in private ... (Luke 9:18)

> One day Jesus was praying in a certain place. (Luke 11:1)

More specifically, Jesus prayed during His baptism (Luke 3:21). He prayed prior to His selection of the disciples (Luke 6:12-13). He prayed before feeding the five thousand (Luke 9:16). He prayed while on the Mount of Transfiguration (Luke 9:28). He prayed as He stood before the tomb of Lazarus (John 11:41-42). He prayed in anticipation of the cross (John 12:28). He prayed on His way to Gethsemane (John 17:1-26). He prayed just prior to His arrest (Luke 22:39-45). He prayed during his crucifixion (Luke 23:34; cf. Matt. 27:46; John 19:30). Jesus prayed—certainly to maintain intimacy with His Father, which included a necessary submission to His Father's will. But also because, as a man, He lived in the clear recognition of His desperate need. The apostles, in turn, witnessed this life of absolute and intentional dependence—and even, on one occasion, requested of Jesus directly: 'Lord, teach us to pray' (Luke 11:1). Now—in emulation of their Master, and as those entrusted with His mission—the apostles ensure that prayer becomes an indispensable activity in the community life of these Christians, a point Luke highlights throughout the entire Acts narrative:

> They all joined together constantly in *prayer*, along with the women and Mary the mother of Jesus, and with his brothers. (1:14)

So they nominated two men: Joseph called Barsabbas (also known as Justus) and Matthias. Then they *prayed*, 'Lord, you know everyone's heart. Show us which of these two you have chosen to take over this apostolic ministry ...' (1:23-25)

On their release, Peter and John went back to their own people and reported all that the chief priests and the elders had said to them. When they heard this, they raised their voices together in *prayer* to God. (4:23-24)

'Brothers and sisters, choose seven men from among you who are known to be full of the Spirit and wisdom. We will turn this responsibility over to them and will give our attention to *prayer* and the ministry of the word ...' They presented these men to the apostles, who *prayed* and laid their hands on them. (6:3-6)

So Peter was kept in prison, but the church was earnestly *praying* to God for him. (12:5)

While they were worshipping the Lord and fasting, the Holy Spirit said, 'Set apart for me Barnabas and Saul for the work to which I have called them.' So after they had fasted and *prayed*, they placed their hands on them and sent them off. (13:2-3)

Paul and Barnabas appointed elders for them in each church and, with *prayer* and fasting, committed them to the Lord, in whom they had put their trust. (14:23) About midnight Paul and Silas were *praying* and singing hymns to God, and the other prisoners were listening to them. (16:25)

When Paul had finished speaking, he knelt down with all of them and *prayed*. (20:36)

The resolute persistence in prayer on the part of Jesus and these early Christians causes me to recollect an acknowledgment I commonly hear from gospel ministers and seminary students who are dissatisfied with the paucity of their praying: 'I really need to become more *disciplined* in my prayer life.' I understand what they mean by this claim because I, too, have felt this dissatisfaction. In response, I seek for ways of applying gospel encouragement and motivation to their concerns. On occasion, however, I have been *tempted* to respond to such folk in a way that reflects a practical reality I have experienced with regard to prayer: 'I don't think *discipline* is the answer. I think *dependence* is the answer. Your need is to become more acutely aware of how desperate you truly are. Were God to make you more sensitive to this, a lack of fervent and persistent prayer would cease to be your problem. In fact, it is not beyond your heavenly Father to bring about something in your life providentially that will *make* you more keenly aware of your need: a spot of cancer, a wayward teenager, an unexpected financial crisis.' What tends to result from such situations? Strength surrenders to weakness and self-sufficiency gives way to humility. Suddenly the perfunctory prayer clichés that can be recited catatonically yield to persistent and heartfelt cries. No longer is it necessary to talk about '*discipline*' in prayer. A heightened sense of dependence has forced it into existence. Prayer becomes:

> ... a renunciation of human means. It is not merely the point beyond which I could not go, the limit of my power which dissolves into impotence, but it is indeed a stripping bare, the abandonment of all human apparatus in order to place myself, without arms or equipment, into the hands of the Lord, who decides and fulfills.[14]

May I ask: Have your own experiences of desperation proved this to be so? More specifically, do you live in the awareness that your role in the mission Jesus has assigned to the church is a *heaven-and-earth* enterprise? This is a point clearly made in a text to which some attention has already been given in an earlier chapter:

> Very truly I tell you, whoever believes in me will do the works I have been doing, and they will do even greater

---

14. Jacques Ellul, *Prayer and the Modern Man* (Eugene: Wipf & Stock Publishers, 2012), p. 30.

things than these, because I am going to the Father. And I will do whatever you ask in my name, so that the Father may be glorified in the Son. You may ask me for anything in my name, and I will do it. (John 14:12-14)

The accomplishment of 'the greater works' is a privilege Jesus grants to those who believe in Him. It is grounded upon two phenomena: 1) His departure to the Father that results in the advent of the Spirit; and, 2) His response to the petitions of His people that are in keeping with His name.[15] The second of these merits close scrutiny, not only because it calls attention to the significance of prayer (for the sake of gospel advancement no less!), but also because it establishes an important continuity in the accomplishment of these works—*a continuity of source*. While the physical presence of Jesus will be removed via the resurrection and ascension, these greater works will continue to be sourced in Him. The new distinction is to be found in the *instrumentality* through which *He* will achieve them: His praying people, a fact highlighted in the statement made twice by Jesus: '*I* will do whatever you ask in my name ... *I* will do it.'

Christians have been given the distinct honor of being the channel through which the mission of Jesus advances. As such, prayer is not a token expression that serves to contribute a spiritual tone to an otherwise efficient operation. It is an act of desperate dependence upon Him to achieve what is impossible apart from Him. Acts 2:42, along with the entire Lukan corpus:

> ... constitutes a powerful encouragement and prophetic call to the church to be a church of prayer: not just to pray for its own perseverance as the people of God under pressure in this age, and for salvation at the end ... but for continual faithfulness in witness to the gospel now, and for fresh inbreakings of God's grace

---

15. The Greek text in John 14:13 begins with 'and,' a coordinating conjunction that serves to further explain the ground for accomplishing the greater works (left untranslated in the ESV).

and power now, such as points to the mercy, glory and power of the ascended Lord until he comes.[16]

A Necessary Admonition

> They devoted themselves to the apostles' teaching and to fellowship, to the breaking of bread and to prayer (v. 42).

In its powerful simplicity, this is an exceedingly crucial text for a contemporary church that is perpetually tempted to rest its confidence in the possibilities of its own sophistication. *But it is also a text with which the church must be extraordinarily careful.* When Acts 2:42 is isolated from its context and left to stand on its own, it provides a portrait of the church that is decidedly lopsided and, without much effort, can quickly degenerate into a terrible distortion. Why is this the case? *It is a verse that displays the interior life of the church only.* Consequently, when it is preached as the exclusive fixation of sermons, it easily becomes an inadvertent entrapment—a snare that inevitably *confines* the church to Acts 2:42. This is an ever-present susceptibility of Christian congregations, one they must consciously resist lest they awaken to find themselves an island of irrelevant piety. To cloister themselves in church buildings, even in the name of Bible study and fellowship and prayer, is a betrayal of the assignment that has been tasked to the church by the resurrected Lord. At the risk of overstatement, nothing in Acts should be heard without the echo of its mission statement resonating loudly and clearly:

> ... you will receive power when the Holy Spirit comes on you; and you will be my witnesses in Jerusalem, and in all Judea and Samaria, and to the ends of the earth. (1:8)

---

16. M. M. B. Turner, 'Prayer in the Gospels and Acts,' D. A. Carson ed., *Teach us to Pray: Prayer in the Bible and the World* (Eugene: Wipf & Stock Publishers, 2002), p. 75.

'Doesn't this raise a point of contradiction?' you may ask. 'How are we to give serious effort to our mission if, as in Acts 2:46, we meet together with Christians every day? Doesn't a persistent devotion to the aforementioned activities exclude the possibility of consistent and meaningful interaction with unbelievers?' Certainly these are the proper questions to ask. Three considerations must be kept in mind.

First, this is revival—an unusually heightened experience of the Spirit's influence and power. Such seasons throughout church history have, at times, required pastoral leaders to remind Jesus' followers of His intention that they live among the people of this world; that the new creation has not yet come in its final form and, therefore, they must not become self-indulgent in the foretastes that anticipate it. *Second*, this is Pentecost—the unique historical fulfillment of God's covenant promise to Israel that He will effect the renewal of His people in Jerusalem. An attempt to replicate Acts 2:42 *identically* (including assembling together every day)[17] is a failure to appreciate this text within in the larger context of the Bible's redemptive storyline. *Third*, the immediate context of Acts 2:42 will not allow for the conclusion that these Christians disengaged from the surrounding community of unbelievers. Luke notes that they were:

> ... enjoying the favor of all the people (v. 47a).

This designation—'*the people*'—is most commonly used in Acts to refer to those outside the Christian community; namely, the people of Israel as those to whom God's message of redemption is initially directed (*e.g.*, 3:11-12, 23; 4:1, 17; 5:12-13). That these Christians are presently experiencing their—'*favor*'—leads to a necessary assumption: they have not disconnected themselves from interaction with unbelievers; rather, their contact with them has been sufficiently meaningful to arouse

---

17. The four activities *described* in 2:42 are *prescribed* in other New Testament texts. As such, Christians must always be persistently devoted to them. Meeting together daily is nowhere reiterated, let alone commanded.

feelings of good will (*cf.* 5:12, 26). An alternative translation makes this point even more forcefully: 'having goodwill *towards* the people.'[18] Assuming its accuracy, this suggests that the joy of these believers was not only expressing itself in praise to God, but also in displays of kindness to their neighbors, undoubtedly contributing to the conversions that were occurring. It is a missionary fulfillment of the great commandment. This is not to infer that unbelievers will always possess a high esteem for gracious Christians. Acts 4-6 will be distinguished by persecution, and martyrdom will follow in Acts 7. Nevertheless, whether it is fickle favor or hostile belligerence, being the recipients of either imply that disengagement from the non-Christian community is not the posture taken by these Spirit-revived followers of Jesus.

Pentecost will not allow for a Christian community that is hermetically sealed, absorbed in its own parochial affairs and detached from contact with the unbelieving world. The Christianity in Acts is sufficiently open and obvious to the point of stimulating definitive feelings on the part of unbelievers. In this instance, Luke enthusiastically notes the conversion to Christianity of many as he draws Acts 2 to a conclusion:

> And the Lord added to their number daily those who were being saved. (v. 47b)

Luke highlights the *regularity* of this saving work—not merely by using the imperfect tense of the verb (literally, '*he was adding* ...'),[19] but also by including the prepositional phrase that is here translated—'*daily.*' This calls attention to the ongoing

---

18. T. D. Anderson, 'The Meaning of ECHONTES CHARIN PROS in Acts 2:47,' *NTS* 34 (1998), pp. 604-610. He shows how *charis pros* is used in extrabiblical writings (Josephus, Philo), and that in each case the object of *pros* is the person towards whom the *charin* is directed. See also Peterson, *The Acts*, p. 164.

19. 'The imperfect is frequently used to indicate a regularly recurring activity in past time (habitual) or a state that continued for some time (general).' Wallace, *Greek Grammar*, p. 548.

progress of conversions. Moreover, this work bears a telling *combination*—a fact made clear in the two verbal ideas: *'added'*— and—*'being saved.'* The grammar suggests that these converts were—'added to the church *as* they were being saved.'[20] In other words, the experience of salvation is the introduction into the Christian community,[21] so that these folk are not added to the church without Jesus saving them—nor are they saved without Jesus adding them to the church, both of which would be an expression of something significantly less than Christian. To be savingly attached to Jesus is to be indivisibly bound to His people. Finally, while it is doubtlessly true that the apostles' proclamation of the gospel was used as a means of effecting this addition (no one is ever saved without hearing the gospel)—and that the joy and kindness displayed by these Christians powerfully enhanced their message in the minds and hearts of unbelievers[22]—Luke, characteristically, draws specific attention to *the sovereign author* of this work—*'the Lord.'* This hearkens back to Peter's plea (v. 40), and even further back to Joel's promise (v. 21). But it especially demands a return to the earlier, unforgettable moment of revelation: 'God has made this Jesus, whom you crucified, both Lord and Messiah' (v. 36). Stott says:

> ... he is the head of the church. He alone has the prerogative to admit people into its membership and to bestow salvation from his throne. This is a much needed emphasis, for many people talk about evangelism today with reprehensible self-confidence and even triumphalism, as if they think the evangelization of the world will be the ultimate

---

20. The present participle *sozomenous* is iterative in emphasis, rather than an ongoing state. While it is conceptually true that salvation is a process, there is nothing in the context to suggest this as Luke's intended meaning here.

21. The Greek text reads: 'the Lord was adding ... *to itself.'* Given the way this phrase—*epi to auto*—is used in the LXX, it can be translated here as 'community' or 'church.' See T. Johnson, *The Acts*, p. 60.

22. Witherington says that their 'presence and witness were infectious.' *The Acts*, p. 163.

> triumph of human technology. We should harness to
> the evangelistic task all the technology God has given
> us, but only in humble dependence on him as the
> principal evangelist.[23]

Here is a most important component for understanding the
dynamic of the Christian mission: the church is the ordained
instrument through which Lord Jesus will achieve His saving
purpose. She must recognize and embrace her direct responsibility for taking the gospel to the unbelieving people of this
world. At the same time, any failure on her part to recognize
Jesus' sovereignty in grace will not only diminish her appreciation of what transpires when a person experiences salvation,
it will tragically keep her from a necessary dependence on the
one who, exclusively, can achieve it. Its author is always the
resurrected, ascended, and enthroned Jesus–'the Lord.'

The Epoch of the Holy Spirit

My friend, have you ever paused to imagine the extraordinary
events of Pentecost? Have you ever attempted to conceive of
what it must have been like to daily witness the exhibition of
the saving power of the exalted Lord? I have. And I often do–
though, admittedly, I myself have never had the privilege of
witnessing firsthand this kind of revival. Nevertheless, a reality
remains that fills me with expectancy to this very hour: though
Pentecost is a uniquely unrepeatable event, it has ushered in
an epoch of salvation history that is not retractable. This is the
epoch of the Holy Spirit, the missionary Spirit who has been
given to the followers of Jesus Christ for the sake of achieving
God's intention to bring salvation to the ends of the earth.
Surely this means that Christians must engage in this mission
with the expectation of success. This is not to imply that every
congregation embracing this mission in fidelity to Jesus will
grow to become a mega-church. Nor does this deny the unique
providential assignments given to individual congregations by

---

23. Stott, *The Message*, p. 86.

the Chief Shepherd with regard to sowing and reaping. Least of all does this mean that missionary success can be expected regardless of the church's negligible evangelistic efforts. Having set forth these caveats, however, it is safe to assume that gospel success will be the ordinary experience of most congregations; that to the extent Christians faithfully declare the gospel in the power of the Spirit, the Lord Jesus Christ will be in the process of saving sinful human beings—whether this is manifested immediately and overwhelmingly as in the revival at Pentecost—or whether this remains to be made evident until the great and final day.

What are the distinguishing activities of a Spirit-revived community? By this point, you are well aware of them: the community persistently learns, the community selflessly shares, the community joyfully eats, and the community intentionally prays. Here, now, is a vital *postscript* that unites the entirety of Acts 1-2: *The community divinely prospers.* The mission that has been assigned to us is achieved: people, mindful of their sin, find deliverance from every expression of condemnation in the saving sufficiency of Jesus Christ.

Do you desire to see the church prosper in this way? Is this the aim to which your praying is directed? Are you expecting to see the answers to these prayers as a result of your own missionary efforts? Your response of each of these questions should be a hearty 'yes.' Why? The conversion of the human race is *not* a wish dream. It is the purpose of God that will ultimately be achieved through the Spirit empowered mission of the church. Consequently, when Jesus is *not* saving, when unbelievers are *not* being converted, the following questions must be asked: Are we meaningfully and consistently engaging unbelievers with the message of the gospel? Are we compassionately and courageously making unbelievers aware of their sin and guilt that has necessitated the crucifixion of Jesus? Are we explicit about Jesus' resurrection, exaltation, and enthronement as Lord and King—along with the repentance and baptism such events demand in response? Is it possible that we have lost sight of the missionary assignment that has been given to us by Jesus, having substituted the conversion of unbelievers for another task that *we* have subsequently defined as 'the mission of the church'? Have we forgotten that the last days have been inaugurated, that the day of the Lord itself is imminent and, thus, the opportunity for people to call upon the Lord for salvation is not without boundaries? Could it be that we have failed to regard the gift of the Holy Spirit as a missionary gift? Have we been unaware that the Spirit of prophecy is poured out on all of God's people in the new covenant era?

> Where the church today finds itself stagnant, unattractive, humdrum and shrinking—and, sadly, there are many churches, in the Western world at least, of which this has to be admitted—it's time to read Acts 2:42-47 again, get down on our knees, and ask what isn't happening that should be happening. The gospel hasn't changed. God's power hasn't diminished. People still need rescuing. What are we doing about it?[24]

Are you engaged in *the* mission that Jesus Christ has explicitly assigned to the church?

---

24. Wright, *Acts*, p. 47.

BIBLIOGRAPHY

Barrett, C. K., *A Critical and Exegetical Commentary on The Acts of the Apostles*. ICC. Edinburgh: T & T Clark, 1994 (2 vols).

Beale, G. K. and Carson, D. A., eds., *Commentary on the New Testament Use of the Old Testament*. Grand Rapids: Baker Academic, 2007.

Bloesch, Donald G., *The Invaded Church*. Waco: Word Books, 1975.

Bock, Darrell L., *Acts*. BECNT. Grand Rapids: Baker Academic, 2007.

Boer, Harry R., *Pentecost And Missions*. Grand Rapids: William B. Eerdmans Publishing Company, 1961.

Bonhoeffer, Dietrich, *Life Together*. New York: Harper & Brothers, 1954.

Bruce, F. F., *Peter, Stephen, James, and John: Studies in Early Non-Pauline Christianity*. Grand Rapids: William Eerdmans Publishing Company, 1979.

_____, *The Book of Acts*. NICNT. Grand Rapids: William B. Eerdmans Publishing Company, 1988.

Calvin, John, *Commentary upon the Acts of the Apostles*. Grand Rapids: Baker Book House, 2003 (repr. ed).

DeYoung, Kevin and Gilbert, Greg, *What is the Mission of the Church? Making Sense of Social Justice, Shalom, and the Great Commission*. Wheaton: Crossway Books, 2011.

DeYoung, Kevin and Kluck, Ted, *Why We Love the Church*. Chicago: Moody Press, 2009.

Dunn, James D. G., *The Acts of the Apostles*. Valley Forge: Trinity Press International, 1996.

Ellis, David J. and Gasque, W. Ward, eds., *In God's Community: Essays on the Church and its Ministry*. Wheaton: Harold Shaw Publishers, 1978.

Fernando, Ajith, *Acts*. NIVAC. Grand Rapids: Zondervan Publishing House, 1998.

Gooding, David, *True to the Faith*. Coleraine: Myrtlefield House, 2013.

Green, Michael, *Thirty Years that Changed the World: The Book of Acts for Today*. Grand Rapids: William Eerdmans Publishing Company, 2002.

Hughes, R. Kent, *Acts: The Church Afire*. Wheaton: Crossway Books, 1996.

Johnson, Dennis E., *The Message of Acts in the History of Redemption*. Phillipsburg: P & R Publishing, 1997.

Johnson, Luke Timothy, *The Acts of the Apostles*. Collegeville: The Liturgical Press, 1992.

Larkin, William J., Jr., *Acts*. IVPNTC. Downers Grove: InterVarsity Press, 1995.

Lloyd-Jones, D. Martyn, *Authentic Christianity*. Wheaton: Crossway Books, 2000.

Longenecker, Richard N., '*Acts*.' EBC, vol. 10. Grand Rapids: Zondervan Publishing House, 2007.

_____, *Biblical Exegesis in the Apostolic Period*. Grand Rapids: William B. Eerdmans Publishing Company, 1975.

Marshall, I. Howard, *The Acts of the Apostles*. TNTC. Grand Rapids: William B. Eerdmans Publishing Company, 1980.

Pao, David W., *Acts and the Isaianic New Exodus*. Grand Rapids: Baker Academic, 2002.

Peterson, David G., *The Acts of the Apostles*. PNTC. Grand Rapids: William B. Eerdmans Publishing Company, 2009.

Schnabel, Eckhard J., *Acts*. ECNT. Grand Rapids: Zondervan Publishing House, 2012.

Stott, John R. W., *The Message of Acts*. TBST. Downers Grove: InterVarsity Press, 1990.

Thomas, Derek W. H., *Acts*. REC. Phillipsburg: P & R Publishing, 2011.

Thompson, Alan J., *The Acts of the Risen Lord Jesus*. Downers Grove: InterVarsity Press, 2011.

Turner, Max M. B., *Power from on High: The Spirit in Israel's Restoration and Witness in Luke-Acts*. Sheffield: Sheffield Academic Press, 1996.

Wall, Robert W., 'The Acts of the Apostles.' *The New Interpreter's Bible*, vol 10. Nashville: Abingdon Press, 2002.

Williams, David J., *Acts*. NIBC. Peabody: Hendrickson Publishers, 1990.

Willimon, William H., *Acts*. Atlanta: John Knox Press, 1988.

Witherington, Ben, *The Acts of the Apostles: A Socio-Rhetorical Commentary*. Grand Rapids: William B. Eerdmans Publishing Company, 1998.

Wright, N. T., *Acts for Everyone*. Louisville: Westminster John Knox Press, 2008 (2 vols).

SCRIPTURE INDEX

SUBJECT INDEX

Christian Focus Publications

Our mission statement –

STAYING FAITHFUL

In dependence upon God we seek to impact the world through literature faithful to His infallible Word, the Bible. Our aim is to ensure that the Lord Jesus Christ is presented as the only hope to obtain forgiveness of sin, live a useful life and look forward to heaven with Him.

Our Books are published in four imprints:

CHRISTIAN FOCUS

popular works including biographies, commentaries, basic doctrine and Christian living.

CHRISTIAN HERITAGE

books representing some of the best material from the rich heritage of the church.

MENTOR

books written at a level suitable for Bible College and seminary students, pastors, and other serious readers. The imprint includes commentaries, doctrinal studies, examination of current issues and church history.

CF4•K

children's books for quality Bible teaching and for all age groups: Sunday school curriculum, puzzle and activity books; personal and family devotional titles, biographies and inspirational stories – Because you are never too young to know Jesus!

Christian Focus Publications Ltd,
Geanies House, Fearn, Ross-shire,
IV20 1TW, Scotland, United Kingdom.
www.christianfocus.com